MW01070599

Place-Based Learning

Connecting Inquiry, Community, and Culture

Micki Evans

Charity Marcella Moran

Erin Sanchez

Solution Tree | Press
a division of
Solution Tree

Copyright © 2024 by Solution Tree Press

Materials appearing here are copyrighted. With one exception, all rights are reserved. Readers may reproduce only those pages marked "Reproducible." Otherwise, no part of this book may be reproduced or transmitted in any form or by any means (electronic, photocopying, recording, or otherwise) without prior written permission of the publisher.

Cover images created with AI-Assisted Adobe Stock images.

555 North Morton Street
Bloomington, IN 47404
800.733.6786 (toll free) / 812.336.7700
FAX: 812.336.7790

email: info@SolutionTree.com
SolutionTree.com

Visit **go.SolutionTree.com/instruction** to download the free reproducibles in this book.

Printed in the United States of America

Library of Congress Cataloging-in-Publication Data

Names: Evans, Micki, author. | Moran, Charity Marcella, author. | Sanchez, Erin (Project-based learning consultant), author.
Title: Place-based learning : connecting inquiry, community, and culture / Micki Evans, Charity Marcella Moran, Erin Sanchez.
Description: Bloomington, IN : Solution Tree Press, 2024. | Includes bibliographical references and index.
Identifiers: LCCN 2023049068 (print) | LCCN 2023049069 (ebook) | ISBN 9781954631816 (paperback) | ISBN 9781954631823 (ebook)
Subjects: LCSH: Place-based education. | Inquiry-based learning. | Community and school. | Multicultural education.
Classification: LCC LC239 .E93 2024 (print) | LCC LC239 (ebook) | DDC 370.11/5--dc23/eng/20231214
LC record available at https://lccn.loc.gov/2023049068
LC ebook record available at https://lccn.loc.gov/2023049069

Solution Tree
Jeffrey C. Jones, CEO
Edmund M. Ackerman, President

Solution Tree Press
President and Publisher: Douglas M. Rife
Associate Publishers: Kendra Slayton and Todd Brakke
Editorial Director: Laurel Hecker
Art Director: Rian Anderson
Copy Chief: Jessi Finn
Production Editor: Kate St. Ives
Copy Editor: Mark Hain
Proofreader: Laurel Hecker
Text and Cover Designer: Abby Bowen
Acquisitions Editors: Carol Collins and Hilary Goff
Assistant Acquisitions Editor: Elijah Oates
Content Development Specialist: Amy Rubenstein
Associate Editor: Sarah Ludwig
Editorial Assistant: Anne Marie Watkins

In loving memory of Rick Lear.

Your presence, guidance, and unwavering support
resonate within the pages of this book. Though
you are no longer with us, your impact on each
of us, both professionally and personally, remains
immeasurable. Your wisdom, kindness, and
friendship enriched our lives in ways we can never
fully express. This book stands as a tribute to your
legacy, a testament to the profound influence you had
on all of us. You will be dearly missed, but your spirit
lives on in the hearts of those you touched.

With eternal gratitude,
Charity, Erin, and Micki

Acknowledgments

We are forever grateful to Dr. Lisa Delpit for writing the foreword and capturing the essence of our purpose for writing this book. We are so appreciative of Solution Tree for providing us with a platform for sharing our vision with the educational community.

We are deeply grateful for the very soil that birthed us, the ancestors who tether us to place and bless us daily, and our families and friends for their patience and resolute belief in the necessity of our message and justness of our words.

We acknowledge that the land on which we live and wrote this book—Erin and Micki in the South and North Puget Sound regions, respectively, and Charity in the Baton Rouge area—is the ancestral land of the Puyallup, Snoqualmie, and Chahta Yakni and Houma Nations, who have stewarded their homelands since time immemorial. They are thriving and vital sovereign nations, despite more than two hundred years of land confiscation and the denial of rights (hunting and fishing rights, language, spirituality, right to educate, and so on) by the United States government and at the state level. We pay our respects to the elders both past and present. We specifically want to honor Connie McCloud, who has spent decades protecting the culture of her people and educating generations of Puyallup children; Robert de los Angeles, chair of the Snoqualmie, who, in 2022, helped secure the purchase of thousands of acres of the tribe's ancestral forest land; and Theresa Dardar, a Pointe-au-Chien tribal member, who is a strong local leader advocating for the restoration and protection of not just the ecosystem of the Gulf of Mexico and its coastal areas but also the people and communities who call coastal Louisiana home.

We recognize that acknowledgment is only a first step, and we commit to intentionally create inclusive and respectful partnerships that honor Indigenous cultures, histories, identities, and sociopolitical realities.

> If you want to know more about the land you inhabit, visit **https://native-land.ca/** for an interactive map, and find out how you can get involved in the Land Back movement to support tribal land repatriation.
>
> Visit Landback (**https://landback.org/**) to find more resources and Sogorea Te' Land Trust (**https://sogoreate-landtrust.org/shuumi-land-tax/**) to view a rematriation model in the Bay Area.

Finally, we are grateful for the students whom we have been gifted to teach and learn from throughout our careers, and we dedicate this book to them, and to all students, who we pray will come to know their inseparability from the places that call to them and the ones they create. We hope, too, that each student embraces their benevolent power and acts on their purest potential.

Solution Tree Press would like to thank the following reviewers:

Courtney Burdick
Apprenticeship Mentor Teacher
Fort Smith Public Schools
Fort Smith, Arkansas

Charlcy Carpenter
Eighth-Grade Teacher
Burns Middle School
Lawndale, North Carolina

Doug Crowley
Assistant Principal
DeForest Area High School
DeForest, Wisconsin

John D. Ewald
Education Consultant
Frederick, Maryland

Nathalie Fournier
French Immersion Teacher
Prairie South School Division
Moose Jaw, Saskatchewan, Canada

Neil Frail
Instructional Design Lead
Calgary, Alberta, Canada

Shanna Martin
Middle School Teacher and
    Instructional Coach
School District of Lomira
Lomira, Wisconsin

Rea Smith
Math Facilitator
Rogers Public Schools
Rogers, Arkansas

Rachel Swearengin
Fifth-Grade Teacher
Manchester Park Elementary School
Olathe, Kansas

Emily Terry
English Teacher
Kinard Core Knowledge Middle School
Fort Collins, Colorado

Sheryl Walters
Instructional Design Lead
Calgary, Alberta, Canada

Visit **go.SolutionTree.com/instruction** to download the free reproducibles in this book.

Table of Contents

Reproducible pages are in italics.

Part II: Design Place-Based Learning Journeys 115

About the Authors

Micki Evans is a writer and education consultant who focuses on transformative liberatory teaching practices. She is the cofounder of the learning organization and consultancy PBL Path. Micki provides quality professional development focused on place-based learning, project-based learning, culturally responsive teaching strategies, and supporting schools in forging authentic community partnerships.

Micki believes place-based learning is a powerful tool that promotes educational equity by connecting students to place and community, encouraging them to find their voice and express their identity in beautiful ways. Place-based learning is a culturally responsive pedagogy that is transdisciplinary, cross cultural, and intergenerational.

Micki is a member of the National Faculty for PBLWorks, providing professional development to educators throughout the United States. In addition, she has consulted with schools in China, Australia, Guatemala, Russia, and the United Kingdom in adopting pedagogical practices that utilize place-based and project-based learning. She has worked with organizations such as i2 Learning, Center for Native Education, Coalition of Essential Schools, EdVisions, New Horizons for Learning, and Greenpeace International.

Micki is the author of *Chrysalis: Nurturing Creative and Independent Thought in Children* and the coauthor of the *Our Only Earth* series, the *Picturing the Possibilities: What Powerful Teaching and Learning Looks Like* video series, *Teacher Support Materials*, and *No Time to Waste: A Student Guide to Environmental Action*.

Micki holds a bachelor of arts in education and psychology from the University of Washington and a K–12 teaching certificate and a master of arts in educational systems design in curriculum and instruction from Antioch University Seattle.

Charity Marcella Moran is a former high school project-based learning teacher, New Tech Network school development coach, and middle school alternative programs instructional specialist. These experiences, coupled with her work as an elementary school Federal Programs Title I coordinator, provide a sustainability and capacity-building focus to Charity's work. She believes that place-based learning is a powerful and transforming instructional strategy that, when leveraged appropriately, dispels achievement disparities and empowers all stakeholders to become lifelong learners. Charity's focus areas include strategic program development, culturally responsive teaching, educating and empowering Black males, STEM, 21st century skills, project-based learning, and literacy, language, and equity.

Charity currently serves as director of district and school leadership in the state of Kentucky for PBLWorks and is founder and CEO of iDoSchool.com, which trains educators internationally and independently, consulting to meet a variety of school program development needs. As the founder of iDoSchool, Charity's work and research revolves around establishing a safe space for teachers to innovate and develop the skills to decolonize curricula, build culturally responsive learning experiences, and debunk myths around students of color. Together with PBL Path, Charity has facilitated place-based learning projects at Whitney Plantation, with expeditions and experiences crafted for both teachers and students to experience, learn from, and appreciate the place and its history. Service opportunities as an adjunct professor, leading culturally responsive teaching professional development, curriculum design, and STEM curriculum management, afford Charity a unique perspective for each and every service.

A Gates Millennium Scholar, Charity earned her bachelor of science degree in biology from Southern University and A&M College, a master of arts in secondary mathematics education from Centenary College of Louisiana, and an educational specialist certification in educational leadership from Louisiana State University–Baton Rouge.

Erin Sanchez has spent the past twenty-three years working as a high school and continuing education teacher, curriculum writer, video producer, and national project-based learning consultant and coach. Erin has taught in both student-directed and teacher-directed place-based learning environments and knows firsthand that place-based learning is a spectrum, with a vision and journey unique to each school community. In addition to cofounding PBL Path, she has been a project-based learning (PBL) coach for the Puyallup Tribe of Indians, the Washington State Department of Education (OSPI), EdVisions Schools (transforming and starting PBL schools), and a coach of coaches for the Technology Access Foundation.

Erin finds great meaning in guiding leaders' and teachers' identity and equity journeys, building assessment tools side by side with educators and students, and connecting project ideas to community partners.

For the past twelve years, Erin has been a member of the National Faculty at PBLWorks (the Buck Institute for Education), delivering professional development to thousands of teachers across the United States and internationally. Most recently, she's stepped into a lead National Faculty role, affording her the opportunity to work closely with school leaders in district partnerships, readying their systems to support change to allow PBL to flourish.

Erin has worked for numerous organizations as a writer and producer, creating videos and professional development tools that illuminate powerful teaching and learning in action in the classroom. Her publications include the *Experiencing Film* series from Islandwood: *A School in the Woods* (in Partnership with *National Geographic*); *Picturing the Possibilities: What Powerful Teaching and Learning Looks Like*, a video series from the Small Schools Project; and *Planning Resources for Teachers in Small High Schools*, a four-volume collection from the Small Schools Project.

Erin received her bachelor of arts in Native American studies from Evergreen State College and a master in education from Antioch University, specializing in teaching Native American learners.

Foreword

by Lisa Delpit

"So Black people couldn't swim in the pool?"

"Not on your life, honey—and I mean that literally! They built this Olympic pool shaped like a lagoon right here in City Park, and even though Black folk paid taxes for it, we couldn't come near the park, much less the pool!"

"This art gallery right here where we're standing used to be the actual fancy pool house!"

This conversation occurred at the Baton Rouge Gallery, a city-owned art center that was memorializing the sixtieth anniversary of a major Baton Rouge, Louisiana, civil rights protest. Spearheaded by several activists, including Pearl George (who brought her eleven-year-old daughter, Debra) and George's sister, Betty Claiborne, fifty or sixty African Americans showed up at the segregated City Park pool to swim. Someone had tipped off the sheriff, and they were met by a plethora of police cars, policemen with billy clubs, and FBI agents in black suits. They were blocked from entering, and a scuffle broke out when Debra was shoved against a police car. Several protesters were arrested, including Debra, who was taken to the police station and questioned harshly without any family member present, repeatedly being referred to as "you little n____." Debra's mom, Pearl, was also arrested and, when she refused to post bail, was given a six-month sentence. The event was a major episode in the battle for civil rights waged by Baton Rouge citizens.

The Baton Rouge Gallery was honoring the date with a gallery show of local and regional artists and activists, and a panel of some of those involved in the original protest, including Debra. The panelists not only described the "Swim-In," as it had come to be known, but also recounted how the importance of access to a pool by the Black community was at the forefront of everyone's minds. Deprived of access to a swimming pool, a number of Black youngsters had drowned attempting to cool off in unsafe lakes, ponds, and reservoirs. The panel facilitator pointed out that there is a continuing legacy of Black people having been historically excluded from learning to swim in pools across the South, and that a Black child is still today 5.5 times more likely to drown than a White child.

The panel also reminisced about the Black communities of the 1960s. Much to the surprise of some of the younger audience members, during this time Black businesses, doctors, dentists, schools, restaurants, and so forth flourished in the segregated enclaves, ensuring that Black residents could limit their interaction with the sometimes dangerous, usually degrading larger White society.

The entire audience was mesmerized. There were tears in the eyes of many of the older Black attendees, who had dressed in elegant evening attire for the occasion, and rapt attention in the eyes of young Black and White attendees, sporting more casual shorts and khakis.

I listened in on a number of conversations between Black and White, young and old, with elders trying to explain the exact location of historically significant community markers long ago replaced by new businesses, homes, or perhaps just a plot of overgrown weeds. The talk was animated, interspersed with pointed questions, laughter, head shaking, and impromptu map drawing on hastily secured napkins.

Thus is the power of place-based stories, local historical inquiries, and opportunities for public interactions to unite a community. When you share a place, you share a history, but you will not understand that shared history unless the voices of those seldom heard are brought to the forefront.

That experience leads me to this book, for which I am delighted to provide this foreword. As I reflect on the importance of place in our lives, I cannot help but ruminate on the importance of place in classroom learning. And when I think of classrooms and place-based instruction, I must think of my dear friend and colleague, Charity Marcella Moran. Charity, a frequent visitor to my teacher education classes, has transformed the landscape for innovative education in Baton Rouge. Her work with Whitney Plantation (for which I am a board member) has brought new ways of imagining the work of teachers and students. In this book, she, Micki Evans, and Erin Sanchez explore the intersection of place, history, and identity as they detail meaningful place-based learning experiences that have inspired countless educators and changed the lives of countless students.

The world we live in is more complex and interconnected than ever before, and our understanding of how we learn and grow within it is constantly evolving. As we navigate a rapidly changing landscape of social, economic, and environmental challenges, it is clear that traditional approaches to education fall short. We need a new way of thinking about learning, that, like my evening at the art gallery, is grounded in the places where we live and the communities to which we belong. We need a framework that empowers us to explore the stories and voices not included in the local dominant canon. Students and educators alike must learn to ask, "Whose voice is telling the story?" "Whose stories are not being told?"

At the heart of this book is the idea that our places and communities are powerful teachers, and that by engaging with them in meaningful and intentional ways, we can develop the skills, knowledge, and perspectives we need to truly educate the future inheritors of our planet. From the stories of educators who have successfully implemented place-based learning in their classrooms, to the insights of organizers and activists who are working to build equitable communities, this book is a call to action. It challenges us to think differently about the role of education in society, and to embrace a more holistic, integrated, and rooted approach to learning, an approach that excites teachers, honors communities, and inspires students.

Although deeply embedded in theoretical understanding of the learning process, this book is not about theory. Instead, it provides a road map for creating engaging, immersive, and authentic learning experiences; lesson designs that challenge traditional power dynamics and center the voices and experiences of marginalized communities; and invaluable strategies for fairly and equitably assessing diverse forms of knowledge.

I am honored to have the opportunity to introduce this book to readers, and I am confident that it will inspire and empower anyone who is committed to growing wiser and becoming more compassionate citizens, and a more just and sustainable world.

Dr. Lisa Delpit is an American educationalist, researcher, and author. She is the former executive director and Eminent Scholar at the Center for Urban Education and Innovation at Florida

International University in Miami; the former Benjamin E. Mays Chair of Urban Education and Director of the Center for Urban Educational Excellence at Georgia State University in Atlanta, Georgia; and the first Felton G. Clark Distinguished Professor of Education at Southern University and A&M College in Baton Rouge, Louisiana. She earned the MacArthur "Genius" Fellowship for her research on school-community relations and cross-cultural communication. She is the author of Other People's Children: Cultural Conflict in the Classroom, The Skin That We Speak: Thoughts on Language and Culture in the Classroom, The Real Ebonics Debate: Power, Language, and the Education of African American Children, *and* Teaching When the World Is on Fire.

Prologue

All cultures recognize the power of place, their interactions with place, and their willingness to improve place for the good of all. The purpose of this book is to be intentional about our connections to place and about how to build those connections for our students. This notion of place is the premise of our definition of place-based learning. We want to nurture in all students their connectedness to place and community.

Professor Dara Kelly, Leq'a:mel First Nation, and researcher Amber Nicholson (2022), from the iwi of Ngaruahine of Taranaki, Aotearoa, New Zealand, suggest that our "deepest human sense of belonging is rooted in our connection to place. Transcending boundaries of time and space, place offers rootedness in a world we work extraordinarily hard to make familiar, safe and survivable" (p. 2).

It is in good faith and with veracity that we share our place stories as a means of demonstrating that very connectedness that each of us possesses—to land, to community, to our ancestors, to ourselves, and to one another. In addition, our place stories are a small way of building a relationship with you, the reader, before we ask you to do the hard work of studying your own sense of place, learning with and from your students, and creating a way to walk together on this place-based path.

Micki's journey to place-based learning began when she was in high school. After being expelled from two schools, the only alternative school, Strawberry Hill on Bainbridge Island in Washington State, became her last resort. There, she was taught by three teachers who had studied the Foxfire books and applied the pedagogical orientation of the Foxfire core principles that value intergenerational learning, the learning potential of individual stories, self-sufficiency, the relationships of an interdependent culture, and the power of place in teaching. As such, her teachers designed journeys that connected their students to their community and place. One journey explored local citizens of Japanese ancestry who had been incarcerated during World War II. The first group of Japanese Americans forced to leave after Franklin Roosevelt, then president of the United States, signed Executive Order 9066 were from Bainbridge Island. Over two hundred Japanese Americans from Bainbridge Island, many of them strawberry farmers, were sent to the Manzanar internment camp in California in March 1942. Through oral histories and primary and secondary sources, Micki's class created a play to educate Bainbridge Island citizens about this travesty, but also to highlight the stories of survival and resilience.

Micki believes projects need to explore both historical and cultural context to increase student understanding of the issues they will face today. These experiences fueled her passion to become a teacher who leveraged the power of place to reach students who had become disenfranchised in traditional school settings and from their communities. Through place-based learning, she believes students become more connected to self and their community, giving them a voice to create positive change.

Charity grew up going to family reunions on Melrose Plantation. She was fascinated by the stories her grandfather told about his life as a child growing up in that very place. She felt a strong connection to the land, so much so that she went on to study the place as a historical context for projects in a place-based learning classroom. Charity was able to use her family's plantation experience to explore how place can shape and inform our understanding of history. She used stories from her grandfather, uncles, and father to illustrate how the land can be a powerful source of knowledge and how it can yield the stories of those who lived before us. She also looked at the ways in which the land can shape our relationship with the environment and how it can create a deeper understanding of the past. She found that her connection to Melrose Plantation created a powerful lens through which to view history.

She discovered, too, stories that provided a counterpoint to the narrative she was taught in school, stories of Black and Creole people who were often overlooked, dismissed, or forgotten. These stories were an important part of Charity's understanding of the plantation and the people who lived there, and they helped her to gain a more complex and nuanced understanding of her family's history.

In her work as a project-based learning geometry teacher, Charity noticed early on that students were not able to make meaning of mathematics in a long-standing way without proper connections to and consideration of the community. This thread of disconnect continued to weave its way into the fabric of educational consultation as well. Teachers were designing projects in true form, but they were not connecting concepts to the community and not anchoring that content in a place. She seeks to change this through her teaching and consultancy work.

Erin's place story began in her hometown, nestled in the Minnesota River Valley, where she was raised in a converted one-room schoolhouse, playing teacher with the remaining school desks and chalkboard. Due to the rural school consolidations of the 1980s, her town lost their high school and with it the involvement of young people in the life of the town. When the first charter school law was passed in the United States in 1991, community members decided to start their own school that more closely resembled a one-room schoolhouse where students of different ages learned together. Gone were bells; gone were *courses*. The community became the classroom, and students became owners of their own learning through self-directed, project-based learning. In 1993, the Minnesota New Country School (MNCS) opened its doors, and the heart of the community was recovered. Erin graduated from a monstrosity of a high school that same year and went off to college but returned to her hometown to teach in this new school where place ruled.

Working at MNCS spoiled Erin to teach anywhere else, but her undergraduate and graduate focus was on working with Native American learners. She took what she learned in her hometown and applied it to her work as a teacher, curriculum writer, video producer, and school start-up, transformation, and place-based learning coach, never leaving her rural roots too far behind.

Individually and collectively, we have traversed the globe, facilitating workshops to provide consequential professional development as we support teachers in creating meaningful place-based learning experiences for their students. Not one workshop has transpired where we do not notice opportunities for students to connect more deeply to the places and spaces in which they live. Each of us in our own ways has coached educators through the process of connecting students to place, content, and community. Using our unique approaches and our place-based learning framework, we have challenged ourselves and our participants to map out projects and tasks that draw on the wisdom located in places and spaces. No matter if online or in person, there persist inequities in every educational place. We guide educators to examine systems and structures, and we walk together on a journey of unearthing those stories and dismantling inequities in those structures.

Our own personal imperative as a team is to ensure that Black, Indigenous, and students of color see their cultures incorporated into authentic place-based learning journeys, including students in rural, urban, and marginalized communities.

Introduction

We are surrounded by places. We walk over and through them. We live in
places, relate to others in them, die in them. Nothing we do is unplaced. How
could it be otherwise? How could we fail to recognize this primal fact?

—EDWARD S. CASEY

In the *Power of Place* exhibition at the National Museum of African American History and Culture in Washington, DC, visitors learn that place is not just about geography:

> [It is] about memory and imagination. People make places even as places change people. Places are secured by individual and collective struggle and spirit. Place is about movement and migration and dis-placement. Place is where culture is made, where traditions and histories are kept and lost, and where identities are created, tested, and reshaped over time. (National Museum of African American History and Culture, n.d.)

This notion of place as multifaceted, as individual and collective, as existing in physical spaces and in time and memory, in the traditions, stories, and identities of culture, is at the heart of our conception of place-based learning. Place-based learning is both local and global because it emphasizes the criticality of engaging students in learning experiences that are deeply rooted in the local community and environment while also helping them develop a broader understanding of the world around them (Anderson, 2018). Place-based learning falls under the umbrella of project-based learning. Indeed, it shares many academic and learning benefits with project-based learning, such as students applying learning in real-world scenarios, developing personally meaningful projects, and using curiosity-driven investigative questions.

Place-based learning, however, extends the breadth and depth of project-based learning due to a number of additional features. First, its focus on student and teacher collaboration with community members, organizations, and businesses solves real issues by creating plans and crafting products that enhance place and community. Second, it increases student voice through, in part, the examination of identity and cultural history. Finally, it fosters more equitable learning contexts through its inclusivity and valuing all individuals' personal and collective pasts, their imaginings and reimaginings, and their growing understandings and ways of being.

Our many years of collective experience have given us insight into the benefits of place-based learning. We contend that place-based learning offers the following benefits.

- ◆ It provides opportunities to apply newly acquired skills and knowledge in real-life situations.
- ◆ It engages students in authentic learning connected with community and culture.
- ◆ It enhances what is taught in school by extending student learning beyond the classroom and into the community.
- ◆ It provides the framework for decolonizing curricula so that students learn all sides of the story.
- ◆ It strengthens community partnerships and relationships.
- ◆ It promotes social justice and equity.
- ◆ It invokes civic engagement.
- ◆ It builds on student interests, talents, gifts, and passions.
- ◆ It utilizes a broad interdisciplinary approach, showing how knowledge is interconnected and interdependent.
- ◆ It creates pathways for liberatory practices for teaching and learning.
- ◆ It offers student choice and creates ownership in their learning.
- ◆ It creates authentic ways to embed traditional culture, knowledge, and ways of learning.

Other experts in the field of education also point to the ways place-based learning powerfully supports student education. Marwa Elbaz (2023), a professor in the education department at Port Said University in Egypt, reports:

> This education represents a link between learners and society, as it depends on solving real-world problems, with this method; education becomes interdisciplinary, combining history, geography, science, environment, media, and languages which increases the pleasure of learning across different disciplines. (p. 1)

Michigan's Department of Labor and Economic Opportunity (State of Michigan, n.d.) stresses the value of this pedagogy by explaining that "at its core, place-based education is an educational endeavor. So it's not surprising that student benefits are the most frequently researched. But its benefits are not limited to students and, in fact, extend to teachers, schools and communities." The Michigan Department of Labor and Economic Opportunity also elaborates on the community benefits of place-based learning in the following ways:

- More interest in place-making and preserving local heritage
- Expanded capacity to address the needs of community and its residents
- Increased social connectedness, activism, intergenerational learning, and social capital
- Increased engagement in policy, advocacy, and activism
- More numerous, impactful and mutually beneficial partnerships with schools (State of Michigan, n.d.)

Another benefit is that place-based learning is everywhere that students are. It is all-encompassing. It helps students recognize that they don't have to go somewhere else to have an impact, or be impacted; students become, therefore, a vital part of their place. In her blog post for Edutopia, "Place-Based Learning: A Multifaceted Approach," Emelina Minero (2016) points out:

Place-based learning engages students in their community, including their physical environment, local culture, history, or people. With place-based learning, students get to see the results of their work in their community. They build communication and inquiry skills, learn how to interact with any environment, and gain a better understanding of themselves, as well as their place in the world.

Place-based learning is inherently empathic because it requires students to recognize and value the experiences of others as well as their own experiences—influenced by personal and cultural histories. It is disruptive and constructivist because it requires a willingness to challenge and subvert the dominant narratives in our communities. At its best, it is world changing because it offers students a pathway to create more just and equitable circumstances. Individuals follow understandings of pathways—maps—to live their lives. These maps may be literal, or they may exist in the psyche. Either way, the maps tell us who belongs somewhere and who doesn't, where we can go and where we can't, what's true and what's false. These maps can be used to control or to free, to maintain or share power. Place-based learning offers students a way to recreate the maps that guide their lives, to connect academic inquiry to community and culture, and to find, often in partnership with community members, better, more authentic ways to live. Our purpose in offering guidance in this book to implement place-based learning is threefold.

1. To offer the academic benefits of in-depth interdisciplinary learning
2. To guide teachers in making education itself more equitable through the inclusivity and valuing of diversity of place-based learning
3. To foster students' ability and will to, through their learning, make substantive positive changes in their communities for greater equity and justice

Moreover, place-based learning provides opportunities to turn false narratives into truth. It gives students a sense of place by creating connections versus disconnections from their school and their community. Thus, students remap their world and, in doing so, find one that is more authentic.

Turning False Narratives Into Truth Through Mapmaking

Counter mapping is a tool for reclaiming the power and agency of disenfranchised and marginalized groups. Counter mapping enables these groups to create their own narratives and representations of their communities, which are often misrepresented or erased in official maps and historical records. It can involve using geographic information systems (GIS), participatory mapping, and other forms of mapping to gather and represent community-based data, stories, and knowledge. Counter mapping is an important alternative to traditional maps in place-based learning.

Rather than showing true connections, traditional maps often show the *dis*connections of place. As map researcher Annie Howard (2022) notes counter mapping is about:

the awareness of the power dynamics and colonial influences involved in traditional map-making. Choosing to map against dominant power structures is called counter-mapping. Mapping can be an act to (re)claim legitimacy and humanity, and to make visible the places and people that modernity and coloniality attempt to erase. (p. ii)

Howard (2022) suggests that counter mapping is used by "activists, artists and scholars alike who wish to shift the paradigm that has kept a stranglehold on geographical practices through colonial methods of mapping" (p. 26). We explore two specific counter-mapping movements in more depth here because they challenge the dominant structures.

- ◆ Indigenous counter mapping
- ◆ Black counter mapping

Counter maps decolonize how these communities represent spaces and places. Today, Indigenous cartographers are actively working to counter cultural erasure by decolonizing maps. Black counter mapping is a process in which Black communities use mapping technologies and techniques to document their lived experiences, histories, and cultural practices in ways that challenge dominant narratives about their communities.

Indigenous Counter Mapping

The purpose of Indigenous counter mapping is to connect Indigenous peoples to their places, as well as their history, culture, and identity. Indigenous counter mapping provides an opportunity to look at the world from a perspective that honors their way of knowing. It also challenges Western two-dimensional maps, which do not render possibilities to address a sense of identity and place. This mapping movement is about decolonizing maps by Indigenizing maps to provide a greater understanding of ancestral lands.

As shown in the short film *Counter Mapping* by Adam Loften and Emmanuel Vaughan-Lee (2018), the Zuni ground their counter maps in art that taps into the voice of Indigenous peoples with perspectives rooted in place. In its description of the film, the Global Oneness Project (n.d.) explains:

> "Counter mapping" challenges the Western notions of geography and the arbitrary borders imposed on the Zuni world. This perspective is not based on ownership and imposed names, but rather on memory, ceremony, song, and a deep relationship to the land.

Today, Indigenous cartographers are actively working to counter erasure by decolonizing maps. Journalists Tiffany Camhi, Jenn Chávez, and Crystal Ligori (2020) provide one such example: "Indigenous groups in Oregon are using their own mapping techniques to reclaim traditional names, spaces and concepts."

Jim Enote, a traditional Zuni elder and the subject of Loften and Vaughan-Lee's (2018) film, is working with Zuni artists to provide an alternative way to understand and create maps that offer an Indigenous voice and perspective rooted in place. Enote explains:

> Names of places within our territory have been passed down from generation to generation, but in the past 500 years we have been re-mapped. What was once known as Sunha:kwin K'yabachu Yalanne is now called the San Francisco Peaks and many people now call Heshoda Ts'in"a . . . Pescado. (A:shiwi A:wan Museum and Heritage Center, n.d.)

Enote goes on to articulate the important role the new counter maps play in combating the deleterious effects of two-dimensional Western maps that wipe away history and identity:

> Our maps aid our memories, they give reference to our place of origin. Places we have visited, and places we hope to go. They also provide us with a reference of where we are within the universe and help to define our relationship to natural process surrounding us. And because these

maps are ours, they function within our particular cultural sensibilities. (A:shiwi A:wan Museum and Heritage Center, n.d.)

The A:shiwi A:wan Museum and Heritage Center (n.d.) explains that the "A:shiwi Map Art is a collective, revisionist effort to elaborate Zuni history and cultural survival independent from the non-Zuni narrative, using Zuni language and Zuni aesthetics and sensibilities." These maps help the Zuni people understand where they come from as well as how and why their culture has traveled to far points. They include art to communicate the landscape and values of that culture.

In a review of Loften and Vaughan-Lee's (2018) film, the website Daily Good (n.d.) noted the following:

> The Zuni maps are an effort to orient the Zuni people, not just to their place within the landscape, but to their identity, history, and culture. The maps contain a powerful message: you have a place here, we have long traveled here, here is why this place is important. Through color, relationship, and story, the maps provide directions on how to return home.

In Camhi and colleagues' 2020 Oregon Public Broadcasting interview, David Harrelson, head of the Cultural Resources Department with the Confederated Tribes of the Grand Ronde, states that Indigenous people are decolonizing maps in Oregon to reconnect with their traditional lands. Harrelson contends that this action "provides a richness and a depth to the history of a place. Whether you're the Indigenous people of a place, or whether you're new residents to that place, you're both sharing a connection to that place" (Camhi et al., 2020). Harrelson reminds us that we are all connected to place and through the very act of decolonizing maps we forge deeper connections to that place.

Black Counter Mapping

Black counter mapping is a tool for reclaiming power and agency because it allows Black people to create their own narratives and representations of their communities. Black people have used counter mapping in a variety of contexts, including urban planning, environmental justice, and community-based research, as a means of highlighting the experiences and perspectives of Black communities and advocating for social change.

Just like the Zuni and other Indigenous cultures, people who were enslaved also used a form of counter mapping, using songs for maps to escape enslavement. They had very sophisticated methods of communication among one another to hide their communication from those who held power over them. Singing as a form of communication is deeply rooted in African cultures. Africans who were kidnapped and shipped across the Atlantic during the Middle Passage used songs to communicate with each other to locate family members. This tradition continued as a means of achieving freedom. According to an article by Dose Team (2017), "Spirituals contained codes that were used to communicate and give directions. Some believe Sweet Chariot was a direct reference to the Underground Railroad and sung as a signal for slaves to ready themselves for escape."

Consider these lines from the African American spiritual "Follow the Drinking Gourd":

> When the sun comes back and the first quail calls,
>
> Follow the drinking gourd.
>
> The old man is a waiting for to carry you to freedom,
>
> Follow the drinking gourd.

This spiritual is noted as one of the best examples of a map song:

> [It] contains essential directions for those enslaved trying to escape. The first line references the beginning of spring (when the days are longer), which was the best time to set out for the long journey North. The second and most famous clue is the drinking gourd, which refers to the Big Dipper constellation. By following the line of the constellation to Polaris (the north star), travelers had a guide in the night sky that pointed them toward freedom. (Dose Team, 2017)

Enslaved Black women also used traditional braids as a secret messaging system for those enslaved to communicate with one another. According to Amplify Africa (n.d.), "People used braids as a map to freedom. For example, the number of plaits worn could indicate how many roads to walk or where to meet someone to help them escape bondage." Most resistance movements have used cipher and codes such as this to send messages so the people in power could not decipher or decode the message. This allowed people not in power to communicate and rise up against the dominant power. This covert means of communication aided in planning rebellions and escaping slavery.

Authors and professors Derek Alderman and Joshua Inwood (2021), who specialize in race, public memory, civil rights, heritage tourism, counter mapping, and critical place name study—all within the context of the African American struggle for social and spatial justice—seek to understand the social, political, and economic structures that make human lives vulnerable to all manner of exploitations. They explore this, as well as how oppressed populations use social justice movements to change their material conditions, in their article, "How Black Cartographers Put Racism on the Map of America." They explain how the Black Panthers in the 1960s and 1970s stressed the practice of making and using maps to illuminate injustice: "The Black Panthers are just one chapter in a long history of 'counter-mapping' by African Americans" (Alderman & Inwood, 2021). Alderman and Inwood recognize that maps are not neutral and at times are used to exclude marginalized communities, stating that decisions made by mapmakers "can have far-reaching consequences." Further, "When the Home Owners' Loan Corporation in the 1930s set out to map the risk associated with banks loaning money to individuals for homes in different neighborhoods . . . they rated minority neighborhoods as high risk and color-coded them as red" (Alderman & Inwood, 2021). This practice, known as redlining, contributed to housing discrimination for years until the federal government banned this practice. However, the legacy of redlining is still prevalent in many cities throughout the United States.

Katherine McKittrick (2011), professor and Canada Research Chair in Black Studies at Queen's University in Kingston, Ontario, Canada, shares enlightening information about the sense of place for Black communities in the following:

> The complexities of black geographies—shaped by histories of colonialism, transatlantic slavery, contemporary practices of racism, and resistances to white supremacy—shed light on how slave and post-slave struggles in the Americas form a unique sense of place. Rather than simply identifying black suffering and naming racism (and opposition to it) as the sole conceptual schemas through which to "understand" or "know" blackness or race, it is emphasized that a black sense of place, black histories, and communities are not only integral to production of space, but also that the analytical interconnectedness of race, practices of domination, and geography undoubtedly put pressure on how we presently study and assess racial violence. (McKittrick, 2011, p. 1)

McKittrick (2011) argues that maps created by the dominant culture exclude the "culture, humanity, resilient creativity, and agency of Black communities and thus continue to re-isolate the dispossessed and perpetuate a placelessness for people of color" (p. 958).

There are many examples of Black counter mapping used in the past and present. Remember *The Negro Motorist Green Book*? It was a travel guide published from the 1930s to the 1960s for and by African Americans to locate safe, accommodating establishments in the face of Jim Crow racism.

> [Ethan McKenzie] Bottone (2020) argues that the *Green Book*, although it contained not one single standard map, represented a "counter-map" because the spatial data contained within it helped travelers of color move across and inhabit a not-so-open highway in oppositional ways and to locate and participate in major Black urban cultural and political spaces of the day. These segregated spaces were embodied sites of African American knowledge creation and information sharing and later became important incubators of formal political protest during the civil rights movement. The routes and stops realized through the *Green Book* continue to frame place interactions, leading some to trace and reflect critically on what is left (or not) of segregation-era Black neighborhoods and business districts. The travel guide has inspired others to produce or call for contemporary, "new" *Green Books* (for example, Miles, 2017) to protect travelers of color in light of the still unreconciled dangers of traveling, driving, and even jogging while Black. (Alderman, Inwood, & Bottone, 2021)

The Equal Justice Initiative's Community Remembrance Project and Community Soil Collection Project are other examples of counter mapping. For these projects, the Equal Justice Initiative (n.d.) partners with community members "to memorialize documented victims of racial violence throughout history and foster meaningful dialogue about race and justice today."

The Community Soil Collection Project gathers soil at documented lynching sites to use in an exhibit displaying the victims' names. As part of this project, communities participate in the Community Historical Marker Project, in which they erect "narrative markers in public locations describing the devastating violence, today widely unknown, that once took place in these locations" (Equal Justice Initiative, n.d.). As the Equal Justice Initiative's (n.d.) website explains:

> These projects, and the other engagement efforts that community coalitions develop, center the African American experience of racial injustice, empower African American community members who have directly borne this trauma, and invite the entire community to use truth to give voice to those experiences and expose their legacies.

The Community Remembrance Project has erected more than eighty historical markers where lynchings took place. In addition, the Community Soil Collection Project has collected soil from seven hundred locations where lynchings took place. The Legacy Museum in Montgomery, Alabama, exhibits jars of this collected soil. To date there are eight hundred jars of soil.

The Equal Justice Initiative (n.d.) also sponsors an essay contest that asks students to examine a historical racial injustice and consider its legacy today. Each year, students may receive awards up to $5,000 for winning essays. More than nine hundred high schools have participated in the Racial Justice Essays. It's a great opportunity for students to explore racial injustices within their community and get involved in the Community Remembrance Project. Visit https://eji.org/projects /community-remembrance-project for more information.

How Counter Mapping Connects to Place-Based Learning

Counternarratives are stories that tell the experiences and perspectives of those who are historically oppressed and silenced. Understanding place-based counternarratives is critical to students building more authentic knowledge of and connections to the places they inhabit, and counter mapping is a key part of that. One specific organization, Village Earth, a nonprofit and publicly supported 501(c)(3) founded in 1993, uses counter mapping to inform its advocacy and provides a tool you can use in your place-based learning classroom to inform the work you do with students. Its stated mission is to "help reconnect communities to the resources that promote human well-being by enhancing social and political empowerment, community self-reliance, and self-determination" (Village Earth, 2021b). Village Earth (2021b) helps achieve this mission by "strengthening intermediate and grassroots organizations through fiscal sponsorship, networking, training, research, and advocacy." Village Earth (2021a) suggests a variety of ways to use counter mapping to empower communities.

- Defending territorial rights
- Revealing social-economic disparities (low-income housing, gentrification, and crime and policing) within a community
- Individual and community planning
- Monitoring lands
- Discovering or revealing spatial relationships

Village Earth's (2021a) website states, "The proliferation of high-resolution satellite and aerial imagery has made it possible to map previously unmapped geographies from your desktop computer or smartphone." Village Earth shows how individuals can use this type of mapping, for example, to inquire about differences in incidences of police use of force in majority Black communities relative to majority White communities. Imagine the different ways you can use counter mapping in a project with your students to understand disparities that are prevalent in your community and to uncover the untold stories of place.

In place-based learning there is room for diverse perspectives and ways of sharing the untold stories of place. Place-based learning involves using the local environment as a context for learning. By incorporating counter mapping into place-based learning, students can gain a more diverse and nuanced understanding of the places they inhabit, as well as the historical and social forces that have shaped them. Place-based journeys can use mapping to uncover truths and make sense of place. By incorporating Black, Indigenous, and other forms of counter mapping into place-based learning, teachers can help students develop a deeper understanding and appreciation of their local environment and community, while also fostering a sense of social advocacy for change.

A Place-Based Journey to Whitney Plantation

Whitney Plantation is located in Wallace, Louisiana, between Baton Rouge and New Orleans. The guided tour at Whitney Plantation shares narratives of those who were enslaved there and the adults and children who lived and labored on the former plantation. On one of these tours, Charity coincidently ran into a former student of hers who is now studying to be a teacher himself at Southern University (a public, historically Black land-grant university in Baton Rouge). Her former student was there through a partnership PBL Path had facilitated with Whitney Plantation, and which included preservice teachers from Southern University.

As the tour unfolded, the director of research for Whitney Plantation described the process of renaming the human property when they arrived at a plantation. Religions, names, and families were all stripped from the enslaved Africans while their skills, traditions, and talents were exploited and replaced with enforced Christianity and manipulated biblical scriptures, which those who were enslaved were not even allowed to read.

As the tour participants listened, Charity's former student asked her, "What religion do you observe?" Charity hesitated answering. She knew this was a loaded question and that her answer could make or break the trajectory of a conversation they'd begun that felt important and thoughtful. Yet she also knew that this kind of question posed midway through a tour of a plantation focusing on the slave experience signaled that some level of introspection was occurring, and a person experiencing that kind of introspection can often use a thought partner. She was also honored, and thought, "Questions like his give my life purpose!" She answered, "I believe in the universality of one creator and that at the core, major religions have one thing in common: love." She glanced at her former student to see if that answer landed well and quickly added, "But I was raised Baptist and Catholic, so what's up?"

"I'm mad, Ms. Momo!" Charity's former student said. "I don't understand why we didn't learn this history in school. I'm really mad at my people for insisting on maintaining their belief in religion. Religion that's still being used to hold us down!" Then, without hesitation, Charity's former student divulged his worries, explaining why and how he had decided to become a teacher.

The young man's next questions showed Charity that he intended to press on with his challenging thoughts. "So what can we do?" he asked. "How do I change my people's minds?" He was wondering how he could bring awareness about a history of exploitation to friends, family, and future students. The young man's question was his way of processing the legacy of slavery and its impact on his friends, family, and community today.

Eureka! This is the purpose of place-based learning: immersion in place allows students to arrive at purpose-driven inquiry in a culturally relevant way. The conversation between Charity and her former student turned into comparisons of slavery to more contemporary issues like incarceration and the policing of Black bodies, as well as discussion of the many forms of activism, like Black Twitter and the Nap Ministry, that we all can take on as we traverse day to day.

This young student teacher's journey serves as a powerful example of place-based learning, where the physical environment becomes an integral part of the educational experience. The plantation, with its painful history of slavery, offers a tangible and emotionally charged setting for students to engage with historical and social issues. In this context, Charity's former student underwent a transformative experience that reshaped his mental map of a place. By walking through the grounds, witnessing slave quarters, and hearing stories of the individuals who lived and suffered there, he gained a deeper understanding of the historical and cultural layers embedded in the landscape and their relevance to him and his life.

Through various forms of nontraditional mapping, students can visually represent their understanding of the environment, relationships, and histories. Story mapping (page 52), which involves plotting narratives onto a spatial layout, and community asset mapping, which identifies strengths and resources within a community, are two strategies highlighted in this book. What these mapping methods share is their ability to encourage students to actively engage with their surroundings, fostering a sense of connection and empathy. By challenging and revising their worldviews through these mapping activities, students develop a more nuanced and informed perspective on history, culture, and social dynamics, promoting a holistic and place-based understanding of the world around them.

How to Use This Book

We offer this guidebook of place-based learning to educators, curriculum designers, and school and community leaders to inspire the design and implementation of place-based learning experiences in grades 4–12. While the projects we highlight in this book are geared toward students in grades 4–12, younger students can greatly benefit from place-based learning as well. Consider contextualizing the project examples for younger students when possible. Throughout the book, we weave in research frameworks, quotes from the field, and success stories of how projects anchored in place have changed students' lives and communities. We engage in the pursuit of a whole and just society by posing crucial questions in instructional decision making. These questions include, For whom are we making the decisions? Whom are we ultimately serving?

We have no qualms taking up the moral imperative that the systems of education in many countries worldwide were not established for all students to succeed. Blind spots reveal that educators are often still trying to operate within inequitable systems instead of dismantling and reimagining those systems. This guidebook aids educators in dismantling and reimagining by posing questions that confront these systems and work toward changes that lead to greater equity in fourth- through twelfth-grade learning while also challenging students to work toward greater justice and equity in the world at large through learning that is rooted in historical and cultural contexts of places.

This book contains fourteen chapters divided into three parts and a conclusion, as well as an appendix with a reproducible planning tool (page 265). We suggest that you read the book in order. In our combined eighty-nine years of experience, we've learned to recognize and create the guideposts that are most present in projects that change students' lives—and in working through this book, you will too.

In part I, "Understand Place-Based Learning Design Principles" (chapters 1–7), we describe the seven design principles that provide a coherent framework for designing robust, meaningful, and engaging projects. To aid comprehension of what the place-based learning design principles look like in practice, we have interwoven the storyline of one real-world place-based learning project— Baton Rouge's Troubled Waters—into each principle. This project was inspired by a conversation with a Black landscape architecture student at the University of California, Berkeley, who is also a Baton Rouge native and worked to reclaim spaces and places in the Black community while debunking myths surrounding Black people's relationships with swimming. The project was created out of the need to help youth understand intergenerational trauma and raise community members' awareness about the impact of local governmental policy decisions on their culture and way of thinking about certain issues. While students from a southern Louisiana city explored the historical ramifications of decisions made regarding public swimming pools in Black communities in their city (both past and present), they applied the knowledge and historical thinking around institutional segregation now and then.

Chapter 1, "Elevate Ways of Knowing" (page 23), shows readers how to integrate a variety of different ways of learning and understanding by weaving in cultural identity with content knowledge and skills. As a result, students not only meet national standards but are also immersed in cultural understandings and multiple worldviews.

Chapter 2, "Facilitate Purpose-Driven Inquiry" (page 33), guides readers in how inquiry goes beyond research and includes interviewing community members, consulting experts, and conducting surveys, field studies, focus groups, and data collection. Trusting that students will get to where they need to be in a project and then being ready to guide them as needed are what moves place-based educators from presenters to facilitators, and students from receivers to creators and innovators.

Chapter 3, "Build Authentic Community Partnerships" (page 49), helps readers strategize how to build strong community partnerships in which students learn, collaborate, problem solve, and receive feedback from experts, mentors, elders, and organizations within their community or region.

Chapter 4, "Empower Student Ownership" (page 65), articulates how to empower students in their learning by giving them voice and choice in the work they produce.

Chapter 5, "Engage in Feedback, Revision, and Reflection" (page 79), shows readers how to use feedback, revision, and reflection to create high-quality work using the feedback they receive from teachers, peers, experts, and community partners.

Chapter 6, "Co-Create an Authentic Community Product" (page 91), guides readers to embed authentic community products into a project to assess students' understanding of content, concepts, and skills.

Chapter 7, "Embed Culture in Teaching and Learning" (page 101), tells how to build classroom and school climates that honor the beliefs and values of cultures represented in the school and community.

Each of these seven design principles are intricately intertwined and essential in the design and implementation of high-quality place-based journeys.

Part II, "Design Place-Based Learning Journeys" (chapters 8–11), is focused on moving from ideas to action, illuminating how each of the design principles discussed in part I is essential in planning any place-based project. As you explore building projects around these principles, you will likely find it affirming to see some of your current practices already embedded in the design principles, such as in the following list, making it easier to add these design principles to your teaching toolbox.

- **Elevate ways of knowing:** You already design units aligned with your standards. Reflect on how you also incorporate social-emotional learning strategies, social justice standards, and disciplinary skills into social studies, science, mathematics, and literacy.

- **Facilitate purpose-driven inquiry:** Throughout many of your units, students already engage in inquiry through research, field studies, and science experimentation.

- **Build authentic community partnerships:** Perhaps you and your school already have established community partnerships that you can leverage for your place-based learning projects.

- **Empower student ownership:** Think about ways that you already build voice and choice into your teaching practice. Perhaps students co-create rubrics with you or have a choice in what they produce as a final demonstration of learning.

◆ **Engage in feedback, revision, and reflection:** Think about the ways you currently use feedback, revision, and reflection in your teaching practice. Do students have an opportunity to reflect on their learning? Do you already use certain critique protocols for getting feedback from their peers?

◆ **Co-create an authentic community product:** Consider units that engage students in creating an authentic product, such as writing to local representatives, presenting school leaders with a solution to bullying, or creating an authentic piece of writing for a specific audience.

◆ **Embed culture in teaching and learning:** Reflect on how you use culturally responsive strategies in your day-to-day teaching.

The truest intention of part II, "Design Place-Based Learning Journeys," is threefold. First, we aim to empower you to think, feel, and design with place in mind. Second, we guide you to understand that planning and assessing are not isolated acts, as has been the tradition in education. Rather, when done in partnership with students and the community, planning and assessing are acts of liberation. Finally, we elucidate all that place entails. We explore how place-based learning provides a framework to decolonize our curricula and how to leverage the design principles as a tool for decolonization and empowerment.

To that end, we introduce our *place-based learning project-planning tool* (a blank reproducible is in the appendix, page 265). This is the tool you will use to begin to map your students' and community's assets, create liberatory learning and assessment pathways, and include culturally embedded teaching strategies and any materials, lessons, and activities that align with learning outcomes and different ways of knowing. We'll explore the planning tool further in the following section, How to Use the Place-Based Learning Project-Planning Tool (page 14).

Part II of the book is scaffolded so you can begin designing your own place-based learning project with our guidance and the help of the planning tools we further explore in the following section as well as in part II. Think of the project-planning tool as a living document that you build out as you read each of the chapters in part II, using guidance from us along the way as you develop your own place-based journey.

Chapter 8, "Use Liberatory Teaching Practices to Decolonize Curricula" (page 117), shows readers what it means to decolonize curricula and how to do so, which plays a crucial role in empowering students and teachers. This chapter examines how race, identity, worldview, and perspective interact to shape our teaching practices and determine outcomes for students by prioritizing liberatory teaching practices that align with the design principles for place-based learning. This chapter explores the importance of an essential question to guide student inquiry and provides specific tips for crafting an essential question that engages students.

Chapter 9, "Unpack Biases and Assumptions and Uncover Community Assets" (page 129), guides readers in how to increase their awareness of their schema, views, and assumptions in service of their students, their families, and the community, and to recognize that designing with place in mind, in partnership with students and the community, is an act of liberation. This chapter explores how place-based learning provides a framework to decolonize our curricula as a tool for liberation and empowerment. This chapter also introduces part one of the project-planning tool, the *community asset map*.

Chapter 10, "Follow Pathways to Liberatory and Decolonized Assessment Practices" (page 151), shows readers, through cutting-edge research, how to achieve equitable assessment with all students and provides strategies for what a decolonized and liberatory approach to assessment looks like in practice. Here you will complete part two of the project planning tool, *liberatory learning and assessment pathways*. The purpose of this chapter (along with chapter 9) is to provide a scaffolded approach with our guidance as you create your first place-based project design for your students. If you do not have a project idea in mind, you might want preview chapter 11 for project ideas.

Chapter 11, "Plan Place-Based Learning Projects" (page 179), offers readers additional examples of completed project planners, with examples of how to incorporate each of the design principles in a place-based learning journey and *entry points* to examine issues and assets from different angles. This chapter introduces *quality indicators*, which are a means of reflection and assessment for place-based project design. The quality indicators act as a guide to ensure inclusion of each of the design principles in a meaningful and robust manner and as a check for equity in the plan.

In part III, "Support and Sustain Place-Based Learning Implementation With an Equity Lens" (chapters 12–14), we focus on monitoring and assessing the efficacy of place-based learning and look at how to build capacity to carry forward the work of growing place-based learning so the practice is sustainable beyond any one teacher or single project.

Chapter 12, "Sustain Place-Based Learning Through the Practitioner's Round" (page 203), introduces readers to *the practitioner's round*, which is designed to guide teachers, coaches, and leaders through the use of vetted protocols, with an emphasis on equity at every step, from trailhead to summit.

Chapter 13, "Dismantle the Barriers to Place-Based Learning" (page 227), shows readers how to recognize perceived and real barriers for successful place-based learning implementation. The chapter addresses such topics as teachers', coaches', and leaders' realm of influence, the school schedule, and effective ways to establish community partners. This chapter also asks readers to consider their school's theory of action for equity work and how it relates to successful place-based learning implementation. We demonstrate how to use storytelling to make space for stories that might not be heard, providing a platform for individuals who don't feel connected to the more dominant established narratives to participate in the larger conversation around place-based learning.

Chapter 14, "Monitor and Assess the Efficacy of Place-Based Learning and Build Capacity" (page 249), guides readers in strategies for monitoring and assessing the efficacy of place-based learning and capacity building by examining the alignment between a classroom's values and its practices as a vital step in the process of sustaining the practice. This chapter explores how place-based learning supports school reform by providing a framework for educational innovation grounded in the local context and the importance of assessing the effectiveness of educational practices that aim to build capacity and foster place-based learning.

In addition to the unique content of the chapters, each chapter opens with an essential question to help readers frame their thinking around the focus of the chapter. Each chapter then closes with key takeaways that provide brief summaries of the main ideas covered and connect them to the larger themes and the purpose. These takeaways also provide an opportunity for reflection and to chart new inspirations, and aspirations, prior to reflection questions. The Journey Log concludes each chapter. The Journey Log provides you with the opportunity to record your learning, thoughts, and ideas about designing a project and to note how components of place-based learning may already align with your teaching practices.

Begin your Journey Log by grounding yourself in place. Consider your own place story. How does it inform your cultural identity? How has it informed your thoughts about resilience? Sense of place is linked to cultural identity. Sense of place is historical, cultural, and spiritual. The relationship between power of place, storytelling, and oral traditions can also be deeply personal, as our own experiences and reflections on place can influence the stories we tell about ourselves and our lives. Our childhood homes, the neighborhoods we grew up in, and the natural landscapes that have shaped us all have a role to play in the narratives we create. By reflecting on the places that have had the most impact on us, we can gain a deeper understanding of our own personal stories and the way that they intersect with the larger narratives of our communities and cultures. Through this process of reflection, we can tap into the power of place and use it to create stories that are both authentic and meaningful. We build on this foundational understanding of place and weave it into our theoretical framework for place-based learning. Think of these reflection prompts as you log your journey in the spaces provided and capture your ideas and questions along the way.

How to Use the Place-Based Learning Project-Planning Tool

The planning tool consists of the following two linked parts but may be used separately at different points in the project-planning process. We use Baton Rouge's Troubled Waters project as an example here in the tool to illustrate the planning process and what can develop from that process.

- **Community asset map:** In the community asset map portion of the place-based learning project-planning tool (introduced more fully in chapter 9, page 135), we begin with the most important consideration as we plan: our students. Then we describe the *ways of knowing*, *issues*, and *infinite capacities* that we want to connect to the community. The *infinite capacities* of students refer to the potential for students to continue growing, learning, and developing throughout their lives. This includes not only academic abilities but also social-emotional, creative, and physical capacities. Once your planning is grounded in your deep-rooted knowledge of students, you can expand your asset map to families and community.

- **Liberatory learning and assessment pathways:** This part of the planning tool asks you to begin with the end in mind (that end being a community product that includes summative assessment). We begin with the *essential question*, which provides an entry point into and parameters for a subject. Next, you'll find the *project sketch*, where you outline your rough plan. You will also find the *community product* or products that tap into the various ways of knowing that students will need to engage in to successfully produce a product—that is, a service or action that benefits their community, *standards*, *skills*, and *ways of knowing* needed by students to successfully create community products and the specific ones you plan to assess. The tool touches on checkpoints, which we refer to as *journey checks*, and *formative assessments* to support students in creating high-quality work. This may include peer feedback opportunities, exit tickets, journal entries, critique protocols such as a gallery walk, a charrette, graphic organizers, note catchers, a summary of research such as digital or survey data, outlines, drafts, storytelling, narratives, and reflections—to name a few possibilities. Finally, use *culturally embedded teaching strategies* to support your students along the way.

Figures I.1 (page 15) and I.2 (page 17) provide the completed example of both parts of the place-based learning project-planning tool based on our case study, Baton Rouge's Troubled Waters project, which is highlighted throughout part I of the book. The blank reproducible for the tool is in the appendix (page 265).

COMMUNITY ASSET MAP

Who my students are

My students are Black youth living in the community they are learning about. The classroom represents a diverse group of young individuals with unique experiences and perspectives. Some students are parents, and some are caretakers of grandparents or other older relatives. These students bring a rich understanding of the challenges and strengths of their community and can provide valuable insights and ideas to their classmates and teachers. Their diverse backgrounds and experiences also bring a dynamic and inclusive atmosphere to the classroom, fostering a sense of community and respect among all students.

Ways of knowing, issues, and infinite capacities to connect to the community

Ways of knowing:	Issues:	Infinite capacities:
Utilizing the expertise of elders Using community sites for experiential learning Accepting the knowledge and expertise of others, such as teachers, experts, or sacred texts Acquiring knowledge through direct personal experience and reflection on that experience	How local policy impacts communities and reverberates across time	Students have the capacity to learn about and appreciate the cultural diversity of others and to develop intercultural communication skills. Students have the capacity to expand their knowledge and understanding of the world through continuous learning and exploration. Students have the capacity to develop and refine their physical skills and abilities through practice and training, most specifically around the ability to swim.

Connecting academic, justice, and action standards

Academic anchor standards:

Use of language as a tool for communication and knowledge acquisition

Collaborative conversations

Persuasive writing

Revising work based on feedback

History standards:

Exploring impact of policy on local community

Unpacking the historical actions of Jim Crow-era laws and policies

Justice anchor standards:

11. Students will recognize stereotypes and relate to people as individuals rather than representatives of groups

4. Students will recognize that power and privilege influence relationships on interpersonal, intergroup, and institutional levels and consider how they have been affected by those dynamics.

15. Students will identify figures, groups, events, and a variety of strategies and philosophies relevant to the history of social justice around the world.

Action anchor standards:

18. Students will speak up with courage and respect when they or someone else has been hurt or wronged by bias.

19. Students will make principled decisions about when and how to take a stand against bias and injustice in their everyday lives and will do so despite negative peer or group pressure.

20. Students will plan and carry out collective action against bias and injustice in the world and will evaluate what strategies are most effective.

FIGURE I.1: Baton Rouge's Troubled Waters project example—community asset map.

continued →

Who, how, and what		
Who will be involved? (Primary community partners)	**How are they an asset? How will they be involved? How will we connect and reciprocate?**	**What learning will happen as a result of their involvement?**
A landscape architecture student who is from Baton Rouge and was formerly a member of the local middle school's swim club	• As counsel, providing historical context for students • As an interviewee • As a primary resource • As an expert who can provide technical guidance on designs • As a target audience—a community member who could support the calls to action and proposals that students craft	Students will get exposure to a landscape architecture professional who looks like them and grew up in their community. They will learn about the pathway of his career, from middle school swim team participation to high school to college and career. Students will learn firsthand what research, feedback, and revision look like in the field of landscape architecture, as well as consult directly with him to determine whether the ways in which they gather information from the community match up with his professional methods.
City council members	• As counsel, to advise students on their proposals as they're being crafted • As support to give students insight on how city council works • As target audience and recipients of students' proposals • As the primary agents of action for the students' calls to action	Students will learn about the various ways citizens communicate with and share their concerns with their local legislators. Council members will also support students in creating persuasive calls to action.
Local elders who were alive during the 1950s, when the pools were shut down	• As counsel, providing historical context for students • As interviewees • As primary resources • As experts to provide guidance on designs • As a target audience and recipients of honors and homages built into students' proposals and calls to action	Students will learn more about the historical context of their community and the impact that policy decisions have had on their community through the anecdotes of local elders. Students will learn about the power of storytelling and active listening, as well as making connections to the past. Students will learn the art of interview skills and gathering oral histories.
Potential community product, service, or call to action		
Potential products can include public awareness campaigns, proposals for legislation to city council, social media campaigns, landscape architectural designs, and any other options that students may design, based on their selected target audience.		

Source for standards: Southern Poverty Law Center (n.d.a).

Liberatory Learning and Assessment Pathways			
Project title: Baton Rouge's Troubled Waters		**Grade:** 5–12	**Estimated duration:** Fifteen to thirty-five hours

Essential question: How can we plan a public swimming pool that will honor the people and culture in our community?

Project sketch: Baton Rouge's Troubled Waters project aims to address historical disparities in access to swimming pools within the Black community by planning a public swimming pool that honors local culture. Students will engage with community elders, landscape architects, and city council members to develop proposals for a sustainable and meaningful outdoor space. Through participatory design processes, research on community needs, and challenging stereotypes, students will create public awareness campaigns, proposals for legislation, and landscape architectural designs that promote social justice and inclusivity. By emphasizing storytelling, critical analysis of racism's impact, and building collaborative partnerships, students will not only learn about historical injustices but also develop essential skills in advocacy, communication, and cultural understanding.

| Community product or products

Presentations, performances, products, or services | Ways of knowing (in student-friendly language)

Content and skills needed by students to successfully complete products | Journey checks and formative assessments

To check for learning and ensure students are on track | Culturally embedded teaching strategies for all learners

Provided by teacher, other students, experts; includes scaffolds, materials, lessons aligned to learning outcomes, and formative assessments |
|---|---|---|---|
| Architectural designs for the pool and surrounding landscape | Design, technical, environmental, and social aspects of creating sustainable and meaningful outdoor spaces | 1. Sketches and conceptual drawings
2. Site analysis
3. Design reviews
4. Models and renderings
5. Presentation preparation, rehearsal, and final sharing | ☐ **Incorporating Cultural and Historical Significance:** Community leaders, historians, and local experts come to discuss and share the stories of how the Black community has been historically deprived of access to pools due to racism; students craft talking prompts for the experts and historians to share thoughts on the topic; students begin this exploration by viewing the documentary Baton Rouge's Troubled Waters (2008).

☐ **Participatory Design:** Students interview community members to actively engage them in the design and construction of the new swimming pool; students organize community meetings, workshops, and brainstorming sessions. |
| Social media and public awareness campaigns about landscape and pool designs that include the historical significance of the closing of swimming pools and the injustices these communities experienced | Goal setting, messaging, content creation, channel strategy, engagement and interaction, and evaluating or measuring campaign success | 1. Audience analysis worksheet
2. Message development—developing and testing campaign messages
3. Social media metrics and analysis—tracking metrics and using the data to refine the campaign | ☐ **Emphasizing the Power of Storytelling:** Students research and gather stories from the Black community about the impact of the historical closing of swimming pools. They can use these stories to create compelling social media content, such as video interviews, quotes, and personal narratives. By highlighting the stories of those affected by this injustice, students can raise awareness and create empathy toward the issue among the wider community.

☐ **Analyzing the Impact of Racism:** Students learn to critically analyze the historical context of racism that led to the closure of swimming pools in the Black community. They receive encouragement to research and explore the lasting impact of this injustice on the |

FIGURE I.2: Baton Rouge's Troubled Waters project example—liberatory learning and assessment pathways.   continued →

			community's health, well-being, and access to recreational facilities. By educating the public on the negative impact of racism, students can challenge stereotypes and foster a more inclusive society. This lesson not only teaches students about social justice but also enhances their critical thinking and analytical skills.
Proposals to city council	Research and preparation, contacting the city clerk's office, drafting the proposal, reviewing, approval, and presenting the proposal to city council	1. Research 2. Proposal outlines, drafts, feedback, and revision along the way 3. Presentation preparation, rehearsal, and final sharing 4. Assessing stakeholder engagement strategies 5. City council procedure review worksheet	☐ **Understanding the City Council's Cultural Values:** It is important to research the city council's values, beliefs, and priorities to understand how to present the proposal effectively. For instance, if the city council values community engagement, the proposal should emphasize the involvement of the community in the project. Students can analyze city council meeting notes to determine how the council's values align to their project goals. ☐ **Researching Community Needs:** Students should be encouraged to research and understand the specific needs and challenges of the community in question. By doing so, students can identify how the proposed project aligns with community needs and present the proposal in a way that resonates with the community's values and goals.
	Unpacking and debunking the stereotypes associated with Black people and swimming capacities	1. Preassessment survey 2. Reflection journal responses to prompts like, "How has your understanding of Black people's swimming abilities changed through this unit?" or "What stereotypes or misconceptions did you hold before this unit, and how have they changed?" 3. Group discussions using prompts such as, "What are some stereotypes or misconceptions you have heard about Black people and swimming?" or "How do you think we can challenge these stereotypes?"	☐ **Challenge the Stereotypes:** Start by having an open discussion about stereotypes and how they can be harmful. Then, specifically address the stereotype that Black people are not good swimmers. Provide students with examples of Black people who are successful swimmers, such as Olympic gold medalist Simone Manuel. Discuss the reasons why this stereotype exists, and encourage students to think critically about why it is not true. ☐ **Provide Access and Opportunity:** Many Black people may not have had the opportunity to learn how to swim due to historical and ongoing systemic barriers, such as limited access to public swimming pools and swimming lessons. Educate students about these barriers and how they contribute to the perpetuation of the stereotype. Then, encourage them to take action by advocating for greater access to swim programs and resources in their communities. This could include organizing fundraisers to support swim programs, volunteering to teach swimming lessons, or advocating for policy changes that increase access to swimming facilities.

What did you notice and wonder as you read through the completed community asset map and the liberatory learning and assessment pathways? What excites you, and what questions do you have? You are beginning your own purpose-driven inquiry into place-based learning. We welcome you on this journey by providing a framework for understanding the importance of connectedness in education, and we offer practical strategies for implementing this approach in your own classrooms and schools. There is an urgent need for a book about place-based learning. Our current education system often fails to address the complex challenges we face as a society, such as environmental degradation, cultural erasure, and social injustice. These needs should be met with righteous indignation, yes, but also proactive urgency. This is where place-based learning comes in as a powerful tool for empowering students to become engaged, responsible citizens who can work toward building a more just and sustainable world.

This book on place-based learning serves as a rallying cry for educators, policymakers, and parents who are passionate about transforming the education system. It highlights the importance of teaching students not only the core academic subjects but also the ways of knowing, skills, and knowledge they need to understand and address the issues facing their communities and the world at large.

PART I

Understand Place-Based Learning Design Principles

Place-based learning might also be called *connected learning*. This is learning that connects students to place, culture to content, and schools to the communities they are part of. In a world that may appear connected—through technology, ease of travel, a global economy—our systems of education often remain siloed in what sufficed for some during the Industrial Revolution of Europe and North America but has little to do with students' lives and futures today, and nothing to do with equity of access. What place-based learning is great at is bleeding the edges of those antiquated rules that dictate, for example, that mathematics is separate from the study of history, or that chemistry has no relation to art, and so on. Place-based learning reminds us that schools are community hubs, where generations can explore and share their knowledge. Place-based learning also destroys, through the active involvement of every demographic of learner, the notion that only some students deserve to learn in a meaningful and synergistic way.

That is why, when we developed the design principles in this book, we didn't name them and then put them into practice. They were organically born from our experience with this type of connected learning. We put names to them so that you can draw parallels to your current practice and envision what is achievable for you, using familiar schema. We also present these design principles to give you a framework to plan a place-based learning journey in all its fullness. For that reason, there is much interdependence of the design principles. They work in tandem. Embedding culture in teaching and learning (chapter 7) is the fruit on the tree of elevating ways of knowing (chapter 1). Co-creating an authentic community product (chapter 6) is only possible with the pollination from building authentic community partnerships (chapter 3). As you read and gain an enriched understanding of each design principle, think of them as the foundation solidifying the path to start your own place-based journey in part II, and as the reassurance to make it sustainable and spreadable in part III.

We ground you in the principles because, without them, this would only be a how-to book. We want this to also be a *why-because* book, with the rationale and experience embedded in every design element.

CHAPTER 1

Elevate Ways of Knowing

By three methods we may learn wisdom: First, by reflection,
which is noblest; second, by imitation, which is easiest; and third by
experience, which is the bitterest.

—CONFUCIUS

ESSENTIAL QUESTION: How can we elevate cultural ways of knowing to prioritize the strengths, skills, and interests of students, families, and the community?

A student walks into our classroom for the first time. We work hard in those first days and weeks to build a relationship with the student and their family, dispelling preconceptions and developing the foundation of a learning partnership. Through this effort, we learn that this particular student is a spoken word artist and has won local poetry slams. We find out another student works in his parents' Filipino bakery, making buko pie from scratch each morning before school. Yet another student spends summers on her grandmother's sheep ranch on the Navajo Nation, weaving traditional rug designs. Each student has a skill set that is an asset to them personally and to the cultural collective. It is the teacher's role to sit these skills alongside the content standards and turn them into pure place-based learning gold.

In this chapter, we explore how to elevate the diverse array of unique backgrounds and experiences students bring to class by articulating and examining ways of knowing and by looking closely at several specific strategies to elevate these ways of knowing. We then consider "Elevate Ways of Knowing, in Action" through the lens of Baton Rouge's Troubled Waters project. The chapter also offers a chance to think further about its content through the Conclusion and Key Takeaways and Reflection Questions sections. It concludes with the Journey Log for writing down your thoughts and ideas.

What Are Ways of Knowing?

Ways of knowing encompass much more than a curriculum or textbook. Ways of knowing are the methods through which knowledge becomes apparent to us, such as utilizing the expertise of elders, integrating Native language, drawing on Indigenous knowledge systems, and using traditional settings such as waterways, cultural centers, and sacred sites for experiential learning. The Common Core State Standards (CCSS), Next Generation Science Standards (NGSS), College, Career, and Civic Life (C3) Framework for Social Studies State Standards, and Social Justice Standards (Learning for Justice) are standards recognized across the United States that demand a new way of teaching and learning. They require that students not only learn key content, but also learn to think critically, problem solve, and collaborate. Although these national standards have made progress in incorporating skill development, they fall short of acknowledging the importance of cultural ways of knowing.

A handful of state education systems, as well as many individual schools, districts, and Native Nations, have elected to adopt cultural standards, such as Alaska's Standards for Culturally Responsive Schools, to recognize the value of and need to make teaching and learning culturally congruent for students. In 2015, the Hawaiʻi State Department of Education adopted the Nā Hopena Aʻo (HĀ, n.d.), a framework of "six outcomes that are firmly rooted in Hawaiʻi. With a foundation in Hawaiian values, language, culture and history, HĀ reflects the uniqueness of Hawaii and is meaningful in all places of learning." The goal of HĀ is to "honor the qualities and values of the indigenous language and culture of Hawaiʻi" (Nā Hopena Aʻo [HĀ], n.d.) and is a prime example of the implementation of ways of knowing systemwide.

How Do I Elevate Ways of Knowing?

Examples of uplifting students' cultural ways of knowing also abound in individual schools and classrooms. In a second-grade classroom at Porcupine Day School on the Oglala Lakota Nation, the teacher, Nikki, pairs the NGSS's (2013) "Earth's Systems: Processes That Shape the Earth" standards with Joseph Bruchac's (1992) *13 Moons on Turtle's Back*, a children's book explaining the lunar phases and seasons, drawing from Iroquoian, Cree, and Sioux traditions (Nikki K., personal communication, February 3, 2020). Students collect and share their own tribal creation stories. Then, they analyze the similarities and differences between the NGSS, Bruchac's pan-tribal story, and their Lakota stories. Finally, they represent their analysis through an artistic medium. In this way, Nikki is elevating traditional knowledge while at the same time addressing the NGSS. This goes beyond the surface-level concept of *heroes and holidays*, where, as author and educator Zachary Wright (2019) defines it, "teachers 'celebrate' differences by integrating information or resources about famous people and cultural artifacts of various groups into the mainstream curriculum. . . . Student learning about 'other cultures' focuses on costumes, foods, music and other tangible cultural items." In Nikki's classroom, the students become the resource, sharing their cultural knowledge in an original way with peers and members of their tribal community, elevating the cultural responsivity of the project in an authentic way.

The act of elevating, valuing, and integrating ways of knowing that stem from cultural knowledge into learning requires the following critical actions.

- **Agitate in your practice:** Take a neighborhood walk with your students to see from their perspective, share power in the classroom to build students' agency, and widen the classroom with community partners and experts.

- **Weave culture and content together:** When we elevate students' ways of knowing to be of equal value to the content we teach, we open opportunities for students to fully express themselves, and we give our content the context it needs in order to be retained.

 ♦ **Advocate for cultural standards:** Once we see the capability of uniting ways of knowing with what and how we teach, it becomes imperative to ensure it happens for every student across our campus, and beyond.

Agitate in Your Practice

Agitating in your practice means reflecting on what you do and why you do it, then adjusting your teaching to realize possibilities you may not have recognized before. This requires inner focus and a close examination of what you do specifically and what you demonstrate value for in both your classroom and the community in which your classroom exists. What can you do to agitate for cultural standards in your practice? Here are a few suggestions.

Walk With Students

You may not live within the boundary of the school where you teach; even if you do, there's a good chance that your students know their neighborhood differently than how you know it, because of age, race, or a variety of other reasons. Take the opportunity to do a physical or virtual neighborhood walk and empower students to show you a bit of their lived experience entirely from their perspective. You can do this walk as a whole class, give it as an assignment, or use it as a form of project ideation to help map upcoming projects with student input. For example, a fine arts teacher might ask, "What examples do you see of people creating, preparing, and sharing artwork in your neighborhood?" A middle school geometry teacher might ask, "How was geometry used to build your neighborhood block, and how does it serve the people who live there?" An earlier grades teacher might make the question more personal and subjective. For instance, a fourth-grade teacher might ask, "What are your favorite places in your neighborhood? If you could add something, what would you build?" In each of these examples, as students collect and report data, you are finding out where their skills lie, what they are passionate about (and not), and what they have expertise in. These rich data are invaluable to project planning grounded in ways of knowing. You'll have a year's worth of ideas from a few initial activities.

Let Students Lead

In many teachers' first year of teaching, there is a good chance that a well-meaning colleague told us to "show no weakness" in front of our students. Fear, indecision, and admitting mistakes are often seen as akin to a prey animal out of the safety of its warren, doomed to be the predator's next meal. Even though the profession has embraced growth mindset, the notion that teachers should show vulnerability is not mainstream (Karnovsky, 2020). That, however, is exactly what we believe should occur.

As a learning facilitator, letting our students lead is the fastest way to find out what they know, what they need from us, and what they can do individually and through collaboration. The first step is getting them curious, and the second step is getting out of the way. Posing questions to students such as, "I'm having this problem and I need your help with it," or "I've noticed _____, and I'm wondering what you think," are surefire ways to activate students' ways of knowing and show our willingness to give them a voice. It's even better if your problem or curiosity is a genuine one.

As students set out to organize the task, there may be a student who is sidelined or seems disengaged. Because we are freed from being the font of all knowledge, we can have a conversation with this student and find out why. We might ask, "What part of this project, no matter how small, seems interesting to you?" or, "If we could alter this project to include something that you care about, how would we do that?" This could be done as an exit ticket to the whole class, so as not to single out any one student. The issue may also be something more nuanced. For example, it may be a cultural norm to observe an adult do a task before attempting it oneself. That's valuable information for teachers, who can then ask what the next step would be to engage this student and respect their cultural identity.

Share the Classroom

This leads us to the final suggestion for agitating for cultural standards: put someone else in the room. Although teachers pride themselves on being content experts, their field is education, which is different from being active in a profession like architecture or natural medicine. Teachers must sometimes act as the guide or seeker rather than the authority. We can help students produce their best work when we seek out the assistance of people who know more about something than we do.

Using the examples from our neighborhood walk, the art teacher may ask her student whose grandfather owns the local hardware store to come in and talk to students about the murals that have adorned his building for more than fifty years. The geometry teacher might reach out to the city's Black history museum to set up a video interview with a historian who knows about redlining. The fifth-grade teacher could invite an architect to bring blueprints to class to show students how 2-D shapes become 3-D structures, who then asks students to design a structure they would like to see in their neighborhood. Whom could you reach out to for more information, and how does it relate to your content? Figure 1.1 provides an example of a letter you might use when reaching out to members of your community to establish a partnership.

Hello [*insert name here*],

[*Insert school name here*] is a unique environment that prepares students to be tomorrow's leaders while also immersing them in cultural knowledge. One way we do this is through place-based learning—a teaching method in which students work for an extended period to investigate and respond to an authentic and complex problem or challenge.

A critical component of place-based learning is making connections with, and learning from, community partners. Our [*insert class name here*] class is learning about [*insert ways of knowing and core project content*] and designing [*insert product*].

You're a leader in [*insert area of experience*], and we would love to hear about your journey and get a window into what you do.

If you are able to give an hour or two of your time, either in person or virtually, over the next few weeks, our students would be so grateful and would benefit immensely. You can email me, leave me a voicemail, or text. We look forward to collaborating with you!

Sincerely,

[*Insert name*]

FIGURE 1.1: Example community partner outreach letter.

We go into much greater detail about how to establish community partnerships in chapters 3 and 9 (pages 49 and 129). What we emphasize here is the hope that, as much as possible, the connections we make with potential partners are born from students' ways of knowing and being in their respective places and in the way they see the world.

Weave Culture and Content Together

Since place-based learning asks educators to partner with students, their families, and the community to weave cultural identity together with content knowledge and skills, students not only meet national standards but are also acknowledged for and immersed in cultural understandings like community participation, storytelling, honoring, developing spiritual consciousness, mentoring, helping and healing, learning songs, and taking cultural journeys (such as canoe trips, hunting camp, and so on).

For example, in the Pacific Northwest, Pacific Northwest Tribal families traveled their ancestral waterways for weeks, joining with tribes across the region. In this case, students met a writing standard during the canoe journey. Students kept a journal every day. In journaling, students practiced metacognition, using speaking and listening skills, reading the water and weather, and learning ancestral narrative structures. Flexibility is important in learning situations like this one. For example, keeping a journal dry aboard a canoe, where every person is focused on the job at hand, can be impractical. As an alternative, students could reflect on their learning in writing after the canoe journey concludes. The when and how of the learning needs to be flexible and allow both for practical concerns and for the cultural ways of knowing to be elevated above the content standards.

In addition to the canoe journey offering an opportunity to practice writing skills, it was interdisciplinary in nature. It could also include the science of wayfinding, the mathematics of canoe operation, the history of Native Nations fighting for their ancestral right to fish and hunt in usual and accustomed places, and the speaking and listening skills needed to canoe on a team. Because it doesn't fit into the silo of a stand-alone core subject, learning experiences like the canoe journey require a a more nuanced assessment and accreditation plan. The canoe journey is an example of a curriculum born of the people it serves—a place-based experience that is worthy of credit. Unfortunately, much time is often spent between school and state trying to prove the value of a journey such as this, trying to make it fit the dominant framework. In an interview with popular blog writer Larry Ferlazzo, author and professor of curriculum and instruction at Georgia State University Gholdy Muhammad speaks to this when she says:

> We have to stop putting fresh coats of paint on the same debilitating structures of education. We must start fresh with a curriculum that was designed with Black and Brown youths in mind and written by Black and Brown people, too. (as cited in Ferlazzo, 2020a)

To date, very few schools, mostly tribal, have been able to bridge the divide of competing priorities. So how do you do it? By starting with your classroom, your students, and place-based learning.

One way that teachers can advocate for weaving ways of knowing with content standards is to examine their content with a culturally informed eye, then consider how to shift the sequence or alter the scope of those standards to elevate students' strengths, skills, and interests. Consider the following questions to ask yourself.

- Can standards that usually happen at different times in the curriculum be clustered to facilitate a more in-depth study?
- Which standards require more direct application for the content to cement itself into understanding, and how might we combine that with ways of knowing to be the glue of a project?
- How can we make content standards work for us and our students, instead of the other way around?

Our students are brilliant. Our students have experience and wisdom that can make our classrooms and communities bastions of harmony and possibility. It is our greatest privilege to inquire of and learn from them, then see what grows when we fully elevate their ways of knowing.

Advocate for Cultural Standards

There is a graduation from being culturally responsive—acknowledging and incorporating students' cultures, languages, and experiences into teaching—to truly championing ways of knowing inside the classroom and with a wider scope. Primarily, the difference is the persistent advocacy for cultural standards being held in equal regard to content standards, with this advocacy driving instruction. The Alaska Department of Education and Early Development (n.d.) frames it in the following way:

> Cultural standards serve as a complement to content standards. Content standards stipulate what students should know and be able to do, cultural standards provide guidance on how to engage students in learning through the local culture. We recognize all forms of knowledge, ways of knowing, and world views as equally valid, adaptable, and complementary to one another in mutually beneficial ways.

We use the word *advocate* because, regardless of what we believe about the role of standards and standardized testing in our profession, students receive the message time and again that if it isn't on the test, it's not important. Important to whom and for what purpose can sometimes be vague, but what comes through loud and clear is that cultural knowledge, if included at all, is tertiary to the content standards and even to learning how to "do school" (that is, conform to the dominant culture). By advocating, we use our roles as teachers and leaders, with a sense of urgency, to serve our students in a culturally robust environment, to leverage students' ways of knowing and allow these ways to take root. Talking with Instruction Partners, a nonprofit focused on educational equity, Muhammad states, "The need to agitate for criticality historically spoke to the social unrest at the time, and I argue that the need to agitate is still necessary and pressing in classrooms today" (as cited in Freitag & Knight-Justice, 2020). We agree, and it falls to the teacher not only to advocate and agitate for students' ways of knowing, but also to recognize that it is always relevant to do so. It is also relevant to insulate students from the pressures of standards coverage, and to nurture the cultural wisdom that will serve them, and our societies, long beyond the waves of high-stakes tests. A particular example of how teachers can advocate in this way that we noted previously comes from that high school in the Pacific Northwest that serves a large percentage of Native American students and is supportive of students participating in a canoe journey (page 27). While the school is supportive of students' participation, that backing does not fully extend to the larger educational system, and the teachers have spent years in dialogue with the state department of education, using their course accreditation process, trying to help students earn credit for the rigorous undertaking of preparing for and participating in the journey. When Erin was working with this school, teachers in four disciplines designed and submitted syllabi, performance tasks and assessment tools, and student work samples to demonstrate the value of the canoe journey to students and to the community. While their success in gaining official recognition of the educational value of the canoe journey was limited, they did succeed in gaining the ability to offer an elective credit for it.

BATON ROUGE'S TROUBLED WATERS
Elevate Ways of Knowing, in Action

Students conducted research using primary and secondary sources regarding the segregationist laws and practices regarding Black people's access to parks, pools, restaurants, and hotels in their city. Students utilized English language arts, social studies, justice, and critical thinking skills by exploring the essential question: How can we plan a public swimming pool that will honor the people and culture in our community? Students worked in teams to co-create guidelines for the community members they identified for the project. Once students identified community members who were willing to participate, they interviewed the community members to learn the stories of public pools that had been passed down by elders in their communities since the 1940s. Through visits with local historians, structured viewings of the documentary *Baton Rouge's Troubled Waters* (2008), and using local town hall meetings as mentor text opportunities, students explored cultural traditions around swimming in the Black community. Guided explorations, direct instruction, and discussions of various works of art and poetry supported students in learning about storytelling and how it is used as a way of passing down knowledge over generations. Along the way, students explored stereotypes and how they harm people and how these stereotypes show up in their school and community. Then, they made a plan on how to actively debunk those stereotypes. One student remarked in a reflection session, "This project really opened my eyes to why things are the way they are in my city, based on the history we explored right here in town and compared to the nation. It made more sense to me this way" (Student, personal communication, April 2015). Questioning techniques and student-led discussion protocols were used to help students actively build critical thinking skills. Using this knowledge, students leveraged these learning experiences to inform the crafting of their team's call to action.

Conclusion

Every student who enters a classroom comes with experiences, insights, and ideas. They come with hope for connections, for a chance to feel pride, to be valued. Every student wants to be seen. In this chapter, we articulated what it means to teach by elevating students' ways of knowing and bringing them to the forefront of planning and instruction. We went on a neighborhood walk to tap into students' assets, we gained an understanding of what it looks like to combine culture and content, and we heard about people advocating for making ways of knowing prominent across the educational sphere. We gained a window into several specific strategies to take back to your own classroom. We saw our new learning reflected in Baton Rouge's Troubled Waters project, and now, after you reflect, carry this momentum into the next six design principles to plan your own place-based learning journey.

Key Takeaways and Reflection Questions

Consider this chapter's key takeaways and reflect on the following questions as you work to elevate ways of knowing through place-based learning. Use the Journey Log to further reflect, brainstorm, jot down ideas, make observations, or plan.

- ◆ Cultural ways of knowing need to be recognized, validated, and valued. Learning about and incorporating cultural standards is a great place to start.
- ◆ Cultural ways of knowing are just as, if not more, valuable to students traditional academic content, both as young learners and as they become adults who are well grounded in their cultural identity.
- ◆ Cultural ways of knowing require that we build relationships with our students by learning with and from them, share power in the classroom, and let them lead.
- ◆ Cultural ways of knowing encompass the community and give an imperative to connect to the community as a resource.

- ◆ How do I currently learn from and about my students? What might I do to make this facet of my teaching even stronger?
- ◆ In what ways could I show vulnerability, admit privilege, and share power with my students?
- ◆ What does "sharing the classroom" look like for me this year? In three years?
- ◆ How can I teach and assess national and state standards while still honoring different ways of knowing?

Journey Log

Journey Log

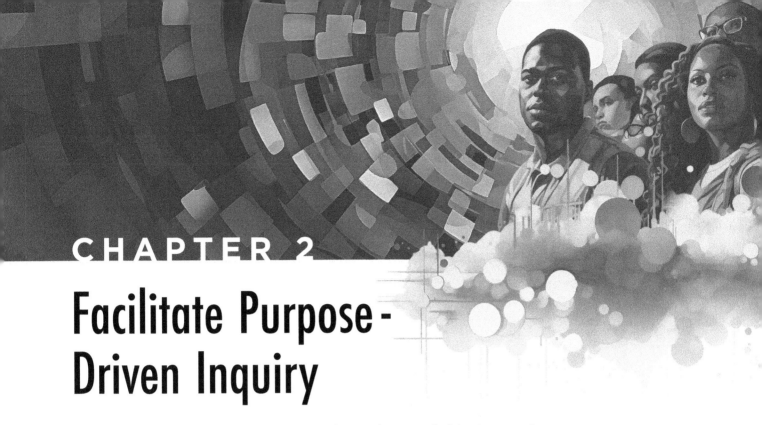

CHAPTER 2

Facilitate Purpose-Driven Inquiry

Give the pupils something to do, not something to learn; and if the doing is of such a nature as to demand thinking; learning naturally results.

—JOHN DEWEY

ESSENTIAL QUESTION: How do I facilitate purpose-driven inquiry to allow students to uncover knowledge, skills, processes, information, and perspectives?

The Sweet Science of Maple Syrup Harvesting: Integrating Native American Traditions in Kentucky project is a unique educational experience for high school students that combines Indigenous ways of knowing, mathematics, and practical skills. The project focuses on the process of maple syrup harvesting, with an emphasis on incorporating the traditions and practices of Native American communities in eastern Kentucky. Throughout the project, students research traditional practices of maple syrup harvesting among Native American communities and learn how they were integrated into the surrounding environment and ecology. They also calculate the surface area and volume of the maple trees and harvest the trees for lumber, using the wood to construct the necessary equipment for syrup production such as taps, buckets, and evaporators. Students document the process of collecting sap and creating maple syrup, and reflect on the interconnectedness of the environment, mathematics, and practical skills, as well as the role that Native American communities have played in the history of maple syrup harvesting in Kentucky. This project provides students with a hands-on learning experience that emphasizes the cultural significance of maple syrup harvesting and the importance of incorporating sustainable practices into the process. It is a great opportunity for students to gain a deeper understanding of the natural world, cultural awareness, and the interconnectivity of subjects.

The purpose of the exploration in this place-based learning experience was to provide high school students with a hands-on, Kentucky-centric learning experience that integrates Indigenous ways of knowing, mathematics (surface area and volume of trees), and practical skills (lumbering) into the process of maple syrup harvesting. The project has a cultural focus, emphasizing the traditions and practices of Native American communities in Kentucky and the importance of incorporating sustainable practices into the process to educate students on the interconnectivity of the environment, mathematics, and practical skills, and to provide a deeper understanding of the cultural significance of maple syrup harvesting, as well as the natural world and cultural awareness. The project seamlessly intertwines cultural appreciation, environmental sustainability, and practical education. By focusing on the traditions and practices of Native American communities in Kentucky, it not only imparts knowledge about cultural heritage but also emphasizes the vital connection between the environment, mathematics, and practical skills. The incorporation of sustainable practices in maple syrup harvesting serves as a tangible example of how education can promote ecological consciousness. Throughout this chapter, readers will gain insights into the intricate design of purpose-driven inquiry in projects, such as the maple syrup harvesting project, learning to facilitate initiatives that not only educate but also foster a deeper understanding of cultural significance, environmental interconnectivity, and practical skills integration.

In this chapter, we define purpose-driven inquiry, explore specific tools and strategies that lead to purpose-driven inquiry, and then dig in to how to build purpose-driven inquiry into projects with intention. We consider "Purpose-Driven Inquiry, in Action" through the lens of Baton Rouge's Troubled Waters project. The chapter also offers a chance to think further about its content through the Conclusion and Key Takeaways and Reflection Questions sections. It concludes with the Journey Log for writing down your thoughts and ideas.

What Is Purpose-Driven Inquiry?

"Why are we learning this, Miss?"

"Sir, what does this have to do with anything I'm going through right now?"

"How am I supposed to know?"

These are questions that students have posed, in our classrooms, in various ways. You certainly have heard these kinds of questions yourself in the course of teaching. However, when using purpose-driven inquiry, these questions are easy to answer, or may never come up at all, because the relevance of what they are learning will be obvious to students throughout the process.

Purpose-driven inquiry is an educational approach that centers on a clear and meaningful objective, aligning learning experiences with a specific purpose or goal to cultivate a deeper understanding, spark critical thinking, and promote engagement among participants. Purpose-driven inquiry is one of the biggest shifts place-based learning asks educators to make in their teaching practice. It shifts the focus from covering content to uncovering knowledge, skills, processes, information, and perspectives. For teachers, purpose-driven inquiry can be a shift in when and how they facilitate learning. They must no longer marry themselves to a strict sequence of lessons. Instruction consists of presenting a question or challenge and then providing the "just-in-time" resources along the learning path. With purpose-driven inquiry, teachers do not begin a learning experience with the traditional sage-on-a-stage lectures and direct instruction.

For example, a high school history teacher in a southern Louisiana town, where there are several oil refineries and factories located in spaces formerly occupied by plantations, might pose this provocative question to students: "If toxic air is a monument to slavery, how do we take it down?" Instead of racing directly into instruction that would ordinarily consist of lectures and reading textbook excerpts, teachers can guide students on a field trip of a local plantation, exposing students to systems associated with chattel slavery. Then, using this place-based exploration, students track the evolution of plantations becoming oil refineries and plants, analyzing historical accounts and maps. Students take on the role of fenceline community activists as they show legislators, community members, and business owners specific ways that each group can combat by-products of colonialism and slavery. The teacher's role here is to offer resources such as simulations for students to explore and gather information.

Teachers do not tell students what and how to think—rather, we facilitate learning in a way that fosters students' discovery of key concepts through purposeful explorations and research. We design this purpose-driven inquiry by anticipating students' needs and questions along the learning journey and inserting resources as necessary. Direct instruction, small-group work, and learning stations still remain relevant in this model of place-based learning; the only difference is that they are all invigorated by the purpose of the challenge or question at hand.

Purpose-driven inquiry is student driven. For the student, purpose-driven inquiry goes beyond research alone and includes interviewing, consulting experts, conducting surveys, undertaking field studies, and collecting data, all while building the necessary knowledge along the way. Proponents of project-based learning argue that it fosters a sense of purpose in young learners, pushes them to think critically, and prepares them for modern careers that prize skills like collaboration, problem solving, and creativity (Terada, 2021). This allows for creativity to be linked to wisdom, distinguishing between ideas and innovations that will have positive social, ecological, and political effects and those that won't (Pisters, Vihinen, Figueiredo, & Wals, 2023). No longer are we simply following a set of arbitrary and often invariant lessons; with purpose-driven inquiry, we utilize place-based project design to mold these lessons into key components of purposeful learning. Specific learning tasks and activities are selected to support and scaffold student-centered learning. All of the traditionally set lessons are now reimagined and made purposeful as the "doing" to which John Dewey refers in the epigraph at the beginning of this chapter. Consider the following tools that you may use to achieve purpose-driven inquiry within your place-based project.

- **Tasks and challenges:** Tasks and challenges serve as strategic catalysts in purpose-driven inquiry, propelling participants to actively engage with the educational process, fostering problem-solving skills, and promoting a holistic understanding of the overarching purpose.

- **Socratic discussions:** Socratic discussions function as a strategic tool in purpose-driven inquiry by fostering critical thinking, encouraging collaborative exploration of ideas, and promoting a deeper understanding of the project's objectives through thoughtful dialogue and inquiry.

- **Writings:** Writings function as a strategic tool in purpose-driven inquiry by providing a reflective platform for participants to articulate, refine, and communicate their understanding of the project's goals, contributing to a deeper integration of knowledge and fostering a sense of purpose-driven engagement.

- **Homework:** Homework acts as a strategic tool in purpose-driven inquiry by extending learning beyond the classroom, allowing participants to delve deeper into the project's subject matter, reinforcing key concepts, and fostering independent exploration to enhance overall comprehension and engagement.

- **Targeted workshops:** Targeted workshops operate as a strategic tool in purpose-driven inquiry, providing focused and hands-on learning experiences tailored to the project's objectives, ensuring participants acquire practical skills and knowledge directly aligned with the overarching purpose.

- **Interactive notebook entries:** Interactive notebook entries function as a strategic tool in purpose-driven inquiry by providing a dynamic platform for students to document their evolving thoughts, reflections, and insights, facilitating a personalized and tangible record of the learning journey aligned with the project's overarching goals.

- **Feedback protocols:** Feedback protocols operate as a strategic tool in purpose-driven inquiry, providing a structured mechanism for constructive critique, reflection, and refinement, thereby enhancing the overall quality and effectiveness of the educational experience.

- **Explorations:** Explorations function as a strategic tool in purpose-driven inquiry, providing learners with hands-on experiences that deepen their understanding of the project's objectives, fostering curiosity, and promoting a practical connection between theoretical concepts and real-world applications.

- **Quizzes:** Quizzes serve as a strategic tool in purpose-driven inquiry by providing formative assessments that gauge participants' comprehension, reinforce key concepts, and guide the iterative learning process toward achieving the overarching educational goals.

- **Field experiences:** Field experiences function as a strategic tool in purpose-driven inquiry, providing participants with real-world immersion, hands-on learning opportunities, and a context-rich environment that enhances their understanding and connection to the project's overarching purpose.

- **Direct instruction:** Direct instruction serves as a strategic tool in purpose-driven inquiry, providing targeted and structured guidance to participants, ensuring they acquire foundational knowledge and skills essential for achieving the project's overarching purpose.

- **Labs and experiments:** Labs and experiments function as a strategic tool in purpose-driven inquiry by providing hands-on, experiential learning opportunities that not only reinforce theoretical concepts but also cultivate a practical understanding of the project's purpose, fostering a dynamic and engaging educational experience.

- **Gallery walks:** Gallery walks operate as a strategic tool in purpose-driven inquiry, allowing participants to visually explore and discuss diverse perspectives, artifacts, and information, fostering a multidimensional understanding of the project's purpose through interactive and immersive engagement.

- **Readings:** Readings act as a strategic tool in purpose-driven inquiry, providing a foundation for knowledge acquisition, stimulating thoughtful reflection, and enabling participants to contextualize their understanding within the broader framework of the project's purpose.

- **Guest speakers:** Guest speakers act as a strategic tool in purpose-driven inquiry, enriching the learning experience by providing real-world perspectives, expertise, and diverse insights that not only align with the project's purpose but also inspire and broaden participants' understanding of the subject matter.

In "What the Heck Is Inquiry-Based Learning?" Heather Walport-Gawron (2016) affirms, "Inquiry-based learning is more than asking a student what he or she wants to know. It's about triggering curiosity. And activating a student's curiosity is . . . a far more important and complex goal than mere information delivery." Purpose-driven inquiry reboots the use of district-mandated curricula; each lesson becomes a key link in a chain of explorations and discoveries, all steeped in curiosity. Students build the skills necessary to achieve a purpose-driven goal: to answer their essential question, which we discuss in the next section.

How Do I Build Purpose-Driven Inquiry Into My Project?

Begin with the end in mind. What do we want students to know as a result of the *doing*? First and foremost, a strong essential question will harness students' inquiry. The essential question helps connect purpose to place and contains specific parameters while also allowing for exploration. Used as an anchor, the essential question can also help us anticipate students' questions. We can then plan for the questions overtly to facilitate and guide the student-centered inquiry. For example, teachers at an elementary school in Baton Rouge, Louisiana, were guided on a tour of Whitney Plantation, their authentic community partner (authentic community partners are discussed at depth in chapter 3, page 49). In this case, the project was anchored in a specific need that the plantation had, so they partnered with the elementary school to achieve the goal. Whitney Plantation needed signage that was child-friendly, and the students were working on informing their community about Whitney Plantation's role in Louisiana heritage, which made for a perfect fit! After the guided tour, teachers then decided that the elementary school students would contribute to an upcoming celebration on site at Whitney Plantation by providing information and an explanation of cultural elements from African and Indigenous people that have contributed to Louisiana's heritage. The purpose of this exploration was for students to experience the place of Whitney Plantation and connect their informative and explanatory writing lessons to contribute to and inform their community.

As a critical piece in crafting their strong essential question, teachers in the elementary school Whitney Plantation project examined the doing they pictured as part of the students' learning experience. They envisioned students gathering artifacts from the plantation tour, interviewing tour guides, surveying other tour participants on their understanding of Louisiana heritage, surveying their family, and leveraging all their research and in-class readings and discussions. With all this inquiry in mind, teachers landed on the project's essential question: "What can we create to educate and inform Whitney Plantation visitors about the ways African and Indigenous people have impacted Louisiana heritage?"

This essential question is strong because it is connected to a specific place, leaving space for students to inquire but also setting parameters for their exploration by focusing on a very specific target. The essential question serves as an anchor in purpose-driven inquiry by providing a foundational focus that guides the exploration of a specific topic. It acts as a central point of reference, allowing teachers to anticipate further questions that naturally arise during the inquiry process. As educators and students delve into the essential question, they often uncover supplementary inquiries that contribute to a more comprehensive understanding of the overarching purpose, creating a dynamic and interconnected framework for learning. The question is revisited daily, and students can connect each day's learning to the purpose as set forth by the essential question.

In addition to crafting a strong essential question, teachers may take the following actions to facilitate purpose-driven inquiry for students.

- **Plan for just-in-time instruction:** In the planning process, the *just-in-time* component involves anticipating students' questions about key context and content, allowing teachers to preemptively identify potential areas of confusion or interest.

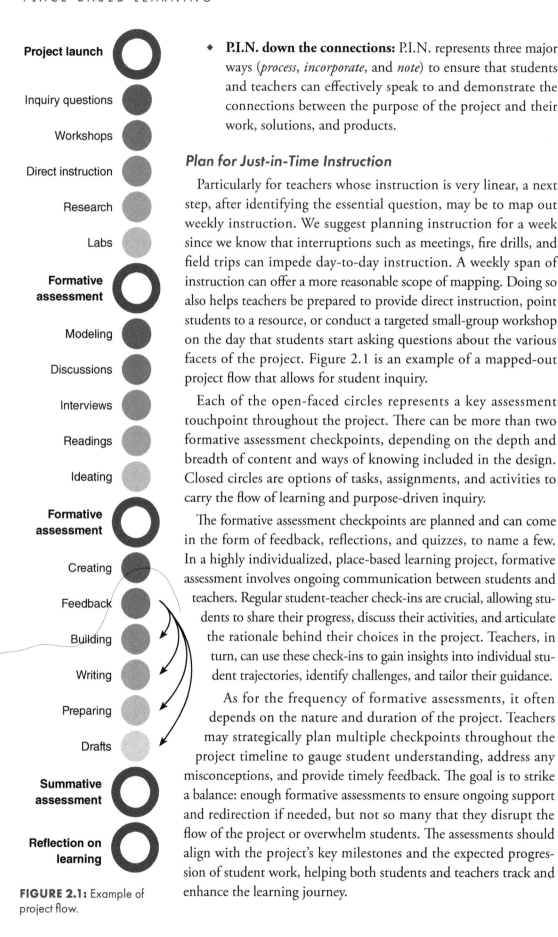

FIGURE 2.1: Example of project flow.

♦ **P.I.N. down the connections:** P.I.N. represents three major ways (*process, incorporate,* and *note*) to ensure that students and teachers can effectively speak to and demonstrate the connections between the purpose of the project and their work, solutions, and products.

Plan for Just-in-Time Instruction

Particularly for teachers whose instruction is very linear, a next step, after identifying the essential question, may be to map out weekly instruction. We suggest planning instruction for a week since we know that interruptions such as meetings, fire drills, and field trips can impede day-to-day instruction. A weekly span of instruction can offer a more reasonable scope of mapping. Doing so also helps teachers be prepared to provide direct instruction, point students to a resource, or conduct a targeted small-group workshop on the day that students start asking questions about the various facets of the project. Figure 2.1 is an example of a mapped-out project flow that allows for student inquiry.

Each of the open-faced circles represents a key assessment touchpoint throughout the project. There can be more than two formative assessment checkpoints, depending on the depth and breadth of content and ways of knowing included in the design. Closed circles are options of tasks, assignments, and activities to carry the flow of learning and purpose-driven inquiry.

The formative assessment checkpoints are planned and can come in the form of feedback, reflections, and quizzes, to name a few. In a highly individualized, place-based learning project, formative assessment involves ongoing communication between students and teachers. Regular student-teacher check-ins are crucial, allowing students to share their progress, discuss their activities, and articulate the rationale behind their choices in the project. Teachers, in turn, can use these check-ins to gain insights into individual student trajectories, identify challenges, and tailor their guidance.

As for the frequency of formative assessments, it often depends on the nature and duration of the project. Teachers may strategically plan multiple checkpoints throughout the project timeline to gauge student understanding, address any misconceptions, and provide timely feedback. The goal is to strike a balance: enough formative assessments to ensure ongoing support and redirection if needed, but not so many that they disrupt the flow of the project or overwhelm students. The assessments should align with the project's key milestones and the expected progression of student work, helping both students and teachers track and enhance the learning journey.

By deliberately including feedback, revision, and reflection within the project's design, we can build in formative assessments in a targeted and intentional fashion, allowing us to let students' curiosity roam freely within the framework of the intended marks along the way. The teacher would view this as an assessment moment while the student would not necessarily know these moments were considered formative assessments, so as not to inhibit them. These checks help us to monitor instruction's efficacy and differentiate accordingly. Most importantly, we can plan to empower students to also track their progress. One way this can take place begins when we introduce the essential question. As we gather and revisit students' inquiry questions (questions that students generate in response to the essential question), we can overtly model this tracking as well. During the project launch, students examine the essential question and respond by generating a list of questions that they need to have answered to achieve the task or challenge at hand. This can occur in myriad ways, using a variety of strategies to guide students through the process of forming questions. These strategies aim to cultivate a dynamic environment where students feel empowered to ask questions, and they promote curiosity, critical thinking, and active engagement in the learning process.

- **Question stems:** Provide students with a set of question stems or starters that prompt critical thinking, such as "How might . . .?", "What if. . .?", or "Why do you think. . .?" These prompts can guide students in formulating inquiries.

- **Think-pair-share:** Encourage students to think individually about a topic, then pair up with a classmate to discuss and refine their questions before sharing with the larger group. This collaborative process fosters idea exchange and the development of thoughtful questions.

- **Question formulation technique (QFT):** The QFT guides students in formulating questions by presenting a provocative prompt, distinguishing between closed and open-ended inquiries, and encouraging the prioritization and refinement of compelling questions, fostering metacognition and inquiry skills.

- **See-think-wonder:** This strategy prompts students to observe (see), interpret (think), and generate questions (wonder) based on visual stimuli or project-related information, promoting critical thinking and curiosity during the project launch.

Once students generate the questions, they can post questions in a whole-group display that they can revisit frequently over the course of the project pathway. Students take ownership of adding questions as they arise, and marking questions that are answered along the way.

As you refine your design, focus formative assessment checkpoints around the knowledge, skills, processes, information, and ways of knowing you intend students to uncover throughout their work. Use these formative assessment checkpoints as the indicators or "I can" statements that students use to reflect on their own learning throughout the course of the project. Having students keep their reflections in one spot (be it in their notebooks, an online data tracker, or a learning log where all project resources are stored) allows them the ability to keep track of how their learning evolves over the course of the project, taking inventory of how they grow and change as they work to answer the essential question.

In another project anchored in Whitney Plantation, a team of students worked with the plantation's social media team to expand the reach, influence, and inclusivity of the information that the plantation has to offer. Figure 2.2 (page 40) illustrates how the project launches with students

Project launch

See-think-wonder

Inquiry questions

Direct instruction

Research

Labs

Quiz on informative writing

Revisiting inquiry questions

Discussions

Interviews

Readings

Ideating

Peer feedback session on products using rubric

Creating

Feedback

Building

Writing

Preparing

Drafts

Unit exam

Product presentation and reflection on learning

FIGURE 2.2: Instructional flow of social media project example.

performing a social media self-assessment. They begin their self-assessment by locating their most viewed and favorite social media profiles and describing the characteristics that make those profiles more engaging, informative, and purposeful. From there, students collaborate as a class to determine a set of criteria that will help guide their work as consultants for the plantation's social media team. The students' challenge is to overhaul the plantation's social media to become more informative and inclusive for visitors of their age group. Each visit they make to the plantation becomes more meaningful, as the students learn about the goals of the plantation's tours and resources, and they think about how to convey the plantation's message to their peers in an informative and intriguing way. Formative assessment along the way consists of checkpoints, quizzes, journal entries, product plans, and social media recommendations that are essential to achieving the goal of the project.

P.I.N. Down the Connections

In a nutshell, to facilitate purpose-driven inquiry, we must pin down the connections daily. For this strategy, that pin is made specific through *P.I.N.*, an acronym that represents three major ways (*process*, *incorporate*, and *note*) to ensure that students and teachers can effectively speak to and demonstrate the connections between the purpose of the project and their work, solutions, and products. Allow this tool to become a pillar of your classroom culture and place-based project design.

P—Process each day's work. For teachers, this means facilitating a conversation or an exit ticket that gets students to call out the process they've undergone that day. For students, processing might be responding to a journal prompt or submitting an exit ticket.

Students overhauling the plantation's social media (page 39) might respond daily on their school or class social media accounts by posting a mini-vlog or going live to process how the day's explorations are adding to their investigations. Students might also explicitly connect historical context and narratives to the posts they recommend to the plantation's social media team by locating specific artifacts on the plantation or on social media sites that accentuate the ideas on which students choose to focus. Students can also pause daily to reflect on their own contributions to their teams, using collaboration tools such as scrum boards to check in on tasks and processes. Students might reflect on the following questions.

◆ *What* did we do today?

◆ *How* did we do that today?

I—Incorporate the day's work into the larger picture. Teachers plan for specific procedures and structures for students to use and show how the day's learning supports the larger purpose of the project. Every day in the place-based project addressing toxic air (page 34), teachers allocated a moment of time to encourage students to articulate how they would use the day's work in their final product. In your project, to incorporate the day's work into the larger picture, students might reflect on the following questions.

- *Why* did we do what we did today?
- *How* does it connect to the product we are creating?

N—Note any connections. Revisit the essential question, the inquiry questions, and the work that students have completed so far. Mark questions that have been answered and any new questions that evolve. Inquiry questions might be kept in students' notebooks, on a whole-class chart (virtually in shared docs or on anchor posters in the room), or in any centralized location where students know their project resources are organized. Students might reflect on the following questions.

- *How* does what we did today help me answer the essential question?
- *Do* I have any new inquiry questions?

The elementary students working with the Whitney Plantation project (page 39) benefited greatly from revisiting their initial inquiry questions on a daily basis. Students reflected each day individually, as teams, and as a whole class, crossing off inquiry questions they addressed and noting new inquiry questions that may have bubbled up in the day's investigations. Not only did this solidify the day-to-day learning for students, but it also served as a formative assessment tool for teachers. As students progressed in their learning journey, there was a gradual increase in the types of questions related more to the informative writing content and historical aspects. The complexity of questions that students posed regarding content and project process became greater in terms of depth of knowledge as the project path unfolded. Students began to think about their target audiences and the types of questions that audience might have when visiting the plantation's exhibits. Instead of asking lower-level questions, such as how long the presentation will be or what should be collected for a grade, students' questions began to reflect deeper levels of thinking about the project process and content as the project pathway unfolded. Technical aspects of the writing and informative pieces became the focus of their questions as the project progressed, as opposed to the questions they asked at the onset of the project, which were more aimed at the logistics of teamwork and determining the why of the project. See figure 2.3 (page 42) for a visual representation of how a project, and students' depth of thinking, progresses.

Pinning down the purpose in place-based learning is necessary to ensure that the doing is not in vain. Daily P.I.N.s can fold into the formative assessment checkpoints we've planned out for the entire project. The more students are allowed to make these connections, the deeper they can understand the project's *purpose*. Trusting that students will *get there* and then being ready to guide them is what moves place-based teachers from presenters to facilitators, and students from receivers to creators and innovators. See figure 2.4 (page 42) for a graphic representation of how P.I.N. can work.

| Beginning of Project | Gradual increase of question complexity | Project Culmination |

	Basic Introductory Questions	More Complex Questions	Evaluative and Reflective Questions
Questions about PRODUCT	What is my product going to be? How many points will it be worth?	How do I know I'm creating the best product? How can I incorporate feedback?	How can I ensure my audience understands my product?
Questions about PROCESS	Will I be working with a team?	How is my team functioning? Do we work well together? How do we overcome any issues? Who are my community members? How do I know what to do?	What are the strengths and weaknesses of my approach? How did my approach change or grow over the course of the project?
Questions about CONTENT	What is this team? What is this about?	What does this term mean? How can I use the term in real life? What are some examples of how this has been done in the past?	How does this topic, content, or concept compare to other, similar concepts?

FIGURE 2.3: How inquiry questions evolve along the project pathway.

	Process	Incorporate	Note
Teacher Action Example	• Facilitate a conversation or an exit ticket.	• Plan for specific procedures and structures for students to use. • Show how the day's learning supports the larger purpose of the project.	• Revisit the essential question, the inquiry questions, and the work that students have completed so far.
Student Action Example	• Respond to a journal prompt or submit an exit ticket.	• Articulate how to use the day's work toward the production of the final product.	• Mark questions that have been answered and any new questions that evolve.
Reflection Questions	• What did we do today? • How did we do that today?	• Why did we do what we did today?	• How does what we did today help me answer the essential question? • Do I have any new inquiry questions?

FIGURE 2.4: The daily P.I.N. method.

The P.I.N. down the connections strategy emphasizes the daily process of facilitating purpose-driven inquiry through three key steps: process, incorporate, and note. This strategy encourages teachers to guide students in reflecting on their daily work, connecting it to the larger project purpose, and noting any new insights or questions that arise. By consistently implementing P.I.N. throughout a place-based project, students deepen their understanding of the project's purpose and progress from receivers to creators and innovators in their learning journey.

BATON ROUGE'S TROUBLED WATERS
Facilitate Purpose-Driven Inquiry, in Action

Purpose-driven inquiry begins with an *essential question*. In this project, part of the teacher's initial planning process centered on generating an essential question. To do so, the teacher took a survey of the intended content, context, and available resources.

- **Intended content:** This includes the impact of policy on local history, how local policy impacts communities and reverberates across time, and primary and secondary resources.

- **Context:** Baton Rouge has a wealth of historical connections to Jim Crow laws and policies historically regulating swimming pools in the area, which pertains to the mostly Black students, who deal with stigmas and preconceived notions of Black people and swimming abilities.

- **Resources:** The school has an immense network of alumni and elders in the community. These resources include an art exhibit dedicated to the local swimming pools protest and a Black landscape architecture student who is also a local swim club alumnus and avid swimmer.

Based on this, the teacher developed the essential question to generate a sense of wondering about the topic of Black swimming pools, reclaiming public spaces, advocating to impact local policy, and landscape architecture. In this case, the essential question became, How can we plan a public swimming pool that will honor the people and culture in our community?

When designing and developing the project, the teacher divided instruction into core conceptual and procedural sections.

- Swimming (self, community, historical context in community)
- Documentary viewing and exploring landscape architecture
- Local policy and our elders
- Finalization of community products
- Presentations of community products in an audience-appropriate delivery method

The roll-out of the project and essential question, and the gathering of students' input, involved students viewing a series of videos, social media posts, and images that played on the notion that Black people do not or cannot swim, as well as counterexamples showing Black people excelling at swimming in various contexts. While viewing, students gathered observations using a see-think-wonder notetaker to gather their initial thoughts. Then, after individually reviewing the project information sheet, randomized student teams worked together to determine what their top questions were that they needed answered to start the task.

Within each of these mileposts, there occurred strategically designed cycles of instruction that followed a distinct path for each section, using repetitive structures within each section. For example, in the "local policy and our elders" section, students experienced the process of surveying their community for locals (both elders and their contemporaries) who were involved in Black swim clubs or in landscape architecture in their area both currently and in the past. Once students located these individuals, they generated a list of questions using the question formulation technique (page 39), to determine the types of questions they could ask the individuals to help students understand more about the local community, local policies historically, and how the two ideas converge to help them formulate how they will answer the essential question.

This same cycle of exploration, inquiry, and research, including instructional strategies such as mini-work sessions, self-paced online learning modules, gallery walks, and feedback protocols, was also built into each of the milepost segments. Students conducted research using primary and secondary resources, created and administered surveys, and analyzed the results to inform next steps. They analyzed the elements of civics and local policymaking processes first by using top hat graphic organizers to compare and contrast the information collected in readings. A *top hat graphic organizer* is a visual tool that divides a top hat shape into two sections, each representing one of the compared elements. This organizer helps students analyze and synthesize information, fostering comprehension by encouraging them to identify similarities and differences between two subjects.

Before they interviewed landscape architecture experts and elders in the community, the students explored StoryCorps' (n.d.) list of "great questions" as a mentor text to come up with a list of what makes a great question. From this list, students determined which types of questions they wanted to pose to their community experts and elders to be sure to elicit the types of information they would need to support crafting their community products.

Conclusion

This chapter on purpose-driven inquiry illuminates the transformative potential inherent in educational approaches that prioritize intentionality, engagement, and depth of understanding. From the strategic incorporation of cultural focus and sustainable practices to the implementation of effective questioning strategies, we have explored the multifaceted elements that contribute to purpose-driven projects. Emphasizing the fusion of content, context, and dynamic instructional strategies, this chapter serves as a guide for educators seeking to cultivate meaningful learning experiences. By anchoring instruction in essential questions, adapting to just-in-time instructional needs, and leveraging diverse strategies like Socratic discussions and guest speakers, educators can empower students to become active participants in their own learning journey. As we delve into the subsequent chapters, the principles outlined here will continue to serve as a foundation, fostering an educational environment where purpose-driven inquiry not only is encouraged but also becomes a driving force for deep, lasting learning experiences.

Key Takeaways and Reflection Questions

Consider this chapter's key takeaways and reflect on the following questions as you work to facilitate purpose-driven inquiry through place-based learning. Use the Journey Log to further reflect, brainstorm, jot down ideas, make observations, or plan.

- The first step to facilitating purpose-driven inquiry is crafting an effective essential question.
- Next, map out the project pathway, designing purposeful inquiry that sparks curiosity along the way.
- P.I.N. down purpose daily.
- Purpose-driven inquiry is essential to creating transformative learning experiences that prioritize intentionality, engagement, and depth of understanding.

- What changes can I make to my planning tools to allow for inquiry?
- How will students use the essential question throughout the project to keep the purpose at the forefront?
- How will students and community partners inquire together?
- How can we effectively incorporate diverse instructional strategies, such as Socratic discussions and guest speakers, to empower students to become active participants in their own learning journey within purpose-driven projects?

Journey Log

Journey Log

Journey Log

CHAPTER 3

Build Authentic Community Partnerships

*If you want to be a true professional, you will do something outside of yourself.
Something to repair tears in your community. Something to make life a little
better for people less fortunate than you. That's what I think a meaningful
life is—living not for yourself, but for one's community.*

—RUTH BADER GINSBURG

ESSENTIAL QUESTION: How do we engage students and partners in an authentic
relationship for the betterment of the community?

One of the most powerful aspects of place-based learning is establishing authentic community partnerships. The Place-Based Education Evaluation Collaboration (2010), which has done extensive
research on the benefits of place-based education, concludes the following:

> The findings are clear: place-based education fosters students' connection to place and cre-
> ates vibrant partnerships between schools and communities. It boosts student achievement and
> improves environmental, social, and economic vitality. In short, place-based education helps stu-
> dents learn to take care of the world by understanding where they live and taking action in their
> own backyards and communities. (p. 2)

Authentic community partnerships empower learners and provide them with the efficacy and
belief that they can transform place for the betterment of the community. Authentic community
partnerships create the conditions for students to expand their horizons. By experiencing different
workplace contexts, be it a business, nonprofit organization, museum, city government, state park,
wildlife sanctuary, or research lab, students can visualize what opportunities might lie ahead of
them. Community partnerships provide pathways to careers students may have never envisioned
for themselves. Having partners who look like the students you serve is often particularly important as it helps students see themselves in different roles, expanding opportunities for their futures.

Emeritus professors of education Gregory Alan Smith and David Sobel (2010), both of whom have contributed immensely to the field of place-based learning, provide a commonly accepted definition of place-based learning. They affirm that place-based learning is "learning rooted in what is local" and that "the community provides the context for learning, student work focuses on community needs and interests, and community members serve as resources and partners in every aspect of teaching and learning" (Smith & Sobel, 2010, p. 23). This definition emphasizes place and the power that results when leveraging authentic community partnerships to uncover the assets and challenges within a place. Place-based learning is about community partnerships in which students learn, collaborate, problem solve, take action, and receive feedback from experts, mentors, elders, and organizations within their community or region.

This chapter outlines strategies for identifying potential partners and experts, for uncovering the stories of the community, and for working together and nurturing each other in the process. It then considers the process of building authentic community partnerships through the lens of Baton Rouge's Troubled Waters project. The chapter offers a chance to think further about its content through the Conclusion and Key Takeaways and Reflection Questions sections. It concludes with the Journey Log for writing down your thoughts and ideas.

What Is an Authentic Community Partnership?

Authentic community partnerships uncover the assets and challenges within a place and foster positive individual and collective changes.

Typically, community involvement in schools happens in the form of field trips or a guest speaker, where someone imparts knowledge to students. This approach unfortunately misses the greater context of what students are learning, and students often have little involvement beyond listening quietly or filling out a worksheet while on their field trip to the local museum. Authentic community partnerships are grown out of a combination of the following.

- Cultivating a relationship between a community member, organization, business, or another partner and a school, teacher, team of teachers, and students
- Aligning learning outcomes (what do we want students to know and be able to do?) with the partner or organization's needs
- Students asking, "What do I need to know to answer the essential question, and who can help me?"

The Highline School District outside of Seattle provides one example of a successful authentic community partnership. Highline students work with biologists from the local aquarium to conduct an annual beach survey. In describing this project, teacher Joe Weiss (2016) writes that students:

> gain valuable experience in intertidal ecology, invertebrate taxonomy and survey methodology. Student work needs to meet accepted scientific protocols. This high standard of data collection is especially satisfying for the students since local scientific organizations will use their work to monitor changes in the relative abundance of flora and fauna.

Partnerships like these can happen at the beginning of a project or throughout the project, driven by teachers, students, and community members. Students can identify partners as part of the inquiry process; partners can be long-standing or identified by teachers during project planning. Because of technology, community partners can be local or across the globe. Global partnerships might occur with organizations working on similar issues in different places, or perhaps students connect with other schools regionally, nationally, or globally working on a similar project. Students may be exploring a global issue but looking at it through the lens of their local context. Jennifer D. Klein, in her 2017 book *The Global Education Guidebook*, explains that:

> An excellent example of a place-based global collaboration comes from This Is Ours, an initiative of e2 Education & Environment (www.e2education.org). In This Is Ours, students in different parts of the world photograph and write about their local environment, identifying the plant and animal species that make it unique, as well as sharing how their environment impacts their lives. Any classroom can use the books of photography and writing each school produces for a deep understanding of place as an element of culture and identity. (p. 28)

This example shows how we can leverage local places to create a global network of places illustrating how interconnected we are.

How Do I Harness the Power of Community Partnerships to Support Place-Based Learning?

How do we build these relationships and sustain these partnerships? Partnerships start with purpose and intention.

Teachers may take the following actions with their students to harness the power of community partnerships to support place-based learning.

- **Encourage narrative inquiry and counternarratives:** Gather stories from a variety of perspectives and see what counternarrative emerges. Narrative inquiry also includes exploring life histories, journals, newspaper articles, artifacts, photographs, and maps as ways to inquire about the past and present-day issues facing students' community.
- **Use story mapping to discover community stories:** Interview different individuals to uncover all sides to an issue within the community.

Encourage Narrative Inquiry and Counternarratives

Projects that leverage authentic community partnerships through narrative inquiry often help students change their own narratives about themselves. Recall our discussion of remapping from the introduction (page 3). Narrative inquiry is a qualitative research method, defined by Deakin University Library (n.d.) in the following way:

> [Narrative inquiry] records the experiences of an individual or small group, revealing the lived experience or particular perspective of that individual, usually primarily through interview which is then recorded and ordered into a chronological narrative. Often recorded as biography, life history or in the case of older/ancient traditional story recording—oral history.

These partnerships and the work produced assist in dismantling false narratives projected onto students, especially students of color. The counternarratives that blossom as a result help children, young adults, and community members see their important contributions to the world. As professor of second language education Raúl Alberto Mora (2014) points out in his blog, *Counter-Narrative*, written for the Center for Intercultural Dialogue:

> The effect of a counter-narrative is to empower and give agency to those communities. By choosing their own words and telling their own stories, members of marginalized communities provide alternative points of view, helping to create complex narratives truly presenting their realities.

Uncovering counternarratives through storytelling is a way that all voices are heard and is the force that shifts apathy to empathy and passivity to action, creating the profound belief that we can make the world a better place. As Muhammad (2020a) so eloquently states in her book, *Cultivating Genius*, "Our students, and arguably adults, are always looking for themselves in spaces and places" (p. 69). Authentic community partnerships and storytelling foster this space for students to see themselves in their community and to understand the narratives of others. Using narrative inquiry is a method of telling the stories of those whose stories are unheard or have no place in the dominant narrative. Engaging students in narrative inquiry broadens their worldview and helps them to recognize there are many sides of a story, not just the dominant story.

Use Story Mapping to Discover the Stories of Your Community

One way to begin the process of engaging students in community partnerships is to help them consider ways to uncover the stories of their communities. To build on the narrative inquiry as a way of learning about place and building relationships with community members, we have adapted strategies from *Community Story-Mapping: The Pedagogy of the Griot* by authors Lynda Tredway and Gretchen Generett (2015) to help communities, schools, teachers, and students to "uncover, recover, tell and retell stories of the community to develop a road map for future action and advocacy" (p. 1). Story mapping lends itself well to project design around issues that matter to the community. Cliff Mayotte and Claire Kiefer (2018), in the introduction of *Say It Forward: A Guide to Social Justice Storytelling*, provide us with the following guiding questions to ask ourselves and our students as we learn about our community: "What are the stories and events that have shaped our community's history and identity? What has impacted how we see ourselves? What is the dominant narrative and how does that complement and contradict personal experience?" (p. 3). They contend that using these questions to guide narrative inquiry can uncover dormant, unseen stories behind the narratives, uncovering unknown or forgotten history. Understanding these stories helps teachers and students to connect the past to the present and content to the community. *Story mapping*, a process that utilizes narrative inquiry to discover assets, issues, and dilemmas in the community, is an effective way to understand these stories and, through that understanding, build relationships with community members as a stepping stone to formal partnerships. A detailed description of the story mapping process in action follows.

Use Story Mapping to Design Projects

In story mapping, as Tredway and Generett (2015) explain it, teachers first identify an essential question centered on a community issue or challenge. Then, they—teachers, students, or both—visit the community to conduct interviews, write, and make sense of the stories they collect. Finally, they design a project action plan. Using this approach, teachers or students collect stories about survival and hope from the past and the present to consider future solutions and improvements. Often, these stories are related to current issues or problems within the community. Think about who the stakeholders are. Ask yourself and your students the following questions.

- "Who is most impacted by this issue?"
- "Who has the greatest influence or power to help resolve the problem or create change?"
- "Who has less influence but can help and support resolving the problem or creating change?"
- "Who else is impacted by the problem, even if indirectly?"

An example problem could be bullying at school. Different perspectives would include students being bullied, the principal, bystanders, teachers, and parents. A student taking the perspective of the principal might note the following.

◆ *I am thinking about the problem of bullying at school from the perspective of the principal and how it impacts our school community.*

◆ *I think bullying is a problem at our school because we don't have a schoolwide policy and have not done training with our teachers and students.*

◆ *A question I have about bullying at our school is, "How can we collect data to recognize the places where bullying happens and keep track of the number of incidents?"*

◆ *I think we might solve this problem with an awareness campaign organized by students, teachers, and the principal.*

You could have students complete a stakeholder chart to further understand influence and impact. Have students brainstorm a list of all those impacted by the problem, issue, or challenge who have an interest in seeing it resolved (this information can easily be derived from their interviews). Next, ask students to categorize each of the stakeholders on the chart. See an example version of this chart in figure 3.1.

Who has the greatest influence to help resolve the problem or create change? *Principal and teachers*	Who is most impacted by this issue? *Students who are being bullied*
Who has less influence, but is interested in the problem and can help and support resolving the problem or creating change? *Parents, bus drivers, bystanders, food servers*	Who else is impacted by the problem, even if indirectly, and would be interested in helping and supporting resolving the problem and creating change? *Other students*

FIGURE 3.1: Stakeholders chart.

*Visit **go.SolutionTree.com/instruction** for a free reproducible version of this figure.*

Once students have identified stakeholders, you might have them use the *circle of viewpoints* strategy from Project Zero (2019a) to understand the issue from a variety of perspectives (see figure 3.2, page 54). Have students review their list of individuals whom the same issue impacts. Students will each choose one perspective from the list to explore, and each takes a turn using these sentence starters to explore the issue and their thoughts on it from the perspective of the individual they are portraying.

◆ I am thinking of _____ (the issue) _____ from the viewpoint of _____ (the viewpoint you've chosen).

◆ I think _____ (describe the issue from your chosen viewpoint).

◆ A question I have from this viewpoint is _____ (ask a question from this viewpoint).

◆ I think the problem might be solved by _____ (describe your ideas for solving the problem).

To use the circle of viewpoints organizer, have students work in teams of four. Provide each student with their own graphic organizer. Have each student start by putting the issue in the circle. From the brainstormed list of stakeholders, ask each team member to select a different viewpoint to consider and individually complete the graphic organizer. Each team member then shares their viewpoint with each other, and the whole team has a discussion about the best possible solutions.

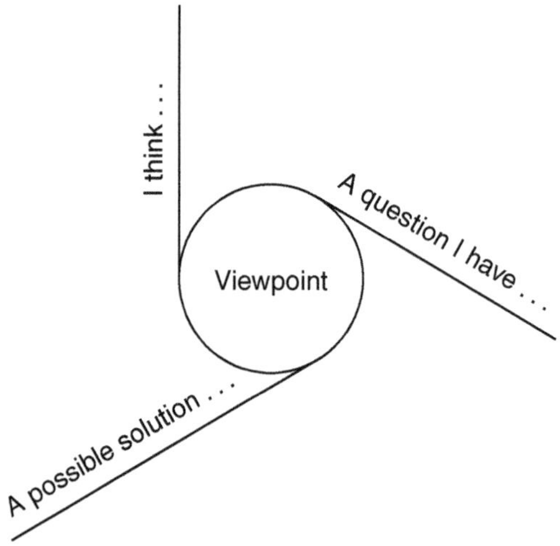

As a final reflection, ask teams to discuss the following.

FIGURE 3.2: Circle of viewpoints graphic organizer.

- What new ideas do you have about the problem that you didn't have before?

- What new questions do you have about the issue?

As a class, refer to the stakeholders chart to identify specific storytellers to shed light on the issue or issues within the community. The storytellers can be anyone from the community. Look to the elders, nonprofit organizations, school community, businesses, and institutions to hear their stories as related to the community. Go beyond the traditional image of storytellers. Adjudicated youth, members of the community who are experiencing homelessness, faith-based organizations, and people representing different ethnicities and cultures all have stories about the community. Tredway and Generett (2015) refer to community storytellers as griots. *Griots* are West African historians and storytellers who have a repository of knowledge—usually oral—and, through repeating the stories, weave the past into the present. They are the oral historians of their community. In the context of community, anyone can be a griot: everyone has a story and a perspective to share about place.

Possible interview questions include the following.

- What are some of the assets and challenges within the community around this issue?

- Describe the assets and how they may be a factor in solving the problem or resolving an issue.

- What changes have you seen in the community that have impacted these challenges?

- What hopes do you have for the community?

- What are some suggestions that might help overcome these challenges?

For example, if students are exploring food scarcity in their community, some of the storytellers they interview may be individuals who work at the food bank, individuals who need the food bank to feed their families, members of a community garden co-op, school officials, and organizations dedicated to ending food scarcity such as The Hunger Project, Rethinking the Food System, and so on. The stories of these individuals help students to better identify and define the issue, problem, or challenge and inform what action the students might take, as well as who might be the best community partner to assist in taking action. Sometimes it might be the organization that has a specific ask of students, furthering the partnership as they work collaboratively together.

Community partnerships often result from these encounters with community storytellers. Once an idea for a project has emerged, it is easy to go back to some of the storytellers to see if they want to engage in a partnership.

Story mapping helps communities and student learners establish strong partnerships in the following ways.

- ◆ **Building empathy:** Story mapping allows individuals to see the world through the eyes of others and understand their experiences, perspectives, and challenges. This helps build empathy and a shared understanding of the community, leading to more effective and inclusive partnerships.

- ◆ **Encouraging collaboration:** By mapping out different stories, communities can identify common themes, goals, and challenges. This information can be used to bring different stakeholders together to collaborate on solutions that benefit the entire community.

- ◆ **Fostering inclusivity:** Story mapping provides a platform for all members of the community to have their voices heard, regardless of their background, status, or influence. This helps to promote inclusivity and ensures that all perspectives are taken into account when developing partnerships.

- ◆ **Improving communication:** Story mapping provides a representation of the community's experiences, perspectives, and goals, making it easier for partners to understand and communicate with each other. This can lead to more productive and effective partnerships.

- ◆ **Strengthening relationships:** By working together on story mapping, communities can build strong relationships and establish a foundation of trust and mutual understanding. This can lead to more sustainable and impactful partnerships over time as they tackle the issue together.

Story mapping is an important tool in building community partnerships because it allows students to visualize the experiences of others, to better understand their stories and, therefore, better appreciate the perspectives of different individuals and groups, and to make sure these perspectives are all honored in a partnership.

Story Mapping in Action

We, the authors, have used the story mapping process to assist teachers in learning about the stories of a place. Micki worked with Dulce Independent Schools, which is in the heart of the Jicarilla Apache Nation and serves 94 percent Native American students. To increase student engagement and preserve cultural identity, these teachers turned to place-based learning, and story mapping became the key to discovering place. In this context, teachers used story mapping to consider project ideas. It was also a way to introduce the teachers to the process and consider how they might use it with students in the future. Teachers received a list of tribal agencies and their responsibilities. Before teachers began their story mapping expedition into the community, they considered their standards, National Indian Education Association National Cultural Standards, and possible project ideas. Then they went out to hear the stories and issues facing the community. Through the story mapping process, teachers learned about the tribe's history, culture, government, racial discrimination, and economy. Following are some project snapshots that resulted from this story mapping process.

- ◆ After teachers met with the Dulce Community Center, elders, churches, a local medicine man, the Department of Health and Wellness, and Traditional Culture and Recreation, they designed a project around creating an interactive community calendar. This calendar emphasized seasonal and cultural activities that lead to a healthier life, be it physical, mental, spiritual, or emotional. The project aligned with English language arts (ELA) and social studies content, as well as cultural standards.

- On the backroads of the Jicarilla Apache Nation, a visit to the Go-Jii-Ya tribal site provided insight into cultural ways of knowing. The teacher group met with tribal biologists and learned more about the big game management and fishing program from an Indigenous perspective. These expeditions led to a deepened understanding of tribal history and how it informs the present. Once the teachers captured these stories through recordings and note-taking, they began designing projects that embedded culture and leveraged traditional ways of knowing. As a result, this teacher group posed the essential question, "How might our wildlife sanctuary teach others about the Jicarilla Apache culture?" This project increased students' pride in their history and culture and led to insights about what their tribe has accomplished today amid the many barriers set in its way over the years. This project aligned with ELA, social studies, and science standards.

In these two projects, teachers connected students with the different tribal agencies who supported them, provided expertise, and helped in providing feedback on their work. These partnerships helped students see that there are meaningful careers available for them on the reservation. They also learned what sorts of higher education would help them in pursuing a career as a tribal biologist, working in the fisheries or the Department of Health and Wellness.

How Do I Capture Stories From My Community?

Consider the following steps to capture the stories in your community and to guide your students in doing so.

Step 1: *Identify an essential question around a central theme.*

When we led a group of educators and students to Whitney Plantation, we asked, "What stories does this place tell?" This is an essential first question when beginning the work of building student-community partnerships. Other essential questions might include, "What is the role of justice and injustice in my community?" and "How can we reimagine a more equitable community?" You can identify the storytellers with your teacher-student teams or use a more organic process in which you introduce the essential question and have teachers and students individually begin the inquiry process to identify the griots within the community.

Step 2: *Prepare teams for community visits.*

Introduce interview protocols, any cultural protocols or areas that might be sensitive to the interviewee, active listening skills, and any other skills that will properly prepare your student teams for capturing stories. You might assign specific roles, such as interviewer, recorder (digital or written), follow-up questioner or clarifier, and videographer or photographer, based on students' strengths and interests. As students become more familiar with the process, you might have them pick a role that challenges them. StoryCorps (2017) shares these four tips on effective interviews.

1. Touch on big and important issues, such as community hunger, racism, housing, and so on. Once students learn about the issue in their community, they can narrow it down to a more specific problem.

2. Use open-ended questions instead of closed questions, which only require a yes or no answer. For example, rather than asking, "Do you like living here?" ask, "What is the best part of living here? Most challenging?"

3. Follow up with more questions. You might ask such questions such as, "How long has your family lived here? How many generations? What compelled your ancestors to move here?"

4. Listen, pay attention, and show that you care. Maintain eye contact, ask follow-up questions, be present and attentive, and don't interrupt the speaker. When you think they are done talking, allow for a few more seconds of silence to see if they have anything else to say. Never insert yourself into an interviewee's story.

Consider the following questions to guide your inquiry as you listen to the stories of the community griots.

- Who are the key holders of history and knowledge of place?
- What cultures are represented in this place?
- What has been important to the history of people in this place, including current residents?
- Who were the Indigenous people who first lived here?
- What has changed in this place over time?

Step 3: *Write the narratives.*

Once teams have completed their interviews, have them write a narrative based on what they learned about that person from the interview. Writing the narrative helps in sense making. Decide on a process for feedback, revision, and reflection. It's important that the griot gets the final word. You might share the narrative with the griot in person or via email. This is especially important if you are collecting oral histories. These narratives can help students understand different perspectives as students consider solutions for resolving a community issue.

Step 4: *Make sense of the stories.*

Have teams read the narratives out loud. Uncover patterns and trends. Tredway and Generett (2015) suggest the following questions.

- "What is the big idea in each story?"
- "What common experiences do storytellers share about themselves and the community?"
- "What historical information is useful for the community?"
- "What are the community's assets?"
- "What are the community's challenges?"
- "What common themes emerge among the stories?" (p. 14)

Step 5: *Design the project or action plan.*

If you are using story mapping with a team of teachers to identify potential partnerships and project ideas, jump into the design process. If you are conducting story mapping with your students, have them address an issue or problem that emerged from the stories and develop or co-create an action plan with the community partner for implementation within the community. Students may also want to consider ways to share the community stories to raise awareness, such as a podcast, website, or video to present their findings as a call to action.

There are many questions that are helpful to consider as you begin project planning. The following are some that may be particularly important.

- Based on the sense making derived from the story mapping process, what do you and your students want to address?

- What content standards, skills, and processes align to the project idea?

- How will you plan the next steps with your students?

- How will you, your students, and community partners identify the product, service, or solution students will lead in their community?

- What will purpose-driven inquiry look like as students learn more about the issue? What voices need to be heard? Who will provide input?

- How will you further the reciprocity with your community partners?

- How will you and your students and community partners know if you've made an impact?

Whether you conduct story mapping with a team of teachers or your students, the outcome results in a list of potential community partners in which you have already established a strong relationship through storytelling. This relationship adds to a collaborative effort to work together to help improve their community.

Finally, in addition to story mapping, conducting effective interviews, and building relationships with community members, consider how you can use technology to help you and your students gather community stories and make sense of them. Geospatial techniques and digital storytelling apps enhance your community stories. Jim Bentley, a fifth-grade teacher and National Geographic explorer, helped to develop the National Geographic *geo-inquiry process*, which asks students to inquire, collect data, and visualize the data that result in a compelling story to drive community action. He has used it with his fifth-grade students for many projects that emphasize place. One project was mapping how plastics move from the suburbs to the sea. In another example, the mapping software ArcGIS (www.arcgis.com), as part of a story mapping project, can provide the historical context of redlining and the changes over time. The ArcGIS app also lets students insert text and photos, as well as audio or video of the storytellers, to enhance the story and allow it to become interactive.

ArcGIS mapping software is free for any school interested in using it to augment storytelling about place. ArcGIS story maps can give your story a stronger sense of place, show spatial relationships, and add visuals to enhance your story.

A Community Story Digitally Mapped

Linnentown was a little-known Black community located along Baxter Street in Athens, Georgia. Built in early 1900, it was a close-knit community that had experienced many hardships as a result of segregation and racial discrimination but thrived as a community. Many of the community members were artisans and professionals, architects, skilled plumbers, and electricians who worked in Athens. Eighty-five percent of the homes in Linnentown were owned by the people who lived there (Adams, 2021).

In 1962, the University of Georgia (UGA) and the city government of Athens received a grant to acquire the property of Linnentown through eminent domain to build a dormitory. None of the residents were informed about the project until renters and homeowners were evicted. By 1966, all residents had been forced to move, and all traces of the neighborhood were erased (Shannon, 2020).

Years later, students at the University of Georgia learned about the story and felt it needed to be told as part of their community GIS (geographic information system) course. Their story map explored the story of Linnentown and the people who lived there, and the total erasure of the community in the late 1960s. The story map describes the resistance efforts from the first descendants of Linnentown, activists, city officials, and community members acknowledging the tragedy and efforts to provide reparations. Using ArcGIS, students mapped out the story using GIS and mapping to understand race relations and segregation and how they influenced Athens in the past and present. One student reflects on his learning:

> Working on the story has enlightened me on ways we can have a positive remembrance of a community and still call out injustices that occurred to it. By digging through records and evidence of what occurred to the community, it has also highlighted the power imbalances that still remain between UGA and the Athens local community. (student reflection from community GIS, spring 2022)

Visit http://www.communitymappinglab.org/Linnentown to learn more about this project.

ArcGIS story maps assist students in mapping a story within the context of their community, provide a road map to think about place, and help breathe life into the creation of communities where all can thrive. This is the power of connectedness and belonging. This is the power of place. This is the power of authentic community partnerships as an integral part of place-based learning.

How Do I Establish, Nurture, and Grow Community Partnerships?

Consider the following tips as you work with your students to build authentic partnerships within your community.

- Some of your best ideas for community partnerships may well come from your students. Give young people a voice. Consider letting them take the lead in designing their projects and establishing community partnerships as appropriate.

- You, your students, and your community partners should all plan for effective collaboration—ask lots of questions and craft the partnership together. Together, come up with the criteria of what measures success. You might get started by asking yourself some of the following questions.
  - "What is our shared vision?"
  - "What role (expert, authentic audience, collaborator on solving a community challenge) can the partner take to support students in their project work?"
  - "Can this expert or organization connect with my students?"
  - "Do the experts and partners reflect the ethnicity of my students?"
  - "How will we communicate regularly?"
  - "How will we assess our impact?"

- Develop a shared vision. This vision is what drives the partnership. Once you have established that shared vision, identify clear roles and responsibilities with a tangible timeline. Some questions to consider when developing a shared vision are the following.
    - "What is your vision for this partnership? Share your vision and together write a vision statement."
    - "What do you need from the school to be successful?"
    - "What would a successful partnership look like?"
    - "What is the best way for us to communicate on a regular basis?"
    - "What are our common goals and outcomes for this partnership?"
    - "How will we measure success?"
- As the teacher, you want to make sure students are engaged in real work and that the work aligns with standards. With place-based learning, students place their work into a real-world context and learn that their own efforts are part of a larger change effort.
- When engaging with your partners, focus on a sustainable relationship rather than a one-time experience.

We want community partnerships to be reciprocal so that it is a win-win situation for everyone. More projects may evolve out of this partnership.

BATON ROUGE'S TROUBLED WATERS
Build Authentic Community Partnerships, in Action

Building authentic community partnerships in this project began with community story mapping. Before launching the project, teachers took a high-level survey of the assets in the community (all people, places, and things like landmarks and buildings) regarding Black swim clubs in Baton Rouge and in the neighborhood surrounding the school.

As the teachers reached out to various community centers and spoke with community members who were either past Black swim club members or the grandchildren of elders who lived during the time, relationships with the community began to form. When it was time for students to engage with the community members, teachers had already laid the groundwork for students to gather the interview responses necessary to support their learning about the state of Black swim clubs and Black swimming pools in their city.

Interview protocols and lessons on how to be an effective interviewer were part of the classroom instruction prior to students engaging with the community stakeholders. Students specifically practiced active listening skills and rehearsed using apps and software on their devices to help them capture the transcriptions of the interviews. Students were trained in the process of switching roles within their groups by practicing reciprocal reading of various texts in their daily lessons. This way, when students were out in the community or interacting with partners via video conferences and FaceTime conversations, they were able to decide roles in advance and switch roles with each person interviewed or even hold the role of an absent classmate as needed.

As a result, students were able to collect narratives and stories of various aspects of Black swim clubs in their city as well as debunk myths and erroneous perceptions about Black people's ability to swim well. One anonymous student even reflected during a recorded session: "After speaking with so many people in my neighborhood and in my city that look like me, who were actually *great* swimmers, I began to think differently about my ability to be able to swim and started to wonder exactly what made me ever think that I couldn't" (student, personal communication, June 2022). In this way, the power of learning about others in the past in their community shone through as this student's self-perception began to change, along with that of many others. In making sense of the stories students and teachers gathered in the community, it was determined that the best plan of action for one particular team of students would be to create an awareness campaign, letting other students know that they, too, can become swimmers.

Conclusion

Using story mapping to build authentic community partnerships helps to dismantle racism and inequities within community, institutions, and structures by changing the story and shifting the narrative. Story mapping helps to build authentic relationships with community members and uncover counternarratives of community members. Building authentic community partnerships provides opportunities to co-create, co-plan, and co-serve in an effort to transform place, communities, relationships, and lives.

Key Takeaways and Reflection Questions

Consider this chapter's key takeaways and reflect on the following questions as you work to build authentic community partnerships through place-based learning. Use the Journey Log to further reflect, brainstorm, jot down ideas, make observations, or plan.

- ♦ Building authentic community partnerships is the pedagogy of connectedness. It connects students to place and those who live there.
- ♦ Authentic community partnerships can happen at the beginning of a project or throughout the project, driven by teachers, students, and community members. Students can identify partners as part of the inquiry process. Partners can be long-standing or identified by teachers during project planning, and technology can connect community partners locally and across the globe.

- Authentic community partnerships create the conditions for students that they may not have considered by working with experts in the field.
- Amplifying the stories of community helps build reciprocal community partnerships to deepen understanding around representation, culture, class, gender, socioeconomics, and ethnicity.

- How does storytelling and story listening deepen our understanding of each other and ourselves?
- Who are the storytellers in my community?
- What places in my community have stories to be heard?
- How do my community partnerships foster storytelling and support the project's story?

Journey Log

Journey Log

CHAPTER 4
Empower Student Ownership

When young people discover they can be agents of change,
wonderful things happen. They start to serve in the neighborhoods,
learn about public issues, create innovative solutions to tough public
challenges and eventually become the voters, community project builders
and leaders in our communities and nation.

—ALMA POWELL

ESSENTIAL QUESTION: How can I foster students' self-management skills in service of efficacy and ownership?

Place-based learning empowers students by giving them a voice in the work they produce. It creates ownership and pride in the process and creation of a meaningful product. It scaffolds the skills for being a change agent in the community and the world. Student ownership is a gradual release, as we create self-managers capable of taking their learning to a new level. It requires that we explicitly teach self-management skills and then step out of the way, allowing students to try out their efficacy in their project work.

In this chapter, you will find an emphasis on trust and practice. This includes trusting students to try things that are hard, grapple with questions and complex tasks, and build their skills over time both inside and outside of project work. We share stories of how student ownership has looked in classrooms we have taught and worked in, and what it looks like to begin this process and move it forward in nurturing, sustainable ways. The chapter offers a chance to think further about its content through the Conclusion and Key Takeaways and Reflection Questions sections. It concludes with the Journey Log for writing down your thoughts and ideas.

What Is Student Ownership?

Student ownership can be as simple as students generating questions they need answers to after working with a community partner. Or, it can be as involved as students forming teams, deciding on the best way to showcase their work to the public, then drafting, revising, and presenting that work, all with minimal teacher intervention. There is an incorrect assumption that age is the defining factor in how much student ownership to allow in a project. Although there are developmental considerations for self-management, fourth-grade (or even younger) students who have place-based learning experience can run independently with a project. Conversely, seniors in high school who have little to no project experience might only be able to handle limited ownership as they learn to be self-managers. The defining key, at any grade level, is how much students have practiced the skills required to manage the project process and produce a community product— the more practice, the more autonomy.

How Do I Empower Student Ownership?

It is of vital importance to challenge your assumptions as you move into the actions of ensuring student ownership in place-based learning. A common error that teachers new to place-based learning make is to swing the student ownership pendulum to extremes in either direction and then blame the resultant failure on the methodology. The refrain goes something like, "I tried place-based learning, but my students couldn't handle the freedom" (think of constructivism on overdrive) or, "My students crave structure, and the room was out of control when we did place-based learning." When attempts at place-based learning don't result immediately in the hoped-for outcome, it is important to examine our attitudes and beliefs about our students' ability to self-manage. Are we expecting our students to instinctively know how to manage their learning because of their age or gender? Likewise, do we think our students need structure because of how they were taught historically? What is at the root of our perceptions? Every student needs freedom, and every student needs structure. Personalizing the project based on a calculated balance of these needs, putting in place appropriate scaffolds and removing them as students gain efficacy, and asking students to reflect on the experience in real time will help us understand that project learning isn't an extreme, but a meeting in the middle of student potential and teacher support.

Teachers can empower student ownership in the following ways.

- **Build efficacy with intention:** Use a gradual approach to infuse your entire practice, year-round, with the skills that are most essential for students to acquire. Then when they begin a project, they are confident and prepared.

- **Map backward and let community need lead:** Plan backward but with students at the helm, taking small, manageable risks so students benefit from the reward of ownership and more authentic collaboration with a community partner.

- **Hone student self-management skills:** Calculate students' readiness for managing their own learning and afford them opportunities to learn and practice self-management skills, both inside and outside of a place-based-learning journey.

- **Find the right starting point:** Set a goal for increasing student ownership in their learning and work toward it, having an unobstructed view of where you want your class to be in the short and long term.

- **Examine structures and lean in:** Leverage infrastructure such as standards clustering, advisories, and asynchronous fieldwork for more student ownership.

Build Efficacy With Intention

How do you build students' efficacy—the ability to do the work the project requires to a high quality—in your classroom when just starting out with a place-based methodology? Educational leader and project designer Kristyn Kamps (2021) describes building efficacy as the *dimmer switch approach*. Instead of place-based learning being an on-off switch, whereby we are "doing" a project in our classroom, think about what skills students need to learn to be successful self-managers in project work and teach those skills throughout the school year in small, meaningful, low-stakes ways, turning the dimmer switch up as you gear up for more complex project work. If students have the opportunity to exercise ownership over their learning only a few select, teacher-orchestrated times a year, there will be limited lasting benefit. Additionally, those necessary self-management skills, such as critical thinking, innovating, metacognition, and collaboration, will be underdeveloped. These skills must be explicitly taught and assessed throughout a student's educational life for the reward to manifest in project output. Picture this scenario: Carlos, a sixth-grade teacher, is preparing for a project where students observe the natural environment surrounding their school. He knows he must teach the skill of translating students' curiosity into researchable and actionable questions. He decides that students, after observing changes or circumstances in the natural environment, will propose a solution to a problem or answer to a question connected to the environment around them (for example, this kind of scenario might lead to an investigation into something related to watershed, animal safety, or native vegetation health). They will then predict the outcome, and discuss it with a local wildlife representative. In this situation, Carlos starts the project with audio and video recordings of coyotes in the forested trails adjacent to the school, then asks students the essential question, "Why are coyotes coming into this neighborhood, and what should we do?" Luckily, Carlos has been using the dimmer switch approach to teach students questioning techniques, so they are prepared for purpose-driven inquiry. Here are a few of the lessons and activities Carlos scaffolded during the months leading up to this project.

- He taught students how to put their wonderings into words and to form different types of questions using the *question formulation technique* from the Right Questions Institute (2024). The class studied an illustration of a plant performing photosynthesis earlier in the year.

- He modeled American Society for Quality's (n.d.) *five whys and hows* questioning strategies to examine a problem and brainstorm solutions. At the time, Carlos and his students were figuring out why the green plants in the class garden bed had gone to seed and what they could do about it. Asking why to get to the cause and then asking how to brainstorm solutions helped them see the progression of their understanding and how asking multiple times got them deeper answers.

- Students kept a question journal, in which they would record things they were curious about, using and coding different types of questions (probing, clarifying, reinforcing, ideating). Carlos would give them time to reflect at key points during a learning experience, and students would periodically turn their journal in for Carlos to give feedback on the quality, purpose, and variety of their questions.

Because Carlos used the dimmer switch approach, infusing the skill of questioning into his science instruction, his students were primed for the challenge of the coyote project.

School communities can use the Coalition of Essential Schools' Habits of Mind (Costa & Kallick, 2009), International Baccalaureate's Learner Profiles (International Baccalaureate, 2023), or a customized framework to determine which skills are most valuable for students to reach their full potential in school and beyond. School communities that have invested the time in making such determinations are more likely to give teachers the permission to devote time and resources to fostering these skills in the classroom. Teachers also have a unified objective, giving students a greater opportunity for growth due to the shared focus and longevity of the mission.

Map Backward and Let Community Need Lead

The opportunity for ownership also impacts the relationship between school, teacher and student, and community partners. So much of the focus of student partnership in the community is on the end product—students showing off a polished *thing* or proposal of a thing to a room full of people who have agreed to be there because they were contacted by a teacher. This kind of showcase of learning has merit, and it encourages students to produce work that reaches beyond the classroom.

What if, however, the product were envisioned and created in true side-by-side collaboration with the community partner? What if the backward planning were of the community partnership—with co-defined outcomes? We know what you're thinking: that sounds big and scary, and my students aren't ready for that! Let's instead think about small, manageable steps that lead to student and community partner empowerment.

We use the following example to show three things. First, we look at how small risks lead to student growth and empowerment. Second, we explore backward design and its three stages: identify desired results, determine acceptable evidence, and plan learning experiences and instruction. Finally, we examine the how the intersection between backward design and student ownership, where students learning about themselves, their community, and their potential empowers the teacher to teach with intention and be responsive to students' deep inquiry (Bowen, 2017).

In Erin's eleventh-grade classroom, she constructed a few lessons where her students learned about noncognitive competencies and examined the difference between growth, maker, and team mindsets. You might know noncognitive competencies better by names such as soft skills, 21st century skills, success skills, or life skills. Her students, using a fist-to-five strategy (indicating agreement or disagreement with the number of fingers raised), agreed that the class was pretty good at navigating systems and understanding and dealing with discrimination (one of the noncognitive competencies). Students also agreed that, although far from mastery, they were getting better at understanding multiple points of view, a feature of a team mindset.

Armed with this new group awareness, Erin's class began to brainstorm community partners who might need people with these specific assets. Erin provided an initial list of potential partners that she had vetted, but the students quickly went beyond her list. She then acted as scribe and redirected when they got off topic. The small risk of putting this step in the hands of students allowed them ownership over what was to come. Using the first stage of backward design— *identify desired results*—Erin's students thought that organizations focused on assisting recent immigrants with gaining access to jobs, housing, and resources might be a place to start. They also considered potential organizations' distance from the school, who they served, and personal connections when selecting potential partners. Their desired result would be to find and collaborate with the right partner. They then composed emails and a phone script. Student teams then reached out to three potential partners, asking to meet with one person from the organization to have a *learning session* focused on the question, How can we be an asset to your organization and its end users? Then they waited, and while waiting they did things unrelated to their project.

After a few weeks, they had a nibble on the line. The director of an immigrant advocacy organization was willing to Skype with Erin's students to talk about possibilities. Students, instead of writing interview questions, crafted team asset statements with Erin's modeling and guidance, highlighting where their strengths lay, along with a few initial ideas for how the organization might benefit from a partnership (based on research students did on the organization). A few more weeks went by, during which time the class again did things unrelated to the project.

Over the next month, students talked to the partner a handful of times as they moved to the second step of backward design: *determine acceptable evidence.* They generated ideas together, clarified need and intent, and decided what was reasonable, spending approximately ten hours on this phase of the project. In tandem with their partner, students found out, through lessons and activities orchestrated by Erin, that immigrants with teen children were often unfamiliar with the realities and nuances of American teen life, such as social media, peer pressure, drugs and alcohol, and personal safety. Students began to think about how to fill this information gap for immigrant teens and their families. Each team (formed with intention by the teacher but with consideration of students' preferences) came up with a different idea and pitched it to the partner. Ideas ranged from an informational website to a documentary film to a phone app. To the surprise of many, the partner decided to go with a no-tech solution of partnering immigrant teens from other schools with teens at Erin's school to have a *scoop session*—a question-and-answer session—at the school or community center. The scoop session would give the immigrant teens an opportunity to ask questions and get much-needed information while also making a face-to-face connection with a peer.

From there, students entered into the third phase of planning backward—*plan learning experiences and instruction*—albeit not in the way we typically think of that phase as teachers. Remember, this is what it looks like when students have ownership over the process. Co-creation demands more flexibility. Students then recruited other students at their own school to get involved with the partnership (to pair with immigrant teens), created a database, set guidelines, compiled information they thought was vital to share, and tested the program. Once these pieces were in place and the first few scoop sessions had taken place, Erin's students reflected with the community partner, individually and as a team, and the project concluded. The class then turned the project over to the community partner and student government to sustain long after this group of students had matriculated, thereby becoming a legacy project.

The students in this example owned the process, with substantial support and scaffolding from the teacher, and the product was co-created with the community partner as a natural result of the relationship they built and the questions they asked. If, after reading this example, granting student ownership is still intimidating, think about how you might take one single aspect of project design and co-create it with students. Can you craft the essential question with students? Can they assist you in identifying places to do fieldwork or people to interview? Can they produce a menu of possible products or actions with the community partner? Start with small risks and gradually work with your students to get to the bigger payout.

Hone Student Self-Management Skills

If there were one word to sum up what students say it feels like to own their learning, that word would have to be *purposeful*. Students say things like, "I know why I'm doing this," and "It makes sense," and "I can figure it out." Walk into any learner-driven classroom and you'll find students who know the why, what, and how of their task, and they are doing that task! You'll see a teacher orchestrating the environment, locating the resources, teaching just-in-time content and skills, and differentiating to meet the needs of all students. And you'll see students who know how to use their teacher to get what they need to further their inquiry. There is a buzz to a student-owned classroom that many have compared to a busy workplace.

An essential part of fostering purposeful students and this kind of purposeful classroom environment is honing students' self-management skills. Tools like management logs and team contracts (readily available with a search at www.pblworks.org), flexible groupings, workshops for teaching and collaborating, and technology (covering everything from practicing discrete skills to making beautiful products) are available to aid teachers in developing self-management skills in students. Teachers should be attentive to addressing a variety of focus areas when honing self-management skills, not just academic skills. This attentiveness should include making sure students are able to self-regulate, interact effectively with others, organize a multistep process, and more. The checklist in figure 4.1 can assist in developing these skills.

As figure 4.1 shows, a student or team of students would complete and present a rigorous proposal, similar to what teachers create for a unit plan, and present it to their advising teacher. A student would revisit the checklist throughout the project, recording progress and updating deadline dates. Individual students can use the project checklist as a self-management tool, or a team of students can adopt it as a team management tool. As with so many of our resources, modeling the use of this or a similar checklist and then progressing to using it together as a whole class will prepare students to use it in a meaningful way with an upcoming place-based learning journey.

At MNCS in Henderson, Minnesota, which is the EdVisions flagship school, design essentials center on self-directed, project-based learning. On average, it takes students there a month to become adept self-managers. This is because the educational model demands this time investment and doesn't send mixed messages by requiring students to operate some of the time in a traditional learning model and some of the time in a self-directed model. All students, all day, every day, act as self-managers, and educators act as guides and advisers. (For more information about this school model, see chapter 13, "Dismantle the Barriers to Place-Based Learning," page 227). Students new to the model need not look any further than a peer to their left or right to see the expectation in action.

As teachers in more traditional school environments, we're taught to think about students' cognitive load. We're asked to be on the lookout for cognitive dissonance in students, when to tap that potential, and when it leads to undue struggle. But we're generally not very familiar with measuring students' preparedness for the place-based learning journeys we hope you'll design. Caution is needed in gauging student preparedness, as Steven Rippe (personal communication, November 2020), EdVisions director of organizational development, explains:

> If [project complexity and current self-management skills] are not aligned, the student doing the project can become frustrated, anxious, and potentially freeze up on their productivity. The inverse can happen if the project is too easy and the student is essentially floating along, not really

Project Checklist

Make a personal plan for how you will complete this project on time, doing your best work. Then, break your plan down by the phases on the checklist. Fill in the projected completion date now and the real completion date as you progress.

"I think I/we will be done with this project by _____."

A. Ideation Phase (Projected date _____, Real date _____)

☐ Complete Ideation using mind map, thinking routine, storyboard, or other tool.

☐ Meet with teacher or peers to create Essential Question and quality indicators.

B. Project Plan Phase (Projected date _____, Real date _____)

☐ Complete Project Plan, including this checklist.

☐ Meet with teacher or peers to get feedback and revise.

Research Phase (Projected date _____, Real date _____)

☐ Contact experts and consult primary sources.

- Scholarly journals: _____
- Interviews: _____
- Events: _____
- Books: _____
- Blogs, tutorials, or other: _____
- Websites: _____
- Videos: _____
- Cultural artifacts: _____
- Government documents: _____
- Stories: _____
- Music or sounds: _____
- Works of art: _____

☐ Gather sources, checking them for relevance to the Essential Question.

☐ Read and take notes on all sources, using strategies like *Reciprocal Reading* and *The Seven Strategies of Highly Skilled Readers*.

☐ Develop questions (Identify what you don't yet know).

☐ Refine questions.

Planning Phase (Projected date _____, Real date _____)

☐ Brainstorm product ideas; create sketches, outlines, plans, storyboards, and so on.

☐ Meet with teacher, peers, and community partner to review research, revise questions, and determine products.

☐ Complete supply and resource list.

C. Production Phase (Projected date _____, Real date _____)

☐ Create draft, prototype, or pilot.

☐ Review with peer; collect and incorporate feedback. Revise as necessary.

☐ Revise and review until quality is achieved; meet with your teacher for status check.

☐ Complete final revision of product(s).

D. Result Phase (Projected date _____, Real date _____)

☐ Write End-of-Project Reflection. Assess whether you answered the driving question.

☐ Evaluate your growth and understanding of the content standards and ways of knowing.

☐ Arrange all project components, including proposal, notes, drafts, time-management tools and documentation, product(s), works cited, and end-of-project reflection.

☐ Plan and practice presentation; perfect your final product; share with all stakeholders.

G. Postassessment Phase (Projected date _____, Real date _____)

☐ Organize your completed project to easily find and share your best work.

Source: Adapted from EdVisions Schools. Used with permission.

FIGURE 4.1: EdVisions Schools project management checklist.

*Visit **go.SolutionTree.com/instruction** for a free reproducible version of this figure.*

challenging themselves and is at risk of becoming bored. This is when it is important to let students explore more complexity with potentially more self-direction.

We cannot always be sure if students are ready to take ownership over a particular phase of a project. However, we can collect data using low-stakes activities to see how students perform. For instance, a high school mathematics teacher designing a place-based learning journey that culminates in students producing a manual for a video game they create may identify the enduring understanding of writing using extended definitions and concrete details. If she is unsure whether her students are equipped for this prominent project task, she can give these stealth assessments a week prior to beginning the project.

1. **Monday:** Set a cell phone (or other familiar object) on the desk or overhead projector and ask students to write a definition and describe it to a partner.

2. **Tuesday:** Display a diary or notebook and ask students to write a sequence of how the object was made.

3. **Wednesday:** Display a soccer ball and have students practice, in pairs, explaining from a bank of mathematical vocabulary how the object is used.

4. **Thursday:** Give a three-question geometry preassessment and invite students to quickly share which "object of the day" they connected to and why.

With the data from the stealth assessments, the teacher can return to the project plan with a clearer picture of what students need for successful self-management and command of the content of the upcoming project. Similarly, by investing time before and during a project for these pre- and formative assessments, you will gain an understanding of the lessons, resources, scaffolds, and support students need to reach project objectives (Sanchez, 2023).

Every facet of self-management discussed so far uses the dimmer switch approach (page 87), building students' self-management skills throughout the school year and really cranking up the wattage during place-based learning journeys. It is helpful to have students early in the school year self-identify skills they need to work on, using a skills inventory or success skills rubric, then track their progress over time. When it is time for project work, you and the student can use this self-awareness to differentiate team tasks, roles, and activities based on what each individual student knows they need to improve on.

Erin fondly remembers a day toward the end of a project when a team of her tenth graders called her over to their table and asked if she had procured a particular resource from the community partner that they needed for a prototype they were building. When she informed them that she hadn't received it yet, one student said, "OK, then we don't need you. Come back when you have it." Although a little harsh, Erin was pleased that she had taught herself out of the equation. They really didn't need her at that point, and that was a good thing.

Find the Right Starting Point

It's important to remember that student ownership isn't either-or. It's a continuum ranging from teacher centered to learner driven, and it envelops everything from schoolwide structures to teacher autonomy. See figure 4.2, which demonstrates progression along this continuum of choice.

STAGE ONE

Teacher designs project.

Project is a supplement to the curriculum.

- A lesson
- One part of whole

Teacher predetermines product, outcome, and assessment.

Single-disciplined

Real-world impact is incidental.

All project work fits within class period.

Student creativity is involved, but little student choice is allowed.

Teacher acts as director of instruction.

STAGE TWO

Teacher designs project.

Curriculum is taught through project.

- A unit
- A percent of CCSS

Students are given choices regarding process and product(s) within parameters set by the teacher.

Project may cross disciplines.

Some resources are found outside the classroom.

Real-world impact built into project design and implementation.

Teacher acts as director of learning.

STAGE THREE

Teacher designs the driving question with students and community partner(s).

Teacher aligns process and product(s) (formative and summative assessments) to content standards.

Project spans the length of the class (quarter, trimester, or semester), and content standards are taught through the project. The project is the curriculum.

Project crosses multiple disciplines and most likely includes multiple planners (teachers, mentors, community partners) from different disciplines.

Students design projects (or products within).

Project offers attainable, intentional, real-world impact.

Work is constructivist.

Authentic assessment uses multiple assessment targets.

A large portion of project work may take place out of the building (*not* homework).

Work is complex and rigorous.

STAGE FOUR

School leadership designs systems and structures that support project learning as the primary methodology.

Project learning is the basis of the whole school system.

Students design projects.

Students design driving question, focus, and goals.

Students align projects to content standards.

Real-world impact is an inherent component.

Work is constructivist.

Authentic assessment involves students choosing assessment target(s).

Much work takes place out of the building.

Project is not discipline-based.

Work is complex and rigorous.

Teacher acts as facilitator and adviser.

Community partner(s) are active participants in design, management, and assessment of projects.

FIGURE 4.2: Continuum of learner-driven place-based learning.

Work toward developing greater student ownership by starting with honestly self-assessing your current place on the continuum of learner-driven place-based learning. Keep in mind that your place on the continuum is often influenced by factors outside your realm of influence—pacing guides, class size, testing mandates—so this is an opportunity to reflect without judgment. Next, have a conversation with your grade-level team or department about where you would like to be on the continuum. You may set a short-term goal, as in, "One year from now, we want our students to choose the project topic based on their interest or the questions they are asking." You may look to an end goal, such as, "Three years from now, our students will self-regulate learning based on passion and purpose." Once the goal is set, you can begin to explore concrete ways to coach students to own their learning. If your goal is to base project topics on questions students are asking, then teaching questioning strategies, such as the QFT mentioned earlier (page 39) from the Right Questions Institute (2024), becomes paramount, and part of your classroom routine.

When visiting the elementary campus of MNCS (mentioned earlier, page 70) over winter break, Erin ran into a first-grade teacher prepping resources in her classroom. Erin inquired about what project the teacher would be working on when students returned from break. The teacher gave a puzzled look and said, "How would I know? The students haven't told me yet." This classroom was clearly in stage four of the continuum of learner-driven place-based learning. Students as young as first grade were project designers. In project-based classrooms that are truly learner-centered, teaching content and allowing for student ownership are not conflicting goals. It requires teachers to know their standards well enough to teach them in tandem with students driving the project. Teachers provide the parameters, and students own the rest. Whatever your starting point and end goal, for your classroom and your school community, the belief that it is possible to get to this level of student ownership should be encouraging.

Examine Structures and Lean In

Many schools have seen the power that place-based learning has had in transforming student learning, teacher practice, and school culture, opting to make it their primary methodology. Other schools see the value but have yet to filter learning, culture, structures, and leadership through a place-based lens. Regardless of what stage your school is at, there are school structures that can act as pollinators for student ownership. Let's look at a few.

- **Ability to *cluster* content standards to grow student inquiry:** Letting students map the trajectory of learning requires teachers to be flexible about when they teach content. Being able to move standards around and group them for project work allows innovation and the ability to meet the needs of community partners and the learning needs of students.

- **Efforts to personalize the school experience for students:** These efforts include advisories (at secondary level) or circles, connections or morning meetings (at elementary level), learner profiles or personal learning plans, moving as a cohort with core teachers in common, common planning, and working in collaborative teams for teachers who have students in common.

- **Ways for students, teachers, and community partners to communicate about project work outside of the four walls of the classroom:** Communication methods might include Google Classroom, 365 Classroom, Class Collaborate, or Zoom. Whatever the mode, when put in the hands of students and managed and used by teachers, this anywhere, anytime learning can make projects blossom.

◆ **Ways for students to learn outside of the classroom:** Simplify the field trip process by making paperwork manageable and nimble. Consider modifications such as virtual field trips and field trips outside of school hours. Keep a schoolwide partner database to track successful partnerships, as well as willing and potential partners. Get partners cleared to work with students in a safe yet simple way.

No matter where your school is on the continuum of choice, we hope you feel empowered to grow autonomous learners in your classroom, year-round, with the tools and examples we've shared.

BATON ROUGE'S TROUBLED WATERS
Empower Student Ownership, in Action

As part of this project, students focused on building self-management skills. Students used a management log to identify major tasks and how they would accomplish them. They used the log to set up what their next task would be during work time and where they needed help and resources.

The management log also became a powerful reflection tool along the way. Students had ownership of which resources they explored for their historical research and had some choice in who they would interview. They used visible thinking routines to dig deeper into ideas as well as to practice taking on multiple perspectives. Students also used Google Classroom and the local district's online learning management system to keep track of resources, as well as communicate outside of school about the project.

Being able to navigate project resources outside of the classroom enabled students to take pride in the work they were accomplishing. They explored digital media sources as an option for sharing their narratives. With the help of the local community outreach teams, students created their various products based on what they learned about effective public awareness campaigns and social media campaigns and how best to tell the story of Black swim clubs. Students identified the purpose behind their work as empowering their peers to become swimmers and to inform the policymaking of local city council members. Noting the pride students took in their work on this project, one of their teachers stated, in an anonymous survey about the project, "Not once prior to this project have I seen students take so much ownership of their learning inside and outside of the classroom."

Conclusion

If you imagine your ideal classroom, the one you dream about teaching in, what does it look like? What are you doing? What are students doing? (Is it even a classroom at all?) Much of what we have written in this book requires you to think about your current state and then envision what you are working toward. If the classroom of your not-so-distant dreams involves students innovating, organizing, asking questions, having fun, learning from each other and the community, and leading, then you are prioritizing student ownership. To get from here to there, let students practice self-management skills, give them the lead on portions of the project, and collect data to make nimble adjustments. You've got the vision and the tools to put student ownership at the front of the class.

Key Takeaways and Reflection Questions

Consider this chapter's key takeaways and reflect on the following questions as you work to empower student ownership through place-based learning. Use the Journey Log to further reflect, brainstorm, jot down ideas, make observations, or plan.

- ◆ The defining factor for how much student ownership to build into your classroom and project, at any grade level, is how much students have practiced the skills required to manage the project process and produce a community product—the more practice, the more autonomy.

- ◆ Think about what skills students need to learn to be successful self-managers in project work and teach those skills throughout the school year in small, meaningful, low-stakes ways, turning the dimmer switch up as you gear up for more complex project work.

- ◆ Let students own the process, with substantial support and scaffolding from you. If they can co-create the product with the community partner around a shared inquiry, even better!

- ◆ Set a goal for how you would like to move on the continuum of choice and begin to explore concrete ways to coach students to own their learning. Project learning is not an extreme, but a meeting in the middle of student potential and teacher support.

- ◆ What preassessments and scaffolding can I put in place now, using the dimmer switch approach, to set my students up for success in project work?

- ◆ What are my own attitudes and beliefs about my students' ability to self-manage? What has influenced these attitudes and beliefs?

- ◆ Where is my classroom currently, and where do I want it to be, on the continuum of choice?

- ◆ What school structures support student ownership, and where is there room for improvement?

Journey Log

Journey Log

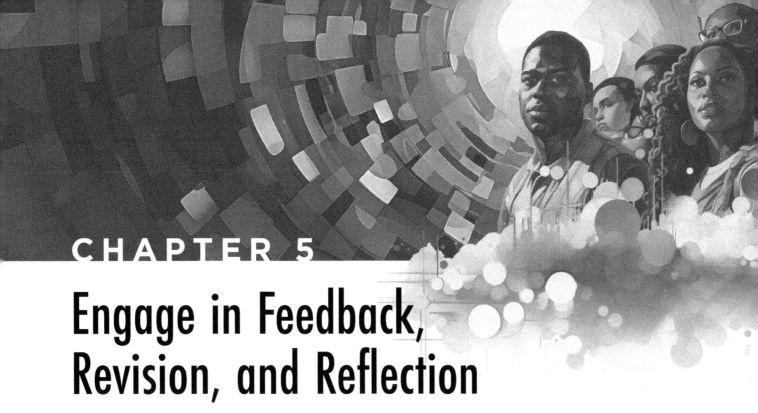

CHAPTER 5

Engage in Feedback, Revision, and Reflection

We do not learn from experience—we learn from reflecting on experience.

—JOHN DEWEY

ESSENTIAL QUESTION: How can we use feedback, revision, and reflection to support students in creating beautiful, transformational products and in building the habit of metacognition?

Reflect on something you have done that you are especially proud of. Maybe it is an athletic feat, or maybe parenting good humans. Possibly it is a piece of art you created. As you think about this source of pride, ask yourself what went into the final product. What was your process? Did you just do it, with no support and little practice, thought, or training? More likely, that source of pride came with time, hard work, practice, an identifiable process, and the wisdom of others who have gone before you. Now ask yourself if those same ingredients—time, hard work, practice, process, guidance—are present for your students and in your teaching.

In this chapter, we accentuate the imperative of giving students the time, processes, and practice to reflect and improve on their work, with the help of feedback from project stakeholders, in order to produce professional-quality products they can be proud of. This chapter also calls out the inequity of a one-and-done, fast-paced curriculum that doesn't allow students to work to mastery. We advocate, instead, imitating what professionals do by carefully seeking feedback and revising a product, creating a habit of learning from one another that is evident within a project and throughout the school year. We will then view "Engage in Feedback, Revision, and Reflection, in Action" through the experience of Baton Rouge's Troubled Waters project. The chapter offers a chance to think further about its content through the Conclusion and Key Takeaways and Reflection Questions sections. It concludes with the Journey Log for writing down your thoughts and ideas.

What Does It Mean to Engage in Feedback, Revision, and Reflection?

Place-based learning asks students to create authentic, high-quality work that is meaningful to the community. As with anything of quality, one's first attempt is typically not one's best, nor do most industries allow professionals to work in isolation without getting feedback from colleagues. If we apply this practice of considering feedback and reflecting to education, then high-quality student work requires revision and reflection on feedback from teachers, peers, and community partners, as well as on the products and services students are creating and producing. Working toward mastery means practice, making mistakes, messiness, constant improvement, and a satisfying conclusion.

From a planning perspective, teachers need to build time into the project calendar for meaningful revision and reflection to take place, and to scaffold critiquing skills throughout the school year to set students up for success in their project work. The skill of critique does not come naturally to many of us but can be explicitly taught, and the benefit of constructive critique is evidenced in the work students produce. Feedback, revision, and reflection are practices that we should infuse throughout our classroom practice and are critical to place-based learning.

How Do I Engage in Feedback, Revision, and Reflection?

Imagine the classroom to be a pride incubator, of sorts, where our actions as teachers result in many opportunities for students to feel capable, empowered, and motivated to do professional-quality work. What if your classroom is the place where students' stories of the work they're most proud of take hold? The opportunity for students to receive feedback, revise, and reflect allows this to happen.

Teachers can engage in feedback, revision, and reflection with students in the following ways.

- **Revise for equity:** By distinguishing the enduring understandings of your content, setting an end goal, and guiding students to work toward it with room for critique, reflection, and revision, we tell students that we are investing time in their ability to produce high-caliber work.

- **Create a habit of feedback, revision, and reflection:** In order for critique, reflection and revision to become a habit, we peek at how to unpack that process as it unfolds before and throughout a project.

- **Heighten collaboration through feedback:** When students care about the work they are producing, there is an engrained need for collaboration with peers and community partners, making it necessary to teach the skills of giving and receiving feedback.

- **Use metacognition to reflect:** Meaningful reflection is metacognitive (thinking about thinking). We can use thinking routines to encourage students to consider their outlook on their process.

- **Imitate what professionals do:** Professionals make corrections and change their minds, produce for a purpose, are transparent about their revisions, and often have voice in the initial ideation. When we emulate this sageness in the classroom, students are more invested in project work.

Revise for Equity

The opportunity for revision is an issue of equity. Without revision, the students who presently perform well will continue to do well, and the students who struggle will continue to do so. It is only with practice and actionable feedback that students can increase skill. Outside of the world of education, we intuitively understand that "practice makes perfect," or at least makes us a whole lot better. We may watch a video tutorial on knitting, give it an initial try with medio-cre (at best) results, and then with repeated practice improve on our initial attempt. If we were judged on our first stitches and then expected to move on to increasingly complex patterns, we would quickly fall into despair, and the knitting basket would get pushed to the back of the craft supply cupboard. This is, however, often what we ask students to do with the content we teach. This expectation, coupled with the varying degrees of exposure students have had to our content, creates an inequitable environment. We therefore ask you not only to make practice one of the key design features in place-based instruction but also to come to an understanding of the value and the equity that revision provides.

There is real and pervasive anxiety in our profession about coverage of content. The anxiety varies in degree from subject to subject, teacher to teacher, but the oft heard refrain is "too much content, too little time." And there is a lot of content. There are also proven and effective ways to standard map and curriculum plan that alleviate the coverage grind. One such example is the *understanding-by-design framework*, which asks teachers to identify the enduring understandings of their content, then use those understandings as the basis of planning and formative assessment, because revision is how we see growth over time and identify areas of need.

Let's talk about assessment for a moment because revision is how we accurately assess student learning. Returning to the knitting example we used earlier, and planning backward, suppose you became interested in this art form because of a fond memory of your grandmother knitting slippers for all her grandchildren. This is a gift you want to pass to the young people in your life, so you set out to knit a scarf for each of them by the holidays. You identify an enduring understanding: knitting is a time-honored family skill you wish to possess, and you are beginning with the end in mind: a goal of knitting scarves. That established, every time you watch a tutorial, read a blog, learn about and buy materials, ask questions of other knitters, and work and rework your scarves you are formatively assessing your own learning. You are able to formatively self-assess because you know what you are aiming for. You have a standard—an attractive, functional scarf—and you are work-ing toward it with purpose because you have an enduring understanding of the value of knitting. That combination of enduring understanding leading to end goal leading to formative assessment is what results in lasting learning. Each time you practice your burgeoning skill, you recognize your progress, seek feedback, and set goals to improve further. We are asking no less in the classroom. Every lesson, activity, resource, draft, prototype, and lab gives us (teachers and students) data on our progress and what we have yet to accomplish. The feedback students receive from peers, com-munity partners, and teachers adds to a robust and valid assessment picture. It is worth repeating: revision is an equity issue. We can give students the seemingly simple gift of time to do their best work, building in the scaffolds and supports they need as their formative assessments reveal real-time progress. As authors and educators Ron Berger, Leah Rugen, and Libby Woodfin (2014) say:

> Motivation is in fact the most important result of student-engaged assessment—unless students find reason and inspiration to care about learning and have hope that they can improve, excellence and high achievement will remain the domain of a select group. (p. 6)

It's amazing that when students have the dueling burdens of time and production lifted and replaced with the expectation of quality through revision, their level of trust in themselves and in their teacher skyrockets, leading to more equitable learning outcomes. Consequently, when mapping out a semester or year of instruction by determining the standards for those enduring understandings, some standards will need to be taught outside of projects, folded into other standards, or given up in favor of a more equitable practice. Something else must be let go in order to ensure the time to make that impeccable scarf.

Create a Habit of Feedback, Revision, and Reflection

What does the feedback, revision, and reflection process look like in a place-based classroom? As you read this section, you'll undoubtedly recognize practices you already do, because what it looks like isn't complicated or a secret. It looks like students practicing, talking about their work, and thinking about their thinking, and doing it so often it becomes a habit. For a practice to become a habit, it should start early in the school year. Start simple so the rationale is evident to students, then make it routine so it's an expectation. By the time students need feedback, revision, and reflection for project work, they have already formed the habit. That said, the skills of giving and receiving feedback, and incorporating that feedback into project work, need to be explicitly, consistently, and patiently taught. Here is a sample timeline of a teacher's plan to build her fourth-grade students' feedback, revision, and reflection skills to prepare for and conduct a project focused on building unique bat houses for a local nature center.

- **Beginning of the semester or quarter:** A teacher co-creates classroom agreements, focusing on how students treat one another and teachers. The class then checks in and reflects each day on how effectively they are adhering to the agreements and what they can do to grow their self-awareness and interdependence skills.

- **Prior to starting the project:** The teacher shares kindness quotes, preferably in a standing circle, and discusses the role kindness plays in friendships, family, workplace, and society. Relating the discussion to bat behavior makes it even better!

- **Beginning of the project:** The teacher introduces visible thinking routines such as see-think-wonder to familiarize students with using specific language to describe, question, and persuade. She uses a provocative image of a bat house and a short video on the loss of bat habitat as her input.

- **Early in the project:** Teacher and students watch EL Education's (n.d.) video *Austin's Butterfly* and discuss. The teacher picks a piece of student work from a previous year related to the content she is teaching and conducts a whole-class tuning protocol. A *tuning protocol* is a structure from the School Reform Initiative (SRI) designed to exchange feedback on a work in progress. For their tuning protocol, the class uses the sentence stems "I like" and "I wonder," along with a word bank or assessment tool for students to draw language from. Students practice giving kind, specific, and helpful feedback on anonymous work. This is a useful formative assessment tool to let the teacher know her students' comfort and competence levels with the habit of giving feedback.

- **As the project progresses:** The teacher conducts a silent gallery walk with students' work in progress on their design ideas for bat houses. Students write their feedback on the back of sticky notes (so peers can't see one another's comments) and include their names. Options for feedback might include *likes* and *wonders* (using the sentence stems, "I like" and "I wonder"), *two stars and a wish* (two positive attributes of the work and one suggestion), and/or a *happy sandwich* (a suggestions sandwiched by two pieces of positive feedback). The gallery walk happens toward the end of class, and the teacher asks students to leave the sticky notes next to the work for her review before students collect them at a later time. After class, the teacher reviews feedback to again check how students are progressing, and she retains feedback that does not meet the criteria (for example, overly negative or unkind). Before students read the feedback they received, she asks them to reflect on how they did as peer reviewers. Were they kind, specific, and helpful? Would they give the same feedback face to face? Finally, she allows students to read the feedback and to sort it into categories such as, "I never thought of," "I'll consider," and "I'm on the right track!"

- ◆ **Midpoint of the project:** Once the teacher is confident that every student knows what kind, specific, and helpful feedback looks like and feels like, she tries a fishbowl tuning of a piece of student work. A *fishbowl tuning* separates students into an inner and outer circle, with the inner circle sharing and the outer circle observing. She asks a student prior to class if they are comfortable sharing their work, then has the student present (as a fish in the bowl), with classmates in the outer bowl jumping in the middle (a few at a time) to share feedback. This is a public critique, and, therefore, it is extra important to adhere to classroom agreements and pause the protocol if issues arise. Students are learning a new process, so they may need in-the-moment guidance on how to frame their feedback (now that they are verbally sharing with peers) and how to engage in the protocol (talk time, moving in and out of the fishbowl, remaining quiet when in the outer bowl).

- ◆ **Midpoint and beyond:** While students practice the skills they've learned and move into smaller group structures for tuning and other critique protocols, the teacher focuses on the skill of revision. How are students taking feedback and making their work better? What is her messaging about this? How many iterations does she hope to see before they can call it their best work? Often, including reflection focused on revision will allow students to see the potential for changes without becoming defensive. The teacher uses simple reflection tools such as Flip, exit tickets, invisible journals (air writing; that is, thinking and moving a finger to shape words only they can see), pre-flections (reflection before peer feedback to anticipate what their peers might say), the GUS method (guessed, unsure, sure) (McDonald, VanCleave, Kim, Salesky, & Green, 2020), and listening dyads which will all build the skill of revision. And, as always, her modeling makes all the difference.

As you work to make feedback, revision, and reflection a habit, keep in mind that each student is unique in their learning, as is each class. We have had high school classes where students were in rival gangs, where it took six months of empathetic practice and scaffolding of feedback skills for those students to make eye contact with each other and say one thing they liked about the other's work. This is an extreme example, but the caution is relevant: start early, start simple, and make it routine.

Heighten Collaboration Through Feedback

When students are reluctant to give, receive, and incorporate feedback on their work, it is usually because they haven't learned how, they haven't built enough trust with their peers or you, or they haven't been given a compelling enough reason to collaborate in this deeply vulnerable way. Meaningful collaboration in the classroom is hard to find . . . unless you're doing place-based learning.

In the example of the high school class that took six months to give each other positive feedback, building skills and trust was the first and slowest part of the process, requiring a great deal of persistence from all involved. What finally made it possible for students to move to giving critical feedback to one another was a class product they all wanted to be proud of. In this case, the product was a series of designs that would be painted on traffic control boxes in their neighborhood. The success of the project hinged on the continuity, originality, and quality of the designs. What students found through the project was that learning how to talk about their work and the work of others was empowering. It was collaboration on a mission!

In place-based learning, students also receive feedback from community partners, and taking that gracefully is a learned skill as well. Putting structures in place so the feedback from community partners falls within their purview and your learning goals is the key to success. A common error is to give your community partner your full rubric, asking them to assess students' work in progress on *all* the criteria. Most people outside of education are unfamiliar with rubrics, and expecting them to understand the tool and assess student work is unrealistic. A better strategy is to look at your rubric, then choose one or two criteria that your community partners have expertise in. Make sure those criteria are exhibited in the work the community partners will be looking at, and create a feedback form using the language of the criteria. This method ensures the feedback students receive will be much more meaningful and actionable.

Use Metacognitive Thinking to Reflect

Reflection provides a mirror into thought processes, deepens understanding, sharpens critical and creative thinking skills, and helps students integrate new knowledge with previous knowledge and experiences. For students, this leads to personal connections to the learning, content, and process, thereby increasing student ownership of new skills and knowledge (Ash & Clayton, 2009).

For reflection to be most meaningful, it should be metacognitive. We want students to be thinking about their thinking. For example, if students are going to be metacognitive about purpose-driven inquiry, they need to think about how to phrase their focus question. As students work collaboratively to take action, they need to consider how they work together, their individual contributions, and ways they can improve team outcomes. And students can use reflection as a way of looking back to process experiences. So how do we ask students self-assessment questions to promote a reflective mindset?

Teachers in the High Tech High network of schools near San Diego, California, offer a list of forty questions to ask students, divided into the following categories.

+ **Inward looking:** What did you learn about yourself as you worked on this project?
+ **Outward looking:** What is the one thing you particularly want people to notice when they look at your work?
+ **Backward looking:** What processes did you go through to produce this product?
+ **Forward looking:** What will you change in the next revision of your work? (Edutopia, 2011)

Establishing thinking routines in your classroom prepares students for metacognitive reflection. We use Project Zero's (n.d.) Thinking Routine Toolbox to help establish a culture of feedback, revision, and reflection:

> A thinking routine is a set of questions or a brief sequence of steps used to scaffold and support student thinking. [Project Zero] researchers designed thinking routines to deepen students' thinking and to help make that thinking "visible." Thinking routines help to reveal students' thinking to the teacher and also help students themselves to notice and name particular "thinking moves," making those moves more available and useful to them in other contexts.

The Thinking Routine Toolbox has over one hundred routines to choose from, for just the right process at the right time in a project.

Imitate What Professionals Do

Although community partners might not know the ins and outs of assessment like teachers do, little explanation is necessary about what feedback and revision are, or why they are necessary, because most professions use revision cycles. That is precisely why we should be using critique and revision in our classrooms: to mimic the practices of professionals so our students are career ready.

In the world outside of school, professionals produce for a purpose. Whether the purpose is manufacturing the aft fuselage for a major airline or composing the score for a new streaming show, people know why they are doing what they are doing, and it gives them the drive to do it well. Students crave the same sense of purpose and a rationale for their learning, beyond the promise of a passing grade or a distant graduation. Revising work becomes a softer pitch when the purpose is within sight. Professionals do something else that is pertinent to our conversation: they bounce ideas off one another, scrapping some and keeping others. When we transfer this to the classroom, we think of a room full of noise, energy, and wild ideas, and it is exactly that. And why not? It is much easier to engage students in a long-term project if they know their initial ideas will be tapped and may influence the end result. At the company Adobe, for instance, they use the *check-in approach*, "where ongoing feedback flows freely," using feedback protocols to bounce ideas off one another and get critique (Adobe, n.d.).

Professionals make corrections and change their minds. If an initial line of inquiry isn't producing results, they enact a new plan. The best organizations, and classrooms, are nimble, able to maneuver quickly when they need something new. We are adept at this as teachers, but our pivoting often happens behind the scenes with students unaware of the changes we make. Place-based learning brings the backstage on stage by asking students to decide when corrections need to be made and what advice they have for what comes next. The revision process applies to the project process as well. "What does our essential question tell us about what we should research next?" "Our original community partner has shared their expertise—who else could help us with this?" These are questions students should be asking, and they occur when we make revisions in learning transparent, when we partner with our students.

How Do I Use Reflection to Improve My Practice?

As we talk about the power in students thinking about their thinking, we want to discuss the role of reflection in our professional practice. Teaching is a relentless job. Finding the time for metacognition, alone or with colleagues, or to ask our students to reflect on how well we are showing up for them, can seem like an unrealistic hope. Now, what if we told you the key to becoming a better teacher has much less to do with professional development or lesson planning and much, much more to do with reflective practice (Rodgers, 2002)?

What is the purpose of developing a reflective practice, and what are some simple ways to do it? The purpose is straightforward. If we hope to teach our students, then we need to hear from them to know if learning is happening. We also need to sit our own reflections side by side with the experience of students and see how they align, how they impact what might come next, and how we might grow. The vulnerability inherent in listening to our students' reflections guides our sense of responsibility so we can refocus on what is most important, which can sometimes be lost if we are practicing in a vacuum.

The simplest rule we've found for building in time for reflection is to model it—when students reflect, you reflect. Whether this happens during a three-minute exit ticket, a Flip video, a brief survey, or a checklist review, the time you allot for your students to reflect will be a gift to you as well. If you ask students to sit quietly with a journal, do the same. If you ask students to share with a partner, send a message to a colleague at the same time, if possible. Make a commitment to build fifteen minutes a week of reflection into your practice, then as you and your students build stamina and see the benefit, increase the time. If you find you are getting stuck in a reflection rut, then use a resource such as the reflection strategies produced by the University of Oklahoma's K20 Learn (https://learn.k20center.ou.edu/strategies), to rejuvenate your tool kit. If fifteen minutes seems like a lot, consider things you do almost mindlessly in fifteen minutes that may not be particularly important to you, and instead use that time to personally reflect. Notice how this change makes you feel and what happens to your practice.

BATON ROUGE'S TROUBLED WATERS
Engage in Feedback, Revision, and Reflection, in Action

"Never in a million years did I ever think I'd actually wind up *asking* my classmates for feedback!" This is a statement from a student telling about their process of reflecting on their learning during the project (student, personal communication, May 2022). Students, through multiple formative assessment opportunities, received ongoing feedback and had class time allotted to make revisions. Students used critique protocols such as a gallery walk of their initial images to get feedback from peers in the form of "I notice" and "I wonder" statements, using the project's rubric in various ways to provide feedback to each other. For example, teachers used rubric indicators for their guiding questions when working with students. Teachers also incorporated exit ticket reflection prompts as indicators throughout the project for students to give peer-to-peer feedback with their teammates. Students met with local public awareness groups, community members, and local historians to get feedback on the research they were conducting. One student team located a local art exhibit that explored themes connected with the local swimming pool protests. The students then used that as a talking point with local elders, soliciting ideas on how to incorporate that history into their final presentations. Students also kept a reflection journal throughout the project to reflect on what they were learning, what they were learning about themselves, and their experience of the project. This reflection journal supported students in seeing how their products were evolving as the project progressed.

Conclusion

When you next sit down to plan a unit or project, think of the student who is always rushing to produce work, right up until the last minute, often leaving portions incomplete. Think of the student who turns in crumpled and torn papers, asks for more time, or immediately throws away papers you return to them. Now envision what it would mean to that same student to know that they are expected to work to fluency on a product and share their work in progress with their peers and a community partner, and that their work was going to matter to someone in the community. What would happen if you showed, through modeling and scaffolding, that you would support that student with every step, until they produced work they were proud of? At first, they may be terrified, but there is something almost mystical when a student understands that, given time and supportive learning structures, they can create or do something well. As you plan, use the tools in this chapter, the project design checklist in chapter 4 (figure 4.1, page 71), questioning strategies, and the processes that professionals use, to build a more equitable learning space for every student to give, receive, reflect on, and incorporate feedback so they may produce their best work.

Key Takeaways and Reflection Questions

Consider this chapter's key takeaways and reflect on the following questions as you work to engage in feedback, revision, and reflection through place-based learning. Use the Journey Log to further reflect, brainstorm, jot down ideas, make observations, or plan.

+ Feedback, revision, and reflection are ongoing processes that require planning, commitment, and time, and should be infused throughout a project and beyond.
+ Revision is how we accurately assess student learning because it allows the teacher to measure growth over time through formative assessment.
+ Opportunities for feedback and reflection move teachers closer to an equitable classroom where there is an expectation of quality through revision.
+ Professionals give each other feedback and revise their work. Students should be modeling and developing these skills as they become interdependent.

+ How might I make reflection a routine in my classroom and in my own reflective practice?
+ How might I scaffold the process and prepare my students for giving and receiving feedback?
+ What structures can I put in place to support students in the feedback, revision, and reflection process?
+ What enduring understandings do I want my students to have about the content and skills I teach?

Journey Log

Journey Log

Journey Log

CHAPTER 6

Co-Create an Authentic Community Product

Educating oneself is easy, but educating ourselves to help the community is much more difficult.

—CESAR E. CHAVEZ

ESSENTIAL QUESTION: What will we need to guide students to create meaningful and authentic community products?

A community product in the context of place-based learning might be an action, such as an awareness campaign, a solution to a local problem, an action plan for the betterment of the community, or a service to address a genuine need. It could also be a product, such as a museum installation about a historical event that impacted the community over time, for example, or a book based on the oral histories of community members, whether to gather the wisdom and knowledge of elders or to interrogate the present. The final community product can take many forms, such as a webpage or website, blog, documentary, or podcast, all meant to engage, educate, interact, or increase awareness.

The community product is a culmination of all that students have learned over the course of the project. It includes evidence of inquiry and feedback, revision, and reflection. You will see elements of student ownership within their approach to inquiry and the final product. You will see indicators of how students embedded culture into their final product, showing an awareness of the racial diversity within their community. The final product will show how they leveraged collaboration with their community partnership and, most importantly, evidence of the standards and ways of knowing that you are assessing.

The community product that students produce and their engagement with community members in this process provide authentic and meaningful ways for the school and the community to move forward with deliberate thought and action around a common purpose. When thinking about final products, make sure, as Sheldon Soper (2017), content writer at the Knowledge

Round Table, puts it, "the product has an authentic purpose, an authentic audience, and an authentic form of personal ownership." In doing so, Soper adds, "Curricular goals are met, real-world skills are fostered, and the process genuinely affects students' thought processes." By engaging students in working toward the betterment of their community, the whole community benefits. The community comes to see students as a valuable resource as they become knowledgeable about the place where they live and better understand the cultural, sociopolitical, economic, environmental, and historical context of their community or region. This in-depth understanding of place guides students in their search for solutions for positive change. When students are engaged in this manner, learning takes on a new dimension. Soper reminds us that:

> from the outset, students need to buy into the notion that their work means something. While the outcome of an authentic [place-based learning] unit may shift throughout the process, students need to believe that the results of their efforts matter.

As students engage with the power of place, they begin to see how they fit into their community and the contributions they can make. Content, skills, and cultural knowledge come alive when rooted in community places.

In this chapter, we'll explore how to ensure the community product is authentic by leveraging your community partners and experts. In addition, we provide tips on how to design authentic products with the support of your students and community partners. We will consider "Co-Create an Authentic Community Product, in Action" through the lens of Baton Rouge's Troubled Waters project. The chapter also offers a chance to think further about its content through the Conclusion and Key Takeaways and Reflection Questions sections. Finally, use the Journey Log to further reflect, brainstorm, jot down ideas, make observations, or plan.

What Is an Authentic Community Product?

Place-based learning asks students to create a product to demonstrate understanding and application of the content. While a product can take a variety of forms, either concrete or abstract, the product is only one part of the place-based learning process. When students, parents, and many teachers think of a project, what they are often thinking of is a product—that thing students create to show what they know, usually after all the content has been taught. In place-based learning, it is essential to help all stakeholders understand that the project encapsulates *all* the learning—from day one to the final reflection—and the products are embedded in a project to assess students' understanding of content, concepts, skills, and cultural knowledge. Once we see products as a single component in the project process, our understanding of place-based learning becomes much richer and more meaningful. An authentic community product is an integrated part of a larger process of learning and making meaningful changes in the community, not simply the end result.

How Do I Increase Authenticity in a Product With Community Partners?

A community partner or partners take on a unique role in the product phase of a project. They often provide the initial idea for the product or even ask students to devise a solution to an issue facing the community. Community partners may give feedback on student works in progress, provide their expertise, or may be the audience to showcase the final product. Community partners increase the quality and authenticity of student work by lending purpose and agency to place-based projects and the products and services students create.

Educator Drew Perkins (2021) explains:

> authenticity includes students working on a real-world problem or creating products for actual clients. For example, perhaps students are creating and administering a water quality testing system for area residents that are concerned whether their drinking water is safe. Or perhaps students are building structures for the U.S. Fish and Wildlife Service.

While it is imperative that the project, and products embedded within, is authentic to students, we also want to make sure the project is authentic to the community and the stakeholders.

Place-based learning provides excellent opportunities for students to use the same tools that professionals use in their work. For example, in an English class, students might use software for creating podcasts that include tools for recording and editing. In a science class, it could be an app that allows for sophisticated data analysis and ways to display the data visually. If students are redesigning a public space, they might use computer-aided design (CAD) or SketchUp, a 3-D drawing tool.

When we connect projects to outside practices, we promote a "a sense of civic purpose and engagement," according to Lucas Education Research (n.d.), "which can be especially powerful when projects result in genuine products or performances for an authentic audience" (p. 5).

Teachers can increase authenticity in a product in the following ways.

- ◆ **Design authentic culminating products:** Begin with the end in mind. Consider the different ways of knowing that students will need to engage in to successfully produce a product, service, or action that benefits their community. Content standards, cultural knowledge, 21st century skills, and understanding the community context are all things to keep in mind as you and your students think about different ways to demonstrate understanding and benefit their community.

- ◆ **Sustain the learning with a legacy project:** Students often create legacy products that continue to inform, create change, and empower members of the community. Sometimes, a legacy project goes beyond local places and moves into regional places. Legacy projects and products often become dependable and sustainable because each year a new class adds to the database, schedules an event, or provides a service to the community.

Design Authentic Culminating Products

To design authentic culminating products, consider ways in which students can demonstrate their understanding, once you have identified the standards and an authentic issue. Whether a community partner has come to you with an issue or a specific request, or students, through inquiry and investigation, have determined an issue and solution for action, you want to ensure that the final product shows evidence of student understanding, application of the content, and being nested in a real-world context. In *Top Ten Tips for Assessing Project-Based Learning*, Edutopia (n.d.) points out:

> over the course of a project, students might take on the roles of scientists, historians, screenwriters, or experts from other disciplines. Look to these disciplines for appropriate end-of-project assessment ideas. What sorts of products would you expect from a biologist, poet, or social scientist?

What do professionals from these fields make, do, or perform? Expect similar products or performances from your students at the culmination of a project to show what they have learned. Authentic products naturally reflect the learning goals and content standards you have identified during project planning. They don't feel fake or forced. (p. 5)

Often, the community product results from collaborative groups where students synthesize their findings to design an action plan, town meeting, or call to action. For example, a team in California created a project on the legacy of the gold rush, creating a newspaper to inform others of the lasting environmental and cultural impacts of the gold rush in their community and what community members could do to help mitigate the ongoing impacts.

In the book *Teaching When the World Is on Fire*, American educationalist, researcher, and author Lisa Delpit (2021) emphasizes the importance of helping students both to understand the broader social context in which they live and to develop critical thinking skills that allow them to analyze and challenge systems of inequality:

For educators, particularly those who teach in communities struggling against the forces of poverty and inequality, the imperative is to help young people not only acquire the tools they need to succeed in the world, but also to develop the capacity to analyze and challenge the social structures that have produced the inequities they face. (p. 7)

With authentic culminating products, students demonstrate their cultural knowledge and awareness, application of the content, and specific skills such as collaboration, critical thinking, communication, and problem solving, all of which teachers can apply in assessing students. This collaborative product is often what students share with the community. In this process of innovation by coming up with a solution, action plan, or product to improve their community, students are now taking what is familiar and making it strange. This is where students hone the skills that will help them succeed beyond the school setting. This is where they understand civic responsibility and the many different ways they can participate in their community. In his blog post "Creating Engaged Citizens Through Civic Education," high school assistant principal Benjamin Washington (2021) emphasizes:

having productive and proactive citizens is fundamental to a functioning society and to the growth of young adults into engaged citizens. Students today need to have opportunities to learn how to work with others with different perspectives. Additionally, students need to learn about the functions of government, how communities operate locally and globally, and social justice issues.

Place-based learning creates the platform for engaging students in the world beyond the classroom. It provides the vessel. Washington (2021) notes:

It is important to create engaged citizens and to develop students who have 21st-century competencies and skills. Creating engaged citizens is important to ensure diverse populations can operate in a society and to empower individuals to build a better community. This can range from understanding how power is divided in the United States government, voting, and how to organize groups for advocacy. Having engaged citizens is important to ensure meaningful roles, discussions, and participation in projects that develop the community and impact stakeholders.

Turning students into engaged citizens so they can continue to advocate for change even after they leave school is one of the outcomes of place-based learning.

We want to leave room for student ownership in the design and implementation of the community product. Think about how you can build in processes that engage the voices of all in identifying next steps. The discovery period, whether it involves research, story mapping, talking with experts, surveying community members, collecting scientific data, or holding town meetings, often leads to the final community product: a solution, action, or other.

Sustain the Learning With Legacy Projects

The students who initially develop and work on a project establish relationships with partners and gather resources that become sustaining pieces of the project. Teachers can then use the lessons, labs, and processes that are already in place. A project's focus might change based on new issues, but the standards and content remain the same in most instances. Additionally, a legacy project may change and grow substantially with time and as new students work on it.

Micki worked with students from the No. 1 Altalanos Iskola in Pomaz, Hungary, on an environmental place-based project. Students launched their project by studying the Barat Brook, a local waterway, and the surrounding wetlands. They cleaned the brook and studied the flora and fauna and the human impact on the stream. This was an integral part of their science and social studies curriculum and a project they did each year in fifth grade. Each year, students and teachers would adapt the project based on new findings or issues surrounding Barat Brook. They showcased their work by sharing the data with the community and created a public awareness campaign providing simple actions community members could take to reduce water pollution.

Armed with these experiences and understanding, students wanted to go beyond cleaning up their immediate environment and explore what they could do on a regional scale. They concentrated their efforts on the pollution of the River Danube from the Black Forest to the Black Sea. Through extensive inquiry and investigation, they identified direct and indirect sources of pollution and created a list of actions that individuals, companies, and organizations could take to decrease sources of pollution. They organized a press conference where they launched an appeal in four languages, asking companies and city councils to stop polluting the Danube and to be part of the solution. They also sent out their appeal in the form of a press release to the media and foreign embassies of the countries through which the Danube flows.

Their local community work expanded to an entire geographical area. They invited schools to join them in their efforts. Students reached out to the University of Budapest, which agreed to partner with the students and provide expertise. Through their outreach efforts, students organized a "water sampling day" where groups of students in the different countries simultaneously took water samples from the areas along the Danube that they had adopted to monitor. The University of Budapest analyzed the samples, and students prepared a report based on the results and presented their findings to the Danube Observation Center.

Students produced a variety of products to demonstrate their content knowledge across all content areas. They wrote press releases, held press conferences, and organized a network of schools to participate in the water-monitoring project and a final scientific report with graphed data that they presented to scientists from the Danube Observation Center. The students' efforts continued under the name of Green Hearts, which became a growing environmental youth movement in Hungary and the legacy of their school, Altalanos Iskola.

As you design a project, consider whether it could become a legacy project that each class, year after year, could work on. A typical example might be a community garden that students improve and add to each year. Once the garden is established, the project focus might change. Perhaps one year, students explore the use of organic fertilizers and pesticides and inform the community about the hazards of using chemical products on the environment and the food they are growing. Students might conduct scientific investigations and provide simple options, such as planting marigolds and nasturtiums that repel insects and attract beneficial insects like ladybugs. Maybe one year, they focus on composting or growing native plants to attract pollinators and butterflies. You can plan out these ideas or let them develop organically, with your students providing ideas. Each year, students would produce a different product with a focus on raising awareness or creating a call-to-action campaign.

Be flexible with this process of creating authentic community products. Allowing in-depth investment in the entire process is how we engage the creativity and hearts of our students. This builds agency, and students recognize that their voices are formidable and that they can use their voices to make positive changes in their community. Create a culture that helps students to discover their strengths and their integral part in the power of place.

BATON ROUGE'S TROUBLED WATERS
Co-Create Authentic Community Product, in Action

In Baton Rouge's Troubled Waters project, students found empowerment by determining which product they would craft to convey their answer to the essential question: How can we plan a public swimming pool that will honor the people and culture in our community? This process looked like teachers presenting the task to the students in true purpose-driven inquiry fashion, then offering students a menu of options to give them an idea of the possibilities. Production possibilities included hosting informative talks at the local healing center, presenting proposals to candidates for local city council positions, and public awareness campaigns. From there, students either selected from the menu of options or chose a different option that most aligned to their audience. In either case, students were led through a process of decision making, using a decision-making protocol.

Using a timed step-by-step protocol, students first worked individually to decide their top idea for a community product, based on their work with the various organizations and experts they interacted with in the community. Students pulled from the repertoire of products they previously made, such as infographics, one-page papers, and formal presentations, as well as new ideas they generated in the project launch. Once individuals decided on their top choice, student teams listened to each other's ideas, focusing on themes or commonalities. Next, the class held a vote to determine consensus; in rare occasions, the teacher served as the tiebreaker vote.

Conclusion

Place-based learning asks students to partner with the community to create a product to demonstrate understanding of the content and community issues or need. Creating community products reminds all stakeholders that the project encapsulates all the learning—from day one to the final reflection—and that the community product or products are embedded in a project to assess students' understanding of content, process, concepts, and skills. Once stakeholders perceive products as one component in the project, our understanding of the process of place-based learning becomes much richer and more meaningful. Community partners ramp up the quality and authenticity of student work, lending purpose and agency to place-based projects.

Key Takeaways and Reflection Questions

Consider this chapter's key takeaways and reflect on the following questions as you work to co-create an authentic community product through place-based learning. Use the Journey Log to further reflect, brainstorm, jot down ideas, make observations, or plan.

- ◆ Place-based learning asks students to create a product to demonstrate understanding and application of the content and process.
- ◆ Community products might be an action, a solution, or a service to the community to address a genuine need.
- ◆ Community partners and members add authenticity to the creation of the final product.
- ◆ Consider sustaining your project ideas by creating legacy projects.

- ◆ How might I design a community product that is authentic and meaningful to the community while providing evidence of learning and deepening students' understanding of major concepts?
- ◆ How do I design culminating products that leave room for student ownership as well as voice and choice?
- ◆ Is what we are asking students to do in alignment with their cultural background?
- ◆ What roles might the community partners and students play in designing the final products?

Journey Log

Journey Log

Journey Log

CHAPTER 7
Embed Culture in Teaching and Learning

*When we connect with our ancestors and put their wisdom into action,
we are evolving our collective consciousness. We are transporting the ancient
truths of our collective past and birthing them into our future. What we create
out of those truths extends the wisdom of all those who have gone before us,
and it provides a guide for all those who will follow.*

—SHERRI MITCHELL WEH'NA HA'MU KWASSET

ESSENTIAL QUESTION: How can I embed culture, traditions, and place-based narratives into my instruction to represent all my students and community?

We are writing from Choctaw and Houma territory in Baton Rouge, Louisiana; Steilacoom territory in Tacoma, Washington; and Snohomish territory in Everett, Washington. Acknowledging the stolen Indigenous land on which we stand and the peoples therein, we take first steps toward truly honoring the place's legacy. Land acknowledgment connects deeply to culturally embedded aspects of place-based learning. Acknowledging the land on which we learn, we actively ground and frame where the learning is taking place. Culturally embedded components are related to how we view, understand, and see the world, and how we position ourselves and draw connections to learning content. Not only in the United States, but also globally, the history of place is the reason why we present these place-based learning principles and strategies.

Who are your students? Where is your community, and what cultures are represented? Upon whose ancestral land do you teach and learn? Whose voice may not be at the table? The power of place is illustrated by the cultures and cultural archetypes represented in that place. This is the essence of the final place-based design principle: embed culture in teaching and learning.

Embedding culture into teaching and learning is a pivotal aspect of fostering a rich and inclusive educational environment. It goes beyond the mere transmission of facts and figures, and delves into the realm of shared values, traditions, and perspectives that shape the fabric of society. In doing so, educators create a bridge between the classroom and the diverse tapestry of students' backgrounds, helping them relate academic content to their own lived experiences. By infusing cultural elements into instruction, educators not only acknowledge the uniqueness of each learner but also cultivate a sense of belonging and mutual understanding. This approach not only enhances the educational experience but also equips students with the cultural competence necessary for navigating an interconnected world. Moreover, embedding culture into instruction serves as a means of promoting empathy, respect, and appreciation for the richness that diversity brings to the learning journey, preparing students to thrive in an increasingly globalized and multicultural society.

In this chapter, we explore what it means to embed culture in teaching and learning and detail specific ways to do so in our project design. We will consider "Embed Culture in Teaching and Learning, in Action" through the lens of Baton Rouge's Troubled Waters project. This chapter also offers a chance to think further about its content through the Conclusion and Key Takeaways and Reflection Questions sections. It concludes with the Journey Log for writing down your thoughts and ideas.

What Does It Mean to Embed Culture in Teaching and Learning?

When we design with culturally embedded concepts in mind, we leverage the archetypes of the place itself and our students' cultures. For example, both oral and written traditions (archetypes) are incorporated and valued within culturally embedded projects. Collaborative, collective efforts are aligned to project tasks as well as individual components. Specifically, in an elementary mathematics project, for example, individual work on scale and proportion contributes to a group or team blueprint of a school playground by leveraging diverse skills, perspectives, and expertise. Each team member brings their unique strengths to the table, allowing for specialized contributions to specific aspects of a project. As individuals work independently, they generate ideas, solve problems, and develop components that, when integrated into the collective effort, enhance the overall quality and effectiveness of the team's output.

This collaborative synergy ensures a comprehensive and well-rounded approach to tackling tasks, leading to more innovative and successful outcomes. Students immerse themselves in a place's culture, which creates the opportunity for students to connect. This can involve participating in community events, volunteering, forming connections with local residents, and being open-minded to new experiences.

Immersing oneself in the local culture, whether through language, cuisine, or traditions, fosters a deeper understanding and appreciation, allowing students to become integral parts of their new environment. This connection comes in the form of connection to place, connection to their own culture, and relativizing the experience to their own culture. Connection to place is about being emplaced in the day-to-day life of a community in a specific geographical location (physically, ecologically, socially, culturally, spiritually, and politically) while being relationally connected to more distanced people and places in an increasingly globalized world (Pisters, Vihinen, & Figueiredo, 2019). This culturally embedded connection can be both direct and indirect—either students can find similarities to the culture of the place, or they can find value in the lessons learned about a new, different culture.

Even when the place is rooted in a culture different from that of the learners, they can forge deep connections by designing with culturally embedded strategies in mind. Not one archetype is valued over another. Delpit (2013) reminds us, "If the curriculum we use to teach our children does not connect in positive ways to the culture young people bring to school, it is doomed to failure" (p. 21).

There is a beautiful interconnectedness between each of the place-based design principles. The design principle of culturally embedded teaching and learning is no exception. In this design principle, we see a key nexus between each of the principles in our designs. True to their name, culturally embedded practices *root*, or embed, themselves in each of the other design principles. For example, in the design principle of feedback, revision, and reflection (chapter 5, page 79), students have access to a variety of both oral and written feedback. This variety in feedback embeds culture in the learning process by reflecting the diverse perspectives, communication styles, and linguistic nuances present within a particular cultural context. The principle of co-creating an authentic community product (chapter 6, page 91) upholds and values both oral and written traditions, which embeds culture by acknowledging and valuing different ways of expressing ideas. It also provides a more inclusive and culturally sensitive approach to assessment and communication in the classroom. To be truly culturally embedded, a project must align to and intentionally incorporate elements of learning that ensure that learning is multidimensional, intergenerational, and built on relationships. Authentic community partnerships and community products—both of which are key to place-based learning—provide the greatest opportunity for project designers to embed culture.

By using the design principle of embedding culture in teaching and learning, we also decolonize traditional curricula by centering projects in a place, literally embedding the learning into the culture of a place. We decenter traditional notions that give preference to the dominant culture and marginalize others. We instead recenter, making certain that we include narratives, events, and sites that have historically been left out of the 4-12 grades canon. Purpose-driven inquiry embeds culture in the core of the project design by emphasizing localized ways of knowing. In sharing power with students, we must design projects that hold sacred student ideas. We must ensure that students share in decision-making, and products are co-created with their very own communities, embedding students into their surroundings in a purposeful and intentional way. Designating a thought-sharing time where students can express their ideas without judgment fosters an environment that cherishes each student's contributions.

Students are empowered to be active participants in decision-making processes through methods such as student-led conferences, class voting on certain topics, or involving students in the selection of classroom projects. This cultivates a sense of ownership and responsibility, making students feel more connected to their learning environment. Engaging students in projects that involve collaboration with their local communities embeds them into their surroundings in a purposeful way. This could involve creating art installations for public spaces, conducting interviews with community members for research projects, or organizing events that address community needs. Such projects not only enhance students' understanding of their community, but also contribute positively to it.

How Do I Embed Culture in Teaching and Learning?

Culturally embedded place-based learning is multidimensional, intergenerational, and built on relationships. It asks us to build a classroom or school climate that honors the beliefs and values of cultures represented in the community. It leverages the cultural ways of knowing represented in the community. Ask yourself these questions.

- "Who are my students?"
- "Where is my community, and what cultures are represented?"
- "Whose voice may not be at the table?"

All of these questions are easily answered as we learn more about and embed ourselves into the students' communities.

When it comes to strengthening our knowledge of our students, we want to make sure that we first unpack our own implicit biases and misconceptions about our students and the communities we serve. It is important that we maintain an asset-based lens as we explore and curate relationships with our students. Doing so helps us to learn more about their worlds as we make connections to content, knowledge, and skills (ways of knowing). An *asset-based lens* in the classroom is an approach that focuses on identifying and leveraging the strengths, skills, talents, and unique qualities that each student brings to the learning environment. Rather than viewing students solely through a deficit or needs-based perspective, an asset-based approach recognizes and values the diverse assets and potential each student possesses.

An asset-based perspective encourages educators to build on students' existing capabilities, cultural backgrounds, and individual experiences, fostering a positive and inclusive learning environment that promotes student growth and success. In *Cultivating Genius: An Equity Framework for Culturally and Historically Responsive Literacy*, Muhammad (2020a) reminds us that "when we frame the stories of people of color as narratives steeped in pain or even smallness, this becomes the dominant or sole representation" (p. 21). As we embed culture into instruction, we must make sure that we share a diverse and cross-cultural array of narratives. Sharing a diverse and cross-cultural array of narratives in instruction involves incorporating various perspectives, voices, and experiences. Here are some examples of how this sharing might take form.

- **Inclusive literature:** Integrate literature from a wide range of authors representing different backgrounds, cultures, and experiences. Include works by authors from various ethnicities, genders, and regions, offering students a rich and diverse collection of narratives.
- **Guest speakers:** Invite guest speakers from diverse backgrounds to share their experiences and expertise with students. This can include professionals, community leaders, or individuals who can offer unique insights related to the subject matter being taught.
- **Multimedia resources:** Utilize multimedia resources such as documentaries, films, podcasts, and online platforms that showcase a variety of cultural narratives. These resources can provide a dynamic and engaging way for students to learn about different perspectives.
- **Personal narratives:** Encourage students to share their own cultural backgrounds and personal narratives. This can be done through written assignments, presentations, or class discussions, fostering a sense of pride in individual identities and creating a space for mutual understanding.
- **Historical perspectives:** Incorporate diverse historical perspectives, ensuring that the curriculum includes contributions and events from different cultures and regions. This helps students develop a more comprehensive understanding of history.
- **Field trips and experiential learning:** Organize field trips or experiential learning activities that expose students to various cultural environments, museums, cultural events, or community spaces, allowing them to engage with diverse narratives in real-world contexts.

Building on the intentional exercise of an asset-based lens, culturally embedded place-based experiences work to decolonize curricula. In the classroom, this means diversifying materials and content. Decolonizing curricula also means that we are designing projects that address power and social justice. Remember the archetypes? Considering the archetypes of oral versus written traditions and the individualistic as opposed to the collectivist within the assessments we design makes practical the decolonization aspect of culturally embedded place-based projects.

How do we design assessments that allow students to demonstrate mastery in diverse ways? The following are several major ways teachers can make culturally embedded instruction practical and doable in their projects and classrooms.

- ◆ **Use literacy strategies:** Culturally embedded literacy strategies allow students to talk about content and verbally process the connections they are making within their projects. Decolonize your curricula by diversifying materials and content and designing projects that address power and social justice. You can also do this by designing assessments that allow students to demonstrate mastery in diverse ways, and that involve students in the creation of knowledge, content, curriculum, and project design.

- ◆ **Diversify course content:** Diversifying course content involves integrating materials, perspectives, and experiences from various cultures, backgrounds, and identities to reflect the diversity of the student population. By doing so, educators can embed cultural relevance into instruction, fostering inclusivity, understanding, and engagement among students with diverse backgrounds.

- ◆ **Employ community mapping:** *Community mapping* is the process of gathering detailed information regarding the assets, resources, and important places in the community that surrounds a school. Community mapping gives you an opportunity to take inventory of the community's assets and resources that you can utilize to enhance instructional and project experiences.

Use Literacy Strategies

Incorporating peer-to-peer feedback, talk stems, visible thinking routines, and discussion protocols does the work of embedding both culture and cultural archetypes, but they also serve as opportunities to connect to multifaceted narratives. Peer-to-peer feedback and discussion protocols provide an opportunity to connect to multifaceted narratives by promoting a more diverse and inclusive perspective. When students give and receive feedback from their peers, they hear different perspectives and viewpoints, which can broaden their understanding of the situation. For example, if a student gives feedback to a peer about a project they are working on, they might share their own experiences and insights, which can add new dimensions to the project. This can also allow for a deeper level of understanding and empathy between the individuals involved, as they are able to appreciate each other's perspectives and experiences. Diana Benner (2021) offers six strategies for building empathy in the classroom.

1. Listen actively
2. Withhold judgment
3. Be understanding
4. Ask open-ended questions
5. Practice mindfulness
6. Show empathetic body language

When we introduce peer-to-peer feedback to our students, it is important that we encourage students to practice each of these six strategies to provide helpful and focused feedback to their peers. Furthermore, by having a diversity of voices in the feedback process, it can help to challenge implicit biases and assumptions, leading to a more nuanced and accurate understanding of a situation. This can result in more creative and effective solutions, as well as promoting a culture of inclusivity and understanding within the team, classroom, and school.

In our place-based learning projects, talk stems and visible thinking routines can also be effective tools for embedding culture into teaching and learning. *Talk stems* are prompts and questions for facilitating conversations and encouraging individuals to share their thoughts and experiences. Students would use talk stems and visible thinking routines anytime there is a conversation about content in the classroom, formal and informal. Using talk stems encourages students to share their perspectives, which can help to build a shared understanding of project content and promote inclusiveness and empathy. See figure 7.1 for examples of talk stems.

Can you explain what you mean by _____?	I see things differently because _____.	I want to build on what you said by adding _____.	What do you think about _____?	You gave me a new way of thinking about that when you said _____.
I agree with you because _____.	To add to what you said, I think that _____.	So, if I understand correctly, you're saying _____?	That reminds me of a time when _____.	I'm not sure I agree with you because _____.

FIGURE 7.1: Talk stem examples.

In the context of embedding culture into teaching and learning, effective discussion strategies play a crucial role in amplifying the impact of multicultural content. These strategies serve as the conduit through which students can engage with diverse perspectives, ask questions, and share their own insights. By fostering open dialogue and encouraging active participation, we create a dynamic learning environment where cultural nuances are explored and celebrated. As we explore the symbiotic relationship between cultural integration and effective discussion methods, it becomes evident that these strategies are essential not only for conveying information but also for cultivating a space where students can authentically connect with the diverse content presented. The success of embedding culture into teaching and learning lies not just in the content itself, but equally in the interactive and inclusive methods employed to ensure that every learner is not only exposed to different cultures but also actively engaged in the enriching tapestry of shared knowledge and understanding.

Diversify Course Content

When designing projects to address power and social justice, teachers should begin by selecting a relevant topic or issue that reflects the experiences and concerns of their students. They should also consider incorporating a diversity of voices and perspectives, including those that are historically marginalized or underrepresented. Teachers can encourage critical thinking and reflection by providing opportunities for students to explore the ways in which power and privilege impact their lives and the lives of others. It's also important to provide students with resources and tools for advocacy and social change, such as opportunities for community outreach or collaborative problem solving. By creating meaningful and engaging projects that address power and social justice, teachers can help students develop a deeper understanding of the world around them and cultivate a sense of agency and responsibility to create positive change.

As a teacher, it is important to recognize that traditional curricula often prioritize certain perspectives and voices while excluding others. Decolonizing your curriculum involves intentionally diversifying your course materials and content to recognize the contributions and perspectives of marginalized communities.

One strategy for achieving this is to incorporate a variety of perspectives. This can be done by including readings and resources authored by writers from different backgrounds, such as people of color, women, LGBTQ+ individuals, and other marginalized groups. Additionally, you can also incorporate sources from a range of disciplines to provide a more comprehensive and inclusive view of the topic you are teaching.

Another strategy is to focus on intersectionality. This approach recognizes the interconnected nature of different forms of oppression and examines how they intersect and compound each other. By discussing the intersection of race, gender, class, and other identities, you can provide a more nuanced understanding of the experiences of marginalized communities. In a classroom setting, an effective strategy to incorporate intersectionality might involve exploring historical events through a lens that considers the simultaneous impact of race, gender, and socioeconomic status. For instance, when studying a period such as the civil rights movement, educators could encourage discussions that highlight the experiences of African American women or individuals from lower socioeconomic backgrounds, shedding light on the multifaceted nature of discrimination and resilience within that historical context. This approach not only deepens students' understanding of the complexities surrounding social issues but also fosters a more comprehensive and nuanced appreciation for the diverse narratives that shape our collective history.

Finally, incorporating critical analysis can encourage students to question what they encounter and who is being represented. Incorporating critical analysis into the classroom involves guiding students to question and deconstruct the information presented, fostering a deeper understanding of perspectives and representation. Teachers can initiate this process by encouraging students to evaluate the sources of information, examining potential biases, and considering the historical or cultural context in which the content was produced. Engaging in Socratic questioning, educators can prompt students to explore underlying assumptions, challenge preconceptions, and identify power dynamics at play in the information they encounter. Additionally, teachers can employ case studies and real-world examples, encouraging students to analyze not only what is presented but also who is included or excluded from narratives.

Through collaborative discussions and reflective exercises, students learn to critically assess information, discern multiple viewpoints, and recognize the impact of representation on shaping societal norms and values. This approach empowers students to become discerning consumers of information, equipping them with the skills to navigate a complex world where critical analysis is fundamental to informed decision making and active citizenship. This approach can help students understand how power operates in society and how marginalized communities are often excluded from mainstream narratives. By incorporating these strategies into your teaching, you can create a more inclusive and equitable learning environment that recognizes the diversity of experiences and perspectives in your classroom.

Employ Community Mapping

Community mapping allows us an opportunity to take inventory of the community's assets and resources that can enhance instructional and project experiences. This notion of community can span as far and wide as the teacher and students can access. Access, in this instance, consists of both in-person and virtual opportunities to learn more about and work within communities. Students might seek to base a project in a community they don't physically live in for various educational and experiential reasons. Virtual exploration allows them to engage with diverse communities, fostering a broader understanding of different cultures, perspectives, and challenges, which is particularly valuable for projects focused on global issues, cross-cultural collaborations, or topics not directly accessible in their immediate surroundings.

Utilizing virtual tools and resources, students can conduct interviews, gather data, and collaborate with individuals from afar, enriching their research and project outcomes. This approach not only enhances technological and research skills but also promotes a global mindset and a sense of interconnectedness, preparing students to navigate an increasingly interconnected and digitally driven world.

To ensure that students don't inadvertently "otherize" the communities they study, educators must emphasize a framework of cultural sensitivity and respect. Encouraging an open-minded approach to virtual exploration and implementing empathy-building exercises, such as personal reflections or empathy interviews, help students connect emotionally with individuals from the studied community, fostering understanding that transcends cultural differences. Collaborative projects involving direct interaction with community members in virtual spaces provide firsthand insights into their daily lives, challenges, and aspirations. Educators should guide students to critically reflect on their biases, fostering a continuous dialogue about cultural humility and the importance of acknowledging diverse perspectives. By promoting a mindset of crossover and unity, students gain a richer understanding of the communities they study and develop crucial skills for effective cross-cultural communication and collaboration.

At a high level, when we make a community map, there are a variety of tools and methodologies that we can leverage to capture information. Boots on the ground, walking the pathways—literally and virtually—educators and students seek out the community organizations, members, and places that are a part of students' everyday lives and historical legacies and infuse those components into instruction. The strategies shown in figure 7.2 can be adapted or modified to fit the specific needs and goals of each community mapping project, but they provide a good starting point for conducting a comprehensive and effective community mapping process.

The community mapping strategy encompasses a multifaceted approach aimed at empowering students to understand, engage with, and contribute to communities in meaningful ways. This involves not only geographical mapping but also the mapping of cultural, social, and economic dimensions. Students learn to identify and analyze community assets, challenges, and connections, fostering a holistic perspective. The end goal of community mapping is to equip students with the skills to navigate and positively impact the complex web of relationships within diverse communities. By honing their abilities to recognize the interplay of various factors and appreciating the nuances of community dynamics, students are better prepared to address real-world

Surveys and questionnaires	Surveys and questionnaires are useful for gathering information about community resources, needs, and priorities. Teachers and students can distribute them to residents, community organizations, and local businesses to gather a comprehensive understanding of the area.
Focus groups	Focus groups can bring together residents, community organizations, and local businesses to discuss their experiences and perspectives on the community. Teachers and students can use this information to better understand the resources and needs of the area.
Asset mapping	Asset mapping involves creating a visual representation of the resources, assets, and strengths of a community. This can include mapping physical resources such as schools, parks, and community centers, as well as mapping intangible resources like community groups and volunteer organizations.
Community meetings	Community meetings can bring together residents, community organizations, and local businesses to discuss community issues and identify potential solutions. This can be a useful tool for building relationships and creating a shared understanding of the community.
Partnering with community organizations	Schools can partner with local organizations to gain a deeper understanding of the community and its resources. These partnerships can also help build relationships between the school and the community, and can lead to collaboration on projects and initiatives that benefit both the school and the community.

FIGURE 7.2: Community mapping strategies.

challenges with empathy, cultural sensitivity, and a commitment to fostering unity. In essence, community mapping serves as a powerful tool for nurturing informed, socially conscious individuals who can contribute meaningfully to the betterment of the communities they engage with.

This section underscores the importance of decolonizing curricula by diversifying materials and content and designing projects that address power and social justice. Incorporating culturally embedded literacy strategies allows students to verbally process connections within their projects, while employing community mapping enables educators to utilize community assets to enhance instructional experiences.

BATON ROUGE'S TROUBLED WATERS

Embed Culture in Instruction, in Action

Throughout this project, students explored the historical impact of local policymaking and segregation on their own perceptions of Black swim clubs across history and connections to their lives today. Students learned about cultural traditions that were lost during the historical period they explored and how the community has worked tirelessly to bring back many of the Black swim clubs of the past, as well as how the students might impact local policy in the future.

Students explored the importance of storytelling and oral traditions as a way of passing on knowledge from generation to generation. They learned the role of storytelling as a traditional method to teach about values, customs, cultural beliefs, history, and ways of life. They explored how to access community resources and how the interviewing and storytelling processes work, and they learned the importance of respecting their elders and the importance of being a contributing member of their community.

Conclusion

In conclusion, the integration of cultural sensitivity, critical analysis, and community mapping strategies into education creates a powerful framework for fostering a generation of globally aware and socially conscious learners. By embedding culture into teaching and learning, students gain not only academic knowledge but also a deeper understanding of the diverse world around them. Moreover, employing critical analysis ensures that students approach information with discernment and empathy, mitigating the risk of perpetuating stereotypes. The implementation of community mapping strategies further enriches this educational journey, enabling students to navigate the complexities of communities with a holistic perspective. Ultimately, this multifaceted approach prepares students to contribute positively to an interconnected world by cultivating a genuine appreciation for diversity and fostering unity. This approach also empowers students to make meaningful and informed contributions to the communities they encounter.

Key Takeaways and Reflection Questions

Consider this chapter's key takeaways and reflect on the following questions as you work to embed culture in teaching and learning through place-based learning. Use the Journey Log to further reflect, brainstorm, jot down ideas, make observations, or plan.

- In place-based learning, embedding culture in instruction represents the considerations and inclusion of students' community and cultures.
- Culturally embedded literacy strategies and community mapping are two important ways in which we can embed culture into our instruction.
- Utilizing culturally embedded literacy strategies and community mapping enhances instructional experiences by allowing students to verbally process connections and leveraging community assets to enrich learning environments.
- Decolonizing curricula involves diversifying materials and content, as well as designing projects that address power dynamics and social justice.

- Are the cultures represented in my classroom present in the project I have designed?
- Does my classroom climate honor the beliefs and values of cultures represented in the community?
- How can I leverage the cultural ways of knowing represented in the community?
- Do I work to decolonize my curricula by diversifying materials and content, designing projects that address power and social justice, designing assessments that allow students to demonstrate mastery in diverse ways, and involving students in the creation of knowledge, content, curriculum, and project design?

Journey Log

Journey Log

Journey Log

PART II
Design Place-Based Learning Journeys

As we embark on the next phase of our exploration into the transformative realm of place-based learning, part II of the book serves as a pivotal transition. Shifting our focus from the broader design principles to a closer examination of place-based learning in practice, we delve into the intricate process of decolonizing curricula. Chapter 8 explores the dynamic interplay of race, identity, worldview, and perspective, illustrating their profound impact on teaching practices and student outcomes. Liberating teaching methods and aligning them with place-based learning design principles, this chapter lays the groundwork for decolonizing curricula. Building on these crucial foundations, chapter 9 provides educators with a nuanced understanding of how biases and assumptions influence the learning environment. It guides educators through the process of addressing these biases with specific strategies, emphasizing the importance of connecting with the community through partnerships and products. By revisiting the creation of an asset map for the classroom community, this chapter underscores the profound connection between our instructional practices and the infinite capacity of our students.

Part I took us on a deep dive into each place-based learning design principle, laying the groundwork for understanding. Now, in part II, we embark on a step-by-step journey through designing place-based learning experiences using the place-based learning project-planning tool. This tool becomes an evolving element in your own story, a guiding force as we navigate the complexities of implementation with an equity lens.

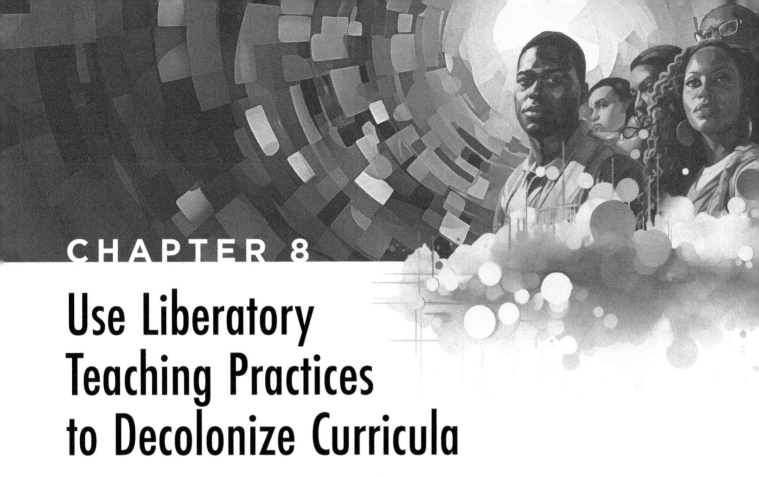

CHAPTER 8

Use Liberatory Teaching Practices to Decolonize Curricula

To teach in a manner that respects and cares for the souls of our students is essential if we are to provide the necessary conditions where learning can most deeply and intimately begin.

—bell hooks

ESSENTIAL QUESTION: What are liberatory teaching practices?

Liberatory teaching practices are educational approaches that prioritize creating a safe and inclusive environment for all students and promoting critical thinking and social justice. In contrast to "programs that center on compliance and whiteness rather than civic engagement and liberation from oppressive systems and policies" (Mayes, Edirmanasinghe, Ieva, & Washington, 2022), liberatory teaching practices aim to empower and liberate individuals by encouraging them to question dominant cultural narratives and challenge oppressive systems. This often involves a focus on student-centered learning, culturally responsive teaching, and creating a supportive community where all voices are valued. The goal of liberatory teaching is to help students develop the skills, knowledge, and awareness necessary to challenge and transform oppressive structures in society. Teacher, educator, and author Zaretta Hammond (2021) emphasizes this when she states that liberatory education "means positioning students to be the leaders of their own learning by helping them increase their ability to actively improve their cognition" (p. 4).

To *decolonize curricula* means to critically examine and transform the ways in which knowledge is produced, taught, and represented in education. This process involves recognizing and challenging the colonial legacies and power imbalances that have shaped the dominant narratives and perspectives in education, and to promote the inclusion and visibility of diverse and marginalized perspectives. In their article "Decolonization Is Not a Metaphor," Eve Tuck and K. Wayne Yang (2012) write, "Decolonization doesn't have a synonym." Building on Tuck and Yang's thoughts, Eric Ritskes (2012) states:

> "Decolonization doesn't have a synonym"; it is not a substitute for "human rights" or "social justice," though undoubtedly, they are connected in various ways. Decolonization demands an Indigenous framework and a centering of Indigenous land, Indigenous sovereignty, and Indigenous ways of thinking.

In essence, decolonization means making fundamental changes and new frameworks. In an education context, decolonizing curriculum involves acknowledging and correcting the ways in which colonialism has influenced the content, methods, and goals of education, and working to create more inclusive and equitable educational experiences for all students. This can involve challenging the Eurocentric and patriarchal biases that have dominated the production and dissemination of knowledge. It can also involve incorporating the histories, cultures, and perspectives of historically marginalized groups, such as Indigenous peoples, people of color, and those from low-income communities. This entails acknowledging and valuing the rich cultural heritage, contributions, and struggles of these groups, and ensuring that the curriculum reflects their histories authentically. It goes beyond mere representation and aims to cultivate a more inclusive and equitable learning environment by examining and challenging biased perspectives. This approach strives to foster a comprehensive understanding among students, encouraging empathy, critical thinking, and a broader appreciation for the multiplicity of human experiences.

By decolonizing curricula, educators aim to create a more diverse, inclusive, and culturally responsive educational experience for students, and to promote a more just and equitable society. This process requires ongoing effort, reflection, and collaboration, as well as a commitment to challenging the ways in which power and knowledge are constructed and transmitted in education. Decolonizing curricula is a critical aspect of place-based learning. Ultimately, the goal is to create a curriculum that respects and honors the cultural diversity of historically marginalized communities, fostering a more inclusive educational landscape that empowers all students.

Chapter 8 explores the synergy between liberatory teaching practices, decolonizing curricula, and the integration of place-based learning. We begin by defining the overarching goal of liberatory teaching, which is empowering students to challenge and transform oppressive societal structures. The chapter emphasizes place-based learning's transformative potential in promoting diverse, culturally responsive educational experiences and empowering students to connect their learning to their communities and the world. Key to the discussion is the role of place-based learning in challenging dominant worldviews during the process of decolonizing curricula.

In essence, chapter 8 provides a holistic exploration of how liberatory teaching practices, decolonizing curricula, and place-based learning converge to create an inclusive and empowering educational environment. Educators will find guidance in examining oppressive structures, challenging dominant narratives, and incorporating students' cultural references into the learning process through the Key Takeaways and Reflection Questions sections. It concludes with the Journey Log for writing down your thoughts and ideas.

How Do Liberatory Teaching Practices and Decolonizing Curricula Connect to Place-Based Learning?

As you know by this point, place-based learning is an educational approach that utilizes the local community and environment as a context for learning. It connects academic learning with real-world experiences, enabling students to make meaningful connections between what they are learning in the classroom and the world around them. Place-based learning can also promote a sense of connection to and stewardship for the local community, as well as encourage students to engage in community-based problem solving.

Inextricably linked, the concepts of liberatory teaching practices and decolonizing curricula form a dynamic partnership in the transformative journey toward place-based learning. Decolonizing curricula serves as the foundational examination phase, probing the deep-seated biases, assumptions, and systemic inequalities that underlie traditional educational structures. This critical examination lays the groundwork for liberatory teaching practices, which can be seen as the action phase of implementing tangible changes informed by a commitment to dismantling oppressive structures and fostering inclusivity. Liberatory teaching practices are the proactive manifestation of the insights gained during the process of decolonization, translating theory into concrete strategies that empower both educators and students in the pursuit of an education system reflective of diverse perspectives and experiences. Together, these concepts create a symbiotic relationship, shaping a pedagogical approach that not only challenges the status quo but also actively works toward a more just and inclusive educational landscape.

Place-based learning aligns with liberatory teaching practices and decolonizing curricula in several ways.

- It recognizes the importance of considering the perspectives and experiences of individuals and communities in the local environment.
- It emphasizes student-centered learning, encouraging students to take an active role in their own education and to consider the ways in which they can make a positive impact on their communities.
- It highlights social, economic, and environmental justice issues, encouraging critical thinking and challenging oppressive structures.

By providing opportunities for students to engage with and understand these issues in their own communities, place-based learning can help promote a more just and equitable society.

How Do I Use Liberatory Teaching Practices and Decolonize the Curriculum Through Place-Based Learning?

To liberate teaching practices and decolonize the curriculum through place-based learning, teachers may take the following actions.

- **Connect project implementation to decolonizing curricula:** Infuse place-based learning with decolonizing curricula to enhance educational inclusivity by incorporating the perspectives of historically marginalized communities, foster critical thinking, empower students to connect with their communities, and promote a more equitable and culturally responsive global society.

- **Recognize Earth as a place and pathway to liberatory and decolonized teaching practices:** Recognize Earth as a place in place-based learning by acknowledging and incorporating the local environment's ecological, cultural, and community dimensions, fostering a holistic understanding of the interconnectedness between nature, education, and lived experiences.
- **Examine race, identity, worldview, and perspectives:** When decolonizing curricula through place-based learning, it is crucial to critically examine and challenge the dominant worldview, including its anthropocentric perspective, by recognizing its limitations and biases, promoting the inclusion of multiple perspectives, and addressing the social construct of race to foster a more inclusive and equitable educational experience for students.
- **Start with essential questions:** Initiate purposeful inquiry through an equity-focused approach commencing with essential questions that foster critical thinking and prompt students to delve into diverse perspectives.

Connect Project Implementation to Decolonizing Curricula

In the context of decolonizing curricula, place-based learning can serve as a powerful tool for promoting more diverse and culturally embedded, culturally responsive educational experiences. By incorporating the perspectives, experiences, and cultural backgrounds of historically marginalized communities into place-based learning projects, educators can help to create more inclusive and equitable learning environments. For example, educators can design place-based learning projects to include the histories and perspectives of Indigenous peoples, people of color, and low-income communities, and to challenge the dominant narratives and biases that have shaped the production and dissemination of knowledge.

Leveraging place-based learning as a tool toward decolonizing curricula can also empower students to take an active role in their own learning and to connect their education to their communities and the world. This can help to build their critical thinking and problem-solving skills, and to promote a more meaningful and relevant educational experience.

Ultimately, the integration of place-based learning into a decolonized curriculum can help to create a more equitable and just educational experience for all students, and to promote a more diverse and culturally responsive global society.

According to Conrad Hughes (2021), campus and secondary principal at the International School of Geneva, La Grande Boissière, here are four reflection points for educators and their instructional support leaders that will help guide the decolonization of the curriculum. This serves as a commendable beginning, though not an exhaustive list; it is intended to steer initial reflections.

1. Review each course outline or scope and curriculum-sequence document. Imagine what it would look like from the perspective of postcolonial thought and try to deconstruct the dominant narrative. What do you see? For example, educators can deconstruct the notion of colonialism as a civilizing mission by incorporating diverse voices in the curriculum, showcasing alternative perspectives that emphasize the resilience and richness of Indigenous cultures. This approach encourages critical analysis, aiming to dismantle hegemonic narratives and foster a more nuanced understanding of historical events. No matter the grade level, this work can be done in a developmentally appropriate way.

2. Investigate the extent to which your curriculum's cultural references, historical facts, authors, and discoveries are presented as Western, male, and European. If they are predominantly Western, male, and European, ask yourself why.

3. Ask what sort of discussions are happening in the classroom to ensure critical thinking and deep reflection on the power of representation in the way that textbooks present materials to learners.

4. Reflect on the extent to which the curriculum offers students views and stories from First Peoples, Africa, Asia, Latin America, the Middle East, and Oceanic regions. What do you see? What can be done to expand the scope of the narratives being explored in the curriculum?

And here are three suggestions for action (Hughes, 2021):

1. Consider project-based learning as an opportunity for students to investigate their own ancestry and to present their findings to their classmates.

2. Consider guiding questions for discussions, presentations, and written assignments that focus on the sociology of knowledge. Pose questions such as, Why do we think this is important? What are other cultural perspectives on this same question?

3. Only present the Enlightenment and the Industrial Revolution with full understanding of and reflection on slavery and colonization.

Decolonizing the curriculum is about being more accurate, more inclusive, and more interculturally responsive. It is not about forcing one ideological perspective on students; it's about telling all sides of the story (Hughes, 2021).

Recognize Earth as a Place and as a Pathway to Liberatory and Decolonized Teaching Practices

When designing place-based learning experiences and decolonizing curricula, it is important to consider the significance of the Earth as a place and to incorporate Indigenous practices, wayfaring, and other related perspectives. *Wayfaring* here refers to the act of traveling or journeying, often with a sense of purpose or exploration. In an educational context, wayfaring represents a deliberate and intentional journey of learning and discovery, where students and educators navigate through diverse perspectives, experiences, and knowledge to deepen their understanding and foster personal and collective growth. Wayfaring can involve the exploration of interdisciplinary topics, the consideration of multiple viewpoints, and the incorporation of reflective practices to guide the educational journey. This term emphasizes the process of traveling and the transformative experiences gained along the way, contributing to a richer and more holistic educational experience. This can help to challenge the Eurocentric and anthropocentric perspectives that have dominated the production and dissemination of knowledge and to promote a deeper understanding of the interconnectedness of all living beings and the environment.

Incorporating Indigenous practices, for example, such as wayfaring, herbal medicine, and resource management, could provide students with a more nuanced understanding of the relationship between humans and the natural world. For instance, students in Alabama might embark on a guided wayfaring journey with members of the Choctaw Nation, native to Alabama, exploring the local landscape. Along the journey, they might learn how Indigenous communities traditionally navigated through the region, identifying edible plants for sustenance and medicinal herbs for holistic well-being. This immersive experience in wayfaring not only imparts practical navigation skills but also fosters a profound connection to the land, enriching students' awareness of the intricate relationships between humans and the natural environment in the specific context of Alabama. By studying the wayfaring traditions of Indigenous peoples, students can gain a deeper appreciation for the interconnectedness of all life and the importance of community and place-based knowledge.

Incorporating these diverse perspectives into the curriculum can help to create a more inclusive and culturally responsive educational experience for students, and to promote a more holistic and sustainable approach to the study of the Earth and its systems. What if the place being studied is our planet, and its place in the surrounding galaxy and universe? The goal is for students to be exposed to and discover a deep sense of unity with the world around them. Can you imagine the sense of purpose that could arise from such a learning experience? By valuing and promoting these perspectives, educators can work toward a more equitable and just educational experience and a more sustainable future for all.

Examine Race, Identity, Worldview, and Perspectives

When decolonizing curricula, it is important to critically examine and challenge the dominant worldview and the ways in which knowledge is constructed and transmitted. This process often involves recognizing the limitations and biases of the dominant perspective and promoting the inclusion of multiple perspectives. One aspect of the dominant worldview is an anthropocentric perspective, which prioritizes human interests and experiences above all others. This perspective can lead to a narrow and limited understanding of the world and can perpetuate systems of oppression and inequality. By incorporating multiple perspectives into the curriculum, educators can promote a more inclusive and equitable educational experience for students.

Another important aspect of decolonizing curricula is the recognition of identity, including race, as a social construct (Criser & Knott, 2019). Race is a complex and multifaceted concept that has been used to classify and categorize individuals based on physical characteristics and to justify systems of oppression and inequality. By exploring the ways race has been constructed and used historically, students can gain a deeper understanding of how identity is socially constructed and the impact that this has on individuals and communities. By incorporating discussions of race as a construct into the curriculum, educators can promote a more equitable and inclusive educational experience for students and help to challenge how race and other aspects of identity have been used to justify systems of oppression and inequality. Ultimately, the process of decolonizing curricula via place-based learning requires ongoing effort, reflection, and collaboration; a commitment to challenging the dominant worldview; and promoting the inclusion of multiple perspectives. By doing so, educators can work toward creating a more diverse, inclusive, and culturally responsive educational experience for all students.

Start With Essential Questions

At the beginning of each chapter of this book, we begin with an essential question to help frame the thinking of the chapter. In part I, we discuss how essential questions are supported by and reinforced by each of the design principles. Essential questions are questions that probe deeply into a subject and encourage students to think critically and reflectively about the topic they're studying. They are open-ended and foster inquiry-based learning, allowing students to construct their own understanding of the subject matter. Essential questions serve as the foundation for inquiry and guide students in their exploration of complex and important topics.

To launch purpose-driven inquiry using the lens of equity, it is important to start with essential questions (chapter 2, page 33) that promote critical thinking and encourage students to explore diverse perspectives.

When crafting essential questions with an equity lens, it is important to consider the following.

- **Promote diversity and inclusion:** Essential questions should promote the exploration of multiple perspectives and the experiences of diverse communities.
- **Challenge dominant narratives:** Essential questions should challenge the dominant worldview and encourage students to explore alternative perspectives and experiences.
- **Foster critical thinking:** Essential questions should encourage students to think deeply and critically about complex issues, and to question their own assumptions and biases.
- **Promote social justice:** Essential questions should encourage students to explore and understand the ways in which systems of oppression and inequality impact individuals and communities.

Examples of essential questions that can launch purpose-driven inquiry using the lens of equity might include the following.

- What are the experiences and perspectives of historically marginalized communities?
- How have systems of oppression and inequality impacted individuals and communities?
- What can we learn from the perspectives and experiences of diverse communities?
- How can we work toward creating a more equitable and just world?

A *project sketch* is a preliminary outline or plan for a project that includes key goals, tasks, and timelines. This is a short, explanatory narrative that describes the project. Imagine if you wanted to quickly describe the project's purpose, essential question, and product to a parent you bump into at the grocery store. What three or four sentences would you tell them? It is not mandatory that teachers start with a project sketch before going to the project-planning form to flesh out the full experience, but the project sketch is a key component of the project-planning form nonetheless. The project sketch is intended to provide a high-level overview of the project and serve as a starting point for further development and refinement.

Moving from a project sketch, which provides a high-level overview of a project's purpose and intended product, to formulating the essential question is a pivotal step in place-based learning. The transition involves a collaborative process between the teacher and students, with variations in the level of guidance and autonomy depending on the educational level. At the elementary level, teachers typically play a more active role in guiding students through the process. The teacher might initiate discussions about the project's overarching goals, potential outcomes, and key concepts. Together with the students, the teacher can explore various aspects of the project sketch, identifying elements that align with the curriculum and the students' interests. Through collaborative brainstorming sessions and guided discussions, the teacher can help distill the project's focus into a clear purpose and potential product. The essential question may be framed by the teacher but can also be co-created with input from the students, ensuring it aligns with their understanding and curiosity.

As students progress to the secondary level, there's an increased emphasis on student agency and independent thinking. While teachers still play a crucial role in facilitating the process, students are encouraged to take on more responsibility. The teacher might present the project sketch, initiate discussions about its purpose and potential outcomes, and guide students in exploring various angles. However, teachers may wish to give secondary students more autonomy in proposing and refining the essential question. Teachers can facilitate group discussions, provide feedback on proposed questions, and guide students in aligning the question with curriculum objectives. This collaborative approach fosters a sense of ownership and engagement, allowing students to connect the project to their interests and perspectives.

Regardless of the educational level, the process involves a cyclical and iterative approach. Teachers and students engage in discussions, refine ideas, and collaboratively shape the essential question. This process not only ensures alignment with curriculum goals but also allows for the incorporation of student interests, making the project more meaningful. The transition from a project sketch to the essential question involves a dynamic interplay between teacher guidance and student input. While teachers provide structure and direction, students are encouraged to actively contribute, fostering a sense of ownership and relevance to the learning experience. The balance between teacher-led and student-driven processes may shift based on the developmental level of the students.

Figure 8.1 provides examples of project sketches and corresponding essential questions at the elementary and secondary levels.

Sample Project Sketch	Sample Elementary Essential Question	Sample Secondary Essential Question
Understanding the impact of migration on a community	How does moving to a new place change our community's traditions?	How does migration impact the cultural identity of our community?
Exploring the diversity of religious traditions	How do the things we believe influence the way we live and celebrate with our families and friends?	How do religious beliefs and practices shape my cultural values and traditions?
Examining the role of food in culture	How does the food we eat tell us about who we are?	How does food reflect and shape cultural identity and community relationships where I live?

FIGURE 8.1: Sample project sketches and possible essential questions.

By incorporating essential questions into the curriculum, educators can promote a more diverse, inclusive, and culturally responsive educational experience for students, and help to build a more equitable and just society. Essential questions and culturally responsive strategies are both related to effective teaching and learning practices.

According to Hammond (2021), any effort to accelerate learning to achieve greater equity and help all students reach their potential must couple the science of learning with culturally responsive practice. Culturally responsive strategies are teaching practices that acknowledge and respect the cultural backgrounds and experiences of students. These strategies help to create a learning environment that is inclusive and welcoming for all students, regardless of their background. Culturally responsive teaching involves incorporating students' cultural references, experiences, and perspectives into the learning process, and adapting instruction to meet the diverse needs of all students. Figure 8.2 gives examples of culturally responsive strategies connected to specific essential question examples.

Essential Question	Culturally Responsive Strategy
How has the history and cultural heritage of my community influenced the world?	Incorporating students' cultural background into the curriculum
What can we learn from the perspectives and experiences of people from different cultures?	Valuing and incorporating multiple perspectives
How do my own experiences and cultural background shape my understanding of the world?	Encouraging self-reflection and cultural awareness
How can we use our understanding of different cultures to create a more inclusive and equitable society?	Promoting social justice and cultural understanding
How do cultural differences and similarities impact communication and collaboration in our community?	Fostering intercultural competence and collaboration

FIGURE 8.2: Culturally responsive strategies that connect with essential question examples.

The connection between essential questions and culturally responsive strategies is that both are effective tools for creating a student-centered learning environment, especially in our place-based learning experiences. By posing essential questions and incorporating culturally responsive strategies, teachers can create a dynamic and engaging learning experience that fosters critical thinking, cultural understanding, and academic success for all students.

Conclusion

In this chapter, we've navigated the initial stages of the wayfaring process of designing place-based learning experiences, exploring its profound connections to liberatory teaching practices and the decolonization of curricula. By recognizing Earth as a dynamic and interconnected educational space, we are prompted to embrace diverse perspectives, fostering a more inclusive and equitable learning environment. The collaborative process of transitioning from a project sketch to the essential question further emphasizes the symbiotic relationship between teacher guidance and student agency, a process that varies in nuance between elementary and secondary levels but consistently aims to cultivate student ownership and meaningful engagement. This chapter underscores the commitment to challenging dominant worldviews, promoting diversity, and fostering a culturally responsive educational landscape through the empowering lens of place-based learning.

Key Takeaways and Reflection Questions

Consider this chapter's key takeaways and reflect on the following questions as you work to liberate your teaching practices and decolonize the curriculum through place-based learning. Use the Journey Log to further reflect, brainstorm, jot down ideas, make observations, or plan.

- ◆ The goal of liberatory teaching is to help students develop the skills, knowledge, and awareness necessary to challenge and transform oppressive structures in society.

- ◆ In the context of decolonizing curricula, place-based learning can serve as a powerful tool for promoting more diverse and culturally embedded, culturally responsive educational experiences.

- ◆ Leveraging place-based learning as a tool toward decolonizing curricula can also empower students to take an active role in their own learning and to connect their education to their communities and the world.

- ◆ When decolonizing curricula, it is important to critically examine and challenge the dominant worldview and the ways in which knowledge is constructed and transmitted.

- ◆ What oppressive structures do you want your students to challenge and transform?

- ◆ While on the journey to answering the essential question, what are some important ancillary key questions that your students can explore that will challenge dominant narratives?

- ◆ How can you add students' cultural references, experiences, and perspectives to the learning process and adapt instruction accordingly?

- ◆ How can educators ensure that essential questions and culturally responsive strategies are effectively integrated to create a truly student-centered learning environment that promotes critical thinking, cultural understanding, and academic success for all students in place-based learning experiences?

Journey Log

Journey Log

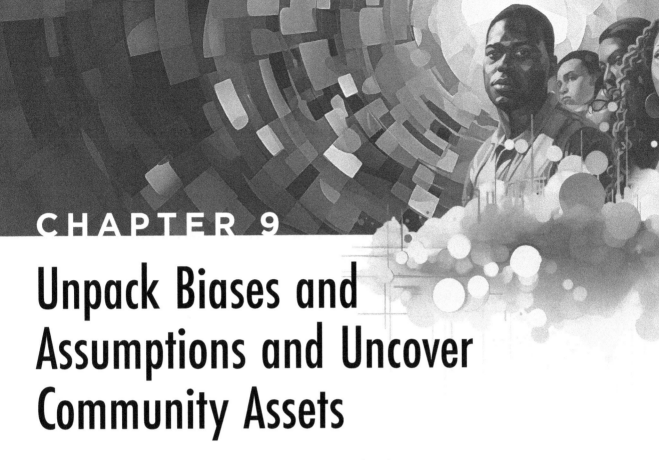

CHAPTER 9

Unpack Biases and Assumptions and Uncover Community Assets

The eye sees only what the mind is prepared to comprehend.
—ROBERTSON DAVIES

ESSENTIAL QUESTION: How do I uncover and uplift the assets of my students and community to build the foundation for a place-based journey?

When we, as educators, uncover and uplift the assets of everyone in our direct influence and in an ever-broadening community circle, we are taking steps that might be very new to us. We might be interacting with people in ways we're not accustomed to. We will probably be walking more slowly, sensing that to hear hidden stories, we must listen with an ear attuned to a place beyond our own making. This chapter asks you to increase your awareness of your schema, tendencies, and assumptions in service of your students, their families, and the community we all belong to. In doing so, you will call on the design principles from part I. That bedrock will give you the confidence to unpack lingering assumptions and confront biases in service of actualizing an equitable vision of education and in making historical contextualization a requisite of building community partnerships rooted in reciprocity and love.

With the effort you put into designing a place-based journey, you will see the community and your students as one and the same, as interconnected as inhalation and exhalation. Therefore, you will want to build the community product, service, or action *with* the community partner. In this chapter, you learn about the practicalities of community outreach and ongoing communication with community partners. You will learn how to generate a community asset map for your classroom and revisit the completed example of the map using Baton Rouge's Troubled Waters project (page 137). The chapter offers a chance to think further about its content through the

Conclusion and Key Takeaways and Reflection Questions sections. It concludes with the Journey Log for writing down your thoughts and ideas.

How Do Biases and Assumptions Influence the Learning Environment?

It is late in the fall semester, and a sixth-grade teacher we'll call Jenna is in her first year of teaching at a public school in a small, majority White agricultural city, bordered by a large Native American nation to the north and Mexico to the south.

Jenna's sixth-grade class of Native, Latinx, and White students is building relationships, establishing routines, and learning to collaborate effectively. As she is planning an upcoming social studies project, she shares with her school coach (whom we'll call Maria) that she is worried about making connections with the students' families because they are absent from school events and conferences. Jenna also anticipates that community partnerships will be equally challenging, given her perception of lack of interest and the political polarization of the area. Jenna's assumption is that her students' families don't value education.

We will come back to Jenna and Maria in a bit. For now, let's talk about how biases (tendencies) and assumptions (beliefs) affect the learning environment, and what can happen when they go unchallenged. Implicit bias, which we all have to varying degrees, is insidious. It is the carbon monoxide of the classroom—odorless, tasteless, and toxic. Unchecked, it can cause negative self-image, learned behaviors (of treating others differently), and lower academic achievement. It can drive assumptions about student ability and behavior, resulting in disproportionate disciplinary action. As content strategist Tiara Smith and curriculum consultant Jennifer Pham (n.d.) point out:

> Teacher bias has the power to deeply affect students in the classroom in multiple ways that affect students' ability to succeed, grow, learn, and feel safe in the classroom. When students see their counterparts being treated differently, they also begin to pick up this learned behavior. The mere act of witnessing the bias that teachers may have has the power to change the way students treat and see one another, and thus, promotes a culture that is anything but inclusive, culturally responsive, or productive.

As it relates to place-based learning, biases can extend beyond the classroom to families and community partners who are impacted by teacher assumptions, resulting in less willingness to be a partner in the learning process.

How Do I Work to Address Biases and Assumptions in the Learning Environment?

It is worth stating again that we all make assumptions, and we all have biases. Some bias is harmless, or a simple matter of preference—a bias toward the beach instead of the mountains, for example. Bias is how we organize information after weighing it against our own experiences, opinions, and the information available to us. Implicit bias, on the other hand, "relies on instinct instead of analysis," writes Adriana Vazquez (2022), summarizing an unconscious bias training session by former teacher, nonprofit leader, and principal Brianne Dotson. Vazquez continues, "So unsurprisingly, the judgments and conclusions people come to are often incorrect, but more importantly, they can be discriminatory." Bias and assumption often work in tandem, affirming erroneous beliefs and resulting in unconscious actions.

Letting go of shame and examining our biases and assumptions are how we build a more equitable learning environment (and world!). In the following pages, we will continue to shadow teacher Jenna and her coach, Maria. We will also tell about a coaching experience Micki had that emphasizes three ways to address biases and assumptions directly related to place-based learning. As you read, embrace a growth mindset, secure in the knowledge that bias is not fixed but malleable as we learn and grow. Assumptions can mature. Talk, too, to your colleagues about their experiences with and understanding of implicit bias in the classroom. Finally, if you are already doing the ongoing work of addressing biases and assumptions, focus on the examples we provide and identify what is familiar and how it can enrich your place-based journeys.

- **Build contextual understanding:** Do the work of assumption-busting through research, listening, and immersing yourself in the context of your students, their families, and the communities in which they reside.

- **Detect biases:** Through reflection and self-assessment, examine your practice and ask your students for their perspectives to modify your biases and mitigate the harm they cause.

- **View students and community as inseparable:** Just like us, students are the whole of their thoughts, feelings, and experiences, and they shouldn't be asked to check parts of themselves at the classroom door. On the contrary, we need the fullness of students to engage in place-based learning.

Build Contextual Understanding

To build contextual understanding in service of scrutinizing assumptions and biases, teachers need to get curious about why students, families, and whole communities operate in a way that may be counter to what dominant (White) culture has deemed correct. Every perceived issue has a deep-seated origin. If we take the time to learn, listen, and ask probing questions, we will come to a more nuanced understanding. When that happens, we are forced to recategorize information and shift our assumptions and confront biases.

Back to the story about Jenna, the sixth-grade teacher. Jenna has shared her frustration about the lack of participation from families with school coach Maria. Maria initiates a conversation aimed to help Jenna remove roadblocks to developing equitable learning opportunities for her students, their families, and the community. She prompts Jenna to think about the historical relationship of the Native community to school and schooling. Jenna admits that she has heard about the boarding school era but doesn't know what it has to do with the families of her students, who are at least two generations removed. However, as Maria points out to Jenna, research conducted on intergenerational trauma indicates the following.

1. Historically traumatic events continue to undermine the well-being of contemporary group members.

2. Responses to historically traumatic events interact with contemporary stressors to influence well-being.

3. The risk associated with historically traumatic events can accumulate across generations (Bombay, Matheson, & Anisman, 2014).

The revelation not only that the parents of her students feel the impact of the original trauma but also that the effects of boarding school trauma are present in her students is unsettling to Jenna.

Maria also asks Jenna if she knows people living in the United States without documents and with an ever-present fear when navigating governmental institutions. Jenna shares that she knows many of her students have family members who lack documentation but she doesn't know anyone without documents in her personal life. This historical contextualization helps her realize why the families of her Latinx and Native students might not see the physical school building as a welcoming environment. The context building, research, and conversations Jenna has with Maria are critical to Jenna developing a more informed understanding of her students' experiences.

Caroline Hill (n.d.), founder of 228 Accelerator and the equityXdesign framework, affirms that "Holding the historical context when designing healing solutions means an acknowledgment of the ways people repair, stitch back, and make themselves whole again" (p. 10). While Jenna's work in understanding the reasons her students' families are reluctant to come to campus has begun with context-building conversations with someone who is able to offer her guidance in examining her assumptions, the work only creates a personal shift with knowledge and acknowledgment. Jenna needs to further build contextual understanding to begin peeling back the layers of her own assumptions. Maria knows she can't just tell Jenna about intergenerational trauma and expect lasting change. She also provides Jenna with an article, a podcast, and a documentary, as well as reflective questions, followed by a conversation.

After Jenna looks at the material Maria has given her, she sees the significance and necessity of revising her project plan. She devises a final product to be organized and managed by students. As part of the project, students' families and people from across the community of differing races, backgrounds, experiences, and ideologies can provide short answers to questions in photobooth listening sessions. Students will be available at various locations—the local Boys and Girls Club, a county park, a cultural center, and a grocery store on the Mexico side of the border—at set times that accommodate different work schedules to record these community members' answers to questions of universal importance. Students will devise their questions and topics to address the spectrum (and polarities) of opinions and beliefs in the community.

Working in small groups for on-site interviews or one-to-one with family members, students will video record their interviews. The videos will then be edited, curated, and showcased to build awareness of collective commonalities and concerns (similar to the story mapping done with adult learners in chapter 3, page 52). Jenna also includes a family survey, conducted by text messaging and in multiple languages, on preferred modes of participation.

Jenna's students and their families don't know the work she has done to build contextual understanding. She doesn't announce, "Now I know about intergenerational trauma and have more empathy." The only people who know about Jenna's influential shift in thinking are Jenna and Maria, but the benefit is far-reaching. Jenna's students see her willingness to go beyond the classroom to include the people they most care about. Families feel seen and valued for the contribution they can make to the project. Community members have a voice and make connections with youth.

Never doubt the significance context building can have for your teaching practice. One first step is to make a list of what you're curious about (for example, "Why do my students of color seem to have a different understanding of what *respect* means?" or, "Why don't my Indigenous students make eye contact with me?"). Put on your student hat and do some research. Head to your local library and grab a copy of Anton Treuer's (2012) book *Everything You Wanted to Know About Indians but Were Afraid to Ask*. Check out the Smithsonian National Museum of African

American History and Culture's educator resources, with a whole section devoted to talking about race. Attend a local cultural event. Conduct a Socratic seminar with your students, using a text you think will provoke an insightful discussion. Talk to a trusted colleague. Admit what you don't yet know and stay curious.

Detect Biases

If an assumption is a poorly formed belief or hunch, then an implicit bias is like a tendency or habit we are unaware of. So, if a bias is unconscious, how are we even aware enough of it to get curious? The bad news is that you might not be aware of your biases, but others are. Your students know your biases and could probably tick them off without much provocation. Southern Poverty Law Center's (n.d.b) Learning for Justice says, in a resource intended for teachers to test themselves for hidden bias, "Studies indicate that African American teenagers are aware they are stigmatized as being intellectually inferior and that they go to school bearing what psychologist Claude Steele has called a 'burden of suspicion.' Such a burden can affect their attitudes and achievement."

As we've established, implicit biases that affect our teaching are far from harmless. The good news is you have a laboratory all set up to conduct experiments and see your biases magnified: the classroom. The Yale Poorvu Center for Teaching and Learning (2021) has curated resources for developing awareness of implicit bias, beginning by self-assessing and reflecting on current practice. They give examples of bias, such as treating students with special needs as lacking intellectual ability, or failing to call on multilingual students as often as students whose first language is English. They then recommend using a tool like a reflection journal to begin noticing biases that may have been previously hidden.

Another method for recognizing biases is to ask a trusted colleague or coach to observe a lesson and objectively record teacher-student interactions, based on a focus area you provide. For example, if your reflection and self-assessment uncovered a predisposition to assume that Hmong students are not listening (because their nonverbal cues may differ from yours or those of your ethnic group), ask your peer to pay special attention to these interactions. This doesn't require a complicated protocol or checklist. It can be a list labeled "I see . . ." followed by direct observations such as, "Teacher asks Chue if he is following along in the text × 3." The observer isn't making inferences or drawing any conclusions, only stating what is visible. The teacher then reviews the data, noticing trends.

Another option is to use a modified Harkness discussion (Christoph, n.d.). The *Harkness discussion* method tracks student participation in class discussions and empowers them to self-manage collaborative talk. It can easily be modified to also track teacher-student interactions. To do so, an observer draws a map of the seating chart, then draws lines from person to person during a set activity, tracking communication. What results is a spiderweb pattern that can aid the teacher in distinguishing who is participating, when, at what rate, and the role the teacher plays in fostering this pattern. The first suggestion, called an *I see* chart, shows types of interactions. The Harkness discussion method shows only quantity. Together, the *I see* chart and the Harkness method can guide a teacher to spot implicit biases.

If approaching a colleague to act as an observer is intimidating at this stage in your equity journey, you can still use these methods by positioning a video recorder in the classroom and reviewing the footage. The only tricky part is you are the least adept at seeing your blind spots. Find a friend outside of school and ask them to watch it with you for that empirical set of eyes.

One final suggestion is to ask your students. Depending on factors such as the age of your students, your relationship with them, their access to technology, and the time of year, this solicitation may take different forms. An anonymous survey (Poll Everywhere, SurveyMonkey, and Google Forms all have an anonymous option) with questions such as these may be useful.

- What helps you learn in this class?
- What makes it hard for you to learn in this class?
- What are one or two things the teacher could do to help you learn?
- What are a few words the teacher would use to describe you?
- Do you think the teacher treats all students fairly? Why or why not?

For older students, share a reading and have a discussion about implicit bias, even connecting it to your English, mathematics, science, or history content. Follow up with one-to-one or small-group discussions focused on what students see in your teaching. You may also consider swapping classrooms with a colleague for an hour, using this suggestion with a group of students who are not your own, as your peer collects the same data for you. The requisite is transparency—students should be fully aware of why you are asking them for this information, they must agree to share it, and they must feel confident that there will not be negative repercussions as a result.

Uncovering biases, like uncovering assumptions, is marathon work. It should be as much a part of a teacher's professional development as literacy strategies and behavior interventions. We don't always see the positive results of our subtle erasure of a bias or assumption, but it is present all the same. It will make the trust quotient rise, make engagement palpable, and improve your relationship with your students. And as we are about to see, overcoming bias makes it possible to more fully see your students for how they live in the world and are inseparable from their surroundings.

View Students and Community as Inseparable

When Micki was coaching at a majority Native American public school near a reservation, she noticed an assumption cropping up in non-Native teachers similar to Jenna in our earlier example. Parents were not attending parent-teacher conferences, so teachers assumed they must not care about education. Non-Native teachers lacked the historical contextualization to know that the tight-knit relations of Native communities prior to boarding schools tasked the whole community with raising the children rather than siloing child-rearing in individual nuclear families. Therefore, even calling the conferences "parent-teacher" failed to represent this broader family structure that Native people are trying to reassert through the process of decolonization.

Micki coached the teachers to unpack the many reasons why parents didn't come to school. One reason was how they had been treated by the district when they were young students themselves. Another was that many on the reservation did not own cars, making it impossible for parents and guardians to make the trek to the school. (This was ascertained by a one-question text survey to families, asking, "What do I [teacher] need to know to make it easier for you to participate even more in your child's education?")

As a result, one teacher asked what might happen if they took student-led conferences to the reservation. Some teachers were hesitant, but the majority thought it was worth a try. Micki formed a committee of teachers to meet with the tribal council about this idea. The council embraced the idea, as did community members and families. The tribal planning team reserved the cultural center to hold the student-led conferences. Participants called them *student-led conferences in the round*. The planning team organized food and a raffle.

The resulting conference was a festive evening, with over 90 percent participation. Not only parents and guardians, but aunties, uncles, and grandparents also attended to hear about their students' progress. Community was built, understanding of each other greatly improved, and a strong sense that it takes a community to uplift their children was revived and felt, perhaps for the first time, by the teachers from the school. The school established additional partnerships with the tribe that further enriched all stakeholders' understanding of each other.

Although the examples throughout this chapter draw from Micki's and Erin's background in Native American education, parallel assumptions and biases show up in almost all settings where the race and culture of the student differs from that of the teacher. This is especially true with marginalized students, and it is exacerbated by White supremacist systems and practices. Few teacher-preparatory programs delve into the impact of *post-traumatic slave syndrome*, a concept developed by Joy DeGruy, renowned author, researcher, and educator. DeGruy (2017) focuses on the intersection of racism, trauma, violence, and American chattel slavery to describe the consequence of centuries of chattel slavery followed by institutionalized racism and oppression that have resulted in multigenerational adaptive behavior.

Likewise, the topic of *epigenetics*, or how the experiences of previous generations affect how later generations live their lives and learn, rarely comes up in staff meetings or professional development. Taking the time to do the interdependent work of seeing the community not as separate from the lives of students and their education, but as part of the whole, is what makes planning a place-based learning journey so bountiful and filled with potential.

Codman Academy Charter Public School in Dorchester, Massachusetts, embodies interdependent work even in the days before the school year begins. Serving 99 percent students of color, with a 100 percent graduation rate, the staff at this project-based school meet each family and enter into a relationship by asking for their child's naming story. What is the legacy of their name? How was it gifted to them? What hopes and expectations are embodied in a name? This tradition started with the founding of the school in 2001 and continues to this day, ensuring each student feels honored and known. As Hill (n.d.) says, "In order to understand the present, we must understand the inherited legacy surrounding the relationships we are designing, the place we are designing in, and the community we are designing with" (p. 6) to better serve students.

Viewing students and community as inseparable isn't an item on a list of tasks to be checked off. It is accomplished by both unpacking biases and assumptions and growing contextual understanding. Even then, there may still be thick walls between your classroom and the community, but keep going. Plan a project using an equity lens and take your first step on the place-based learning path project-planning tool by generating a community asset map, and you will have made the first step toward bringing those walls down.

Generate an Asset Map of Your Classroom Community

In chapter 3, "Building Authentic Community Partnerships" (page 49), we outlined the story mapping process, whereby a group of teachers, students, or both can uncover the stories of their community to illuminate, enrich, and become a part of the narrative. Story mapping can be a project incubator, spawning ideas for projects and products, or the story mapping process can be the project itself. *Community asset maps* are similar to story maps. Community asset maps have been employed in the research and justice fields, as well as in education. The Center for Court Innovation (2011) describes the concept in this way:

> The process of asset mapping can include identifying the institutions, individuals, and citizen associations existing within communities that serve as positive resources. The goal of asset mapping is to document a community's existing resources, incorporating these strengths into community development work. (p. 2)

Planning a place-based learning journey requires a specialization of the project-based learning methodology. Using the project-planning tool can aid in achieving this specialization. The tool begins with a community asset map. Prior to using the project-planning tool, we encourage you, if possible, to conduct story mapping and then move to the more targeted community asset map for a project of your choice. Think of story mapping as the whole nonfiction section of a library and the community asset map as the biography collection. If you are constructing a specific project as you read this text, now is the time to make a copy of the project-planning tool from the appendix (page 265) so that you can begin to fill it out as you make the community asset map.

As we touched on briefly in the introduction (page 1), the community asset map contains distinct and sometimes overlapping sections. These are as follows.

- **Who my students are:** Describe your students in your own words. Paint a picture with those words for someone who has never entered your classroom and met your students. How are they unique? What makes them who they are? How might they describe themselves?

- **Ways of knowing, issues, and infinite capacities to connect to the community:** Expanding on the previous description, list the cultural and individual assets your students bring to the learning, as well as issues they may be uniquely positioned to take on because of these assets. Then, inspect the capacity for growth your students have in relation to possible place-based journeys.

- **Connecting academic and justice standards:** Think about alignment of your students' assets to both academic and justice standards early in project planning, as this will solidify and clarify the direction in which you move.

- **Who, how, and what:** Take stock of the human resources available to you for place-based journeys. Think about how to partner and about what purpose sets the course for the entire project.

- **Potential community product, service, or call to action:** Leave room for your students and community partners to contribute to the deliverable. Conceive of as many viable potential products as you can.

These five components all work together to make it impossible to move to the next section of the planner, liberatory learning and assessment pathways (first visited in the introduction, page 17), without needing to deeply consider again who your students are and how the community will be inherent. This consideration is what gives place-based learning its name.

To provide a sense of how the community asset map works, figure 9.1 again shows the completed version, using Baton Rouge's Troubled Waters project as an example.

COMMUNITY ASSET MAP

Who my students are

My students are Black youth living in the community they are learning about. The classroom represents a diverse group of young individuals with unique experiences and perspectives. Some students are parents, and some are caretakers of grandparents or other older relatives. These students bring a rich understanding of the challenges and strengths of their community and can provide valuable insights and ideas to their classmates and teachers. Their diverse backgrounds and experiences also bring a dynamic and inclusive atmosphere to the classroom, fostering a sense of community and respect among all students.

Ways of knowing, issues, and infinite capacities to connect to the community

Ways of knowing:	Issues:	Infinite capacities:
Utilizing the expertise of elders Using community sites for experiential learning Accepting the knowledge and expertise of others, such as teachers, experts, or sacred texts Acquiring knowledge through direct personal experience and reflection on that experience	How local policy impacts communities and reverberates across time	Students have the capacity to learn about and appreciate the cultural diversity of others and to develop intercultural communication skills. Students have the capacity to expand their knowledge and understanding of the world through continuous learning and exploration. Students have the capacity to develop and refine their physical skills and abilities through practice and training, most specifically around the ability to swim.

Connecting academic, justice, and action standards

Academic anchor standards:

Use of language as a tool for communication and knowledge acquisition

Collaborative conversations

Persuasive writing

Revising work based on feedback

History standards:

Exploring impact of policy on local community

Unpacking the historical actions of Jim Crow-era laws and policies

Justice anchor standards:

11. Students will recognize stereotypes and relate to people as individuals rather than representatives of groups

4. Students will recognize that power and privilege influence relationships on interpersonal, intergroup, and institutional levels and consider how they have been affected by those dynamics.

15. Students will identify figures, groups, events, and a variety of strategies and philosophies relevant to the history of social justice around the world.

Action anchor standards:

18. Students will speak up with courage and respect when they or someone else has been hurt or wronged by bias.

19. Students will make principled decisions about when and how to take a stand against bias and injustice in their everyday lives and will do so despite negative peer or group pressure.

20. Students will plan and carry out collective action against bias and injustice in the world and will evaluate what strategies are most effective.

FIGURE 9.1: Baton Rouge's Troubled Waters project example—community asset map.   continued →

Who, how, and what		
Who will be involved? (Primary community partners)	**How are they an asset? How will they be involved? How will we connect and reciprocate?**	**What learning will happen as a result of their involvement?**
A landscape architecture student who is from Baton Rouge and was formerly a member of the local middle school's swim club	• As counsel, providing historical context for students • As an interviewee • As a primary resource • As an expert who can provide technical guidance on designs • As a target audience—a community member who could support the calls to action and proposals that students craft	Students will get exposure to a landscape architecture professional who looks like them and grew up in their community. They will learn about the pathway of his career, from middle school swim team participation to high school to college and career. Students will learn firsthand what research, feedback, and revision look like in the field of landscape architecture, as well as consult directly with him to determine whether the ways in which they gather information from the community match up with his professional methods.
City council members	• As counsel, to advise students on their proposals as they're being crafted • As support to give students insight on how city council works • As target audience and recipients of students' proposals • As the primary agents of action for the students' calls to action	Students will learn about the various ways citizens communicate with and share their concerns with their local legislators. Council members will also support students in creating persuasive calls to action.
Local elders who were alive during the 1950s, when the pools were shut down	• As counsel, providing historical context for students • As interviewees • As primary resources • As experts to provide guidance on designs • As a target audience and recipients of honors and homages built into students' proposals and calls to action	Students will learn more about the historical context of their community and the impact that policy decisions have had on their community through the anecdotes of local elders. Students will learn about the power of storytelling and active listening, as well as making connections to the past. Students will learn the art of interview skills and gathering oral histories.
Potential community product, service, or call to action		
Potential products can include public awareness campaigns, proposals for legislation to city council, social media campaigns, landscape architectural designs, and any other options that students may design, based on their selected target audience.		

Who My Students Are

Start making your community asset map by generating an asset map of your classroom community. Ask yourself the following.

- "Who are my students?"
- "What are their ways of knowing and being?"
- "What are their interests, strengths, and needs?"

This is where all the classroom culture building you do will take on new importance and become the most valuable lever in project design.

Ways of Knowing, Issues, and Infinite Capacities to Connect to the Community

Ways of knowing, issues, and infinite capacities represent the assets we can connect to the community. While we previously discussed ways of knowing (chapter 1, page 23), we'll define infinite capacities here. Recall from the introduction (page 1) the *infinite capacities* of students refer to the potential for students to continue growing, learning, and developing throughout their lives. This includes not only academic abilities but also social-emotional, creative, and physical capacities. Delpit (2013) contends, "reversing the shallow learning that poor and minority students receive starts with teachers' beliefs in all children's infinite capacities, acknowledging their brilliance rather than focusing on deficiency and reminding them of their rich intellectual and cultural legacies" (p. 79). Because beginning the identification of students' infinite capacities is broad, figure 9.2 offers the following as considerations when planning projects. We ask that you use these considerations as a starting point for describing the intellectual legacies of students on the community asset map. The considerations offer a way to internalize important elements, and the beliefs serve as an internal checklist against which to monitor implicit biases and preconceived notions.

Aspect of Infinite Capacity	Beliefs
Intellectual	Students have the capacity to expand their knowledge and understanding of the world through continuous learning and exploration.
Creativity	Students have the capacity to generate new ideas, perspectives, and solutions to problems, and to express themselves in unique and imaginative ways.
Emotional intelligence	Students have the capacity to understand and regulate their own emotions, as well as to empathize with and understand the emotions of others.
Physical capacity	Students have the capacity to develop and refine their physical skills and abilities through practice and training.
Cultural competence	Students have the capacity to learn about and appreciate the cultural diversity of others, and to develop intercultural communication skills.
Resilience	Students have the capacity to overcome challenges and setbacks, and to develop a growth mindset.
Historical	Students have the capacity to tap into and learn from the accomplishments and wisdom of their ancestors and how they overcame obstacles.

FIGURE 9.2: Considerations regarding infinite capacities when planning place-based-learning projects.

Not every project will address every aspect of infinite capacity. It is up to us, the teachers, to learn as much as we can about our students and their community so we can tease out which capacities are most connected to the ways of knowing, content standards, issues, and justice standards that we hope to have our students explore. By recognizing and nurturing the infinite capacities of students, we can help them reach their full potential and become lifelong learners. This requires creating supportive and inclusive learning environments that value and respect the diverse strengths and abilities of all students.

Don't worry if there is overlap of infinite capacities and ways of knowing in your planner, or if you cannot yet think of an issue. The vital element of this section of the planner is centering who your students are in the conception of the place-based journey.

Connecting Academic and Justice Standards

Typical project planning puts academic standards at the center, often dictating and narrowing the focus of the project. Inversely, place-based planning requires the alignment of students' ways of knowing, issues, and infinite capacities with content and justice standards, without limiting the entry points to or scope of the project. Eventually, that alignment will extend to community partners, products, services, and actions. But for now, look at the standards you must teach and assess, and evaluate, using your familiarity with those standards, which will provoke the ways of knowing, issues, and infinite capacities you have called out. Looking back at figure 9.1 (page 137), the example community asset map based on Baton Rouge's Troubled Waters project, we see that students have the skill of utilizing the expertise of elders as a way of knowing. We then see that there is alignment to the ELA standard of *participating in collaborative conversations* and the history standard of *exploring impact of policy on local community* (Southern Poverty Law Center, n.d.a). This progression then extends to the justice standard of *recognizing stereotypes and relating to people as individuals* (Southern Poverty Law Center, n.d.a). It is not necessary for everything to set up perfectly. At this point in your planning, you are postulating, and you will refine as you gather more information.

Who, How, and What

Once your planning is grounded in your deep-rooted knowledge of students, you can expand your asset map to families and community, although this is not to imply that the process of knowing happens in a linear fashion. Instead, it usually happens in multiple spheres at the same time, as they are all interconnected. For example, since students' identities are often intertwined with their families, you may learn about a student and that student's family at the same time. Don't let the project-planning tool limit you. If you had an amazing conversation with a technician at a kidney dialysis center while standing in line at the bank, and you recall that a group of your students were recently discussing their concern over a friend's diabetes diagnosis, feel free to begin your community asset map with the *who*, the *how*, or the *what*, and then backtrack to earlier sections of the tool.

It is probable when sitting down with the project-planning tool that you know two things well: (1) your students and (2) what you are expected to teach them. The question at this point in the process is, How do you connect your students' capacities and your content learning goals to those community assets just waiting to be contacted? One successful strategy we have practiced is to put a piece of chart paper up in a common area (staff room, hallway in the main office) with a topic circled in the middle (for example, health care). Send out a brief email to all staff, informing them you'd like to design a place-based journey on this topic, and, if they know anyone in this field who they think would be willing to be contacted, promptly add their names to the chart paper. Within a few weeks you will have at least a few potential partners—we've yet to encounter a blank piece of paper. It is unclear why the combination of digital (email) and analog (chart paper) is so magical, but it works better than an either-or approach.

We also recommend asking your students if they have connections. Our students' networks are vast. Ask for the same information from them in the form of an exit ticket or Kahoot!, and you will get connections to family members as well as to YouTubers in other countries and TikTok influencers on other continents. As you progress in your inclusion of family and community partners, the Southern Poverty Law Center (2012) has a detailed guidebook for community asset mapping, with sample surveys, letters, exploratory spreadsheets, and a skills checklist, which we find particularly helpful for inventorying families about their unique capacities. Aligned with our place-based approach in their process, the Alabama Youth Justice Alliance and Southern Poverty Law Center (n.d.) affirm that community asset mapping:

> rejects the habit of describing communities in which many of our children live by listing their problems. Instead of focusing on deficits, asset-mapping spotlights methods of tapping into the hidden wealth of knowledge in all communities for the benefit of children. (p. 5)

Remembering to approach the communities your students live in with an expectation that they hold a wealth of knowledge contributes to positive outcomes for your students and the communities themselves. Doing so will also help you avoid coming up short when creating a list of potential partners. In addition to taking on a wealth mindset regarding what the community has to offer, try any number of these quick actions to produce leads.

- Go to where groups meet.
- Read local papers.
- Take a neighborhood drive.
- See who is hiring. (Their business is growing, and they may need students' help!)
- Attend a city council meeting.
- Research what government agencies work in your area (National Oceanic and Atmospheric Administration or National Trust for Historic Preservation, for example).
- Read flyers posted around town.
- Start noticing community and cultural organizations.

Primed with this list of contacts and a few potential leads from your own networks and research, think about and brainstorm answers to these four questions from the community asset map.

- How are they an asset?
- How will they be involved?
- How will you and your students connect and reciprocate?
- What learning will happen as a result of their involvement?

Viewing students, their families, and community partners as assets and creators, capable of enriching any learning experience, and then approaching the planning process with as much malleability as you can muster will make this section of the planner an evolving yet foundational component as you get further into the tool.

Potential Community Product, Service, or Call to Action

After anticipating community partners in the Who, How, and What section of the community asset map, contemplate the ways in which students, in genuine partnership with the community, might demonstrate their knowledge and skills in authentic ways. This section is figuratively written in pencil, as your isolated brainstorm is just an initial attempt to align the ways of knowing, standards, and product, service, or call to action so that when you begin to discuss the possibilities with your students and community partners, you have laid the groundwork. The product, service, or call to action may change, but your responsibility to align that to ways of knowing and standards does not.

How Do I Get Started Connecting With Community Partners?

In this section, we take a more comprehensive look at connecting with community partners as you create your community asset map, so you will feel as primed as possible for this fundamental part of the planning formula. Beginning with unpacking biases and assumptions was deliberate. In order to sketch a map and make a plan to partner with the community, you must supplant fear, mistrust, and shallow understanding with curiosity, trust, and contextual knowledge. You don't have to know everything about a potential partner before sending out a letter of inquiry, but being reflective, using the strategies we outlined earlier in this chapter and throughout part I, and practicing humility will prime the actions we discuss in this section.

As you consider partnering with community members and organizations for a project, think about how you have partnered with the community in the past. (If you have yet to do this, think back to your own experience as a student.) Many of us rely on experts to impart content knowledge to students or to give them a chance to get off campus and see a play or visit a museum. But place-based learning, as we've shared throughout this book, demands a much more nuanced and in-depth conception of teaching. Sometimes a partnership could very well include an individual coming into the classroom to provide information on discrete content, but in a place-based learning orientation this would happen because students need that information for a project and have sought out (or asked you to find) someone to provide it. Teachers may also establish a partnership during the planning phase, possibly with the goal of solving a shared dilemma, gaining industry experience for students, or garnering feedback. Thus, the establishment of a more project-specific partnership might necessitate teachers making a different initial ask of the community partner.

The following four actions can be useful to start connecting with community partners.

1. **Write a community partner letter:** Tap into your personal connections and those of your colleagues to cast a wide net for community partners who are excited to work alongside your students.

2. **Keep a database:** As early into your place-based journey as possible, record data on your community connections to build lasting partnerships that can become a legacy, minimize redundancy, and indicate patterns and gaps in your partnerships over time.

3. **Reciprocate:** Contemplate how you hope students and community partners will show reciprocity toward one another at the conclusion of a place-based journey, and what each can learn from the other that will last well beyond the project.

4. **Practice beloved community:** As you plan, entertain both how you encourage respectful examination of differences in beliefs and ideas and how you model an attitude toward community partnerships that teaches students that they are part of something much greater than one project in one classroom—that they are beloved.

Write a Community Partner Letter

In the following example community letter to a potential partner (figure 9.3), Erin introduced the school and the teaching methodology (in accessible language). She then engaged the potential partner with several ways they could be involved, acknowledging that this might be different from the relationships they've had with schools in the past. Finally, Erin followed up with a phone call shortly thereafter.

Dear Community Partner,

Squatahan School is a unique environment that prepares students to be productive members of today's world while at the same time immersing them in traditional cultural knowledge. One way we do this is through place-based learning—a teaching method in which students work with the community for an extended period of time to investigate and respond to an authentic and complex need or challenge. A critical component of place-based learning is making connections with, and learning from, community partners. You've been identified as someone who might be willing to be a part of this exciting work. What does it mean for you, and how can you contribute? Great questions!

<u>Students can help solve</u> a problem that requires an innovative solution.

Maybe you are curious about why something is happening: *"Why are the spring salmon runs so much larger than the fall runs?"* Maybe you have a nagging issue: *"How do we ensure our waiting room can accommodate all our patients comfortably at peak hours?"* Maybe you need data collected to improve your work: *"How can we find out if our target market knows about the services we provide?"* You pose the question, problem, or challenge, then students research, innovate, collect, and solve.

<u>You can provide</u> students a window into what you do.

A guest speaker at the front of the classroom, telling students what they do, was probably a part of your school experience. A far more effective means of teaching students what happens in the professional world is to invite individual or small groups of students to spend time where you do your work, watching you communicate, collaborate, create, and navigate obstacles. This might be for an entire day or a few hours. Because the immersion would be tied directly to their project, students are guided by their teacher beforehand to be as unobtrusive as possible while collecting valuable information they'll need to complete the project.

<u>You can be an expert</u> eye on students' work.

Often, schools ask community partners to view student work once it's all polished, but there's even greater value when students can receive feedback on their works in progress. This feedback might happen in person, with a few hours spent talking to student teams about their initial efforts, such as designs, drafts, storyboards, proposals, blueprints, or surveys. Your feedback may happen virtually using Google Docs or a Zoom call, sharing what you see in students' work. It might happen by example, sharing with students samples of what high-quality work looks like in your industry.

I encourage you to think about the possibilities. If you can't wait to add your name to our list of willing partners, you can email me at <u>xxxxx@squatahanschool.org</u>, or leave me a voicemail or text at (xxx) xxx-xxxx. We look forward to collaborating with you!

Sincerely,

Erin Sanchez, place-based learning instructional facilitator, Squatahan School

---

FIGURE 9.3: Sample community partner letter.

The sample community partner letter is fairly generic, as you will want to cast a wide net when you are first fishing for partners. You want them to know why you are contacting them; how your students, school, or teaching is unique; and how they might be involved. If you have personal connections or a specific request of a potential partner, then by all means make the email more subjective. Despite the amazing students you teach, you will get rejections from potential partners, so strike a balance between sending out numerous queries and conducting personal outreach to people in your network. This combination of wide net and personal angling will produce more yeses.

Keep a Database

One of the most useful actions a teacher, instructional coach, or leader can take when partnering with the community is to build a schoolwide community partner database. It need not be elaborate. Your database can be just a spot to record existing and potential human resources so that, as your place-based learning network grows, there is a historical repository of partners for everyone within the school to draw and learn from. It may look something like the example in figure 9.4.

In our experience, this data collection is generally an afterthought, coming years into the implementation of place-based learning, and the refrain is always the same with educators: "Why didn't we start collecting this information earlier?" After building a database, include a link to it on your project-planning tool template so every time you begin ideating on a new project, the database is at your disposal.

The database can also be a reflective or analytical tool to examine project elements such as the following over time and across grade levels or departments.

- Cultural representation of community partners (Do our partners look like the students we serve?)

- Gaps in community representation (What members of our community are unrepresented or underrepresented in our database?)

- Partner retention (Which partners are we retaining and working with across disciplines or grade levels? Why?)

Reciprocate

What does it mean to you to connect and reciprocate with community partners? We've included a question in the community asset map that addresses reciprocity in an effort to consider, at the beginning of the planning process, how the partnership can be transformative rather than transactional. Students excel at defining ways to reciprocate with community partners. Erin's fifth-grade students who had spent months working with their tribe's salmon hatchery, raising salmon from roe to maturity, then releasing them into a restored creek, decided to also learn how to bead and gifted the three partners with beautiful medallion necklaces featuring a chinook salmon at the center. However, reciprocity isn't always a tangible thing. Giving of time and trust or helping with a difficult task could be a means of reciprocating. If the product is co-determined with the partner, it is judicious to gift them the model, design, film, podcasts, or art, for example. Including students in the effort to reciprocate necessitates your initiation of ideas on the community asset map and then being flexible as students add their voices to the plan.

Grade level/ Teacher/ Project	Who? (Business/ Organization/ Family)	Who is the contact?	Contact information	What are they like to work with? Might they be an asset? How are they connected to my students' cultures and lives?	Have they been a partner in the past? In what capacity? Was the partnership successful?	Date contacted	What else do we need to know about this partner?	Did you secure a confirmation of willingness?

FIGURE 9.4: Sample community partner database.

Visit go.SolutionTree.com/instruction for a free reproducible version of this figure.

Practice Beloved Community

As you reach the point in connecting to potential community partners where you begin to ponder potential products, services, or a call to action, we implore you to call forth bell hooks's (1996) practice of *beloved community*: "Beloved community is formed not by the eradication of difference but by its affirmation, by each of us claiming the identities and cultural legacies that shape who we are and how we live in the world" (p. 265). Beloved community beseeches us to make a vast and compassionate commitment to one another—through conflict, through ambiguity, through hardship—*throughout* the work that needs to be done, not just at its possible conclusion. We raise this practice here because (1) as often as possible, we urge you to build the community product, service, or action *with* the community partner, and (2) the journey—the process—is as important as the destination, or the product. Having ideas is wonderful; having preconceptions can cause us to abandon partnerships when differences arise, instead of seeing those differences as the cultural reservoir that they are. So jot down some malleable ideas, aligned to your standards and students' ways of knowing, and then see how these original product, service, and action ideas are made more exceptional when students and community partners come into the work.

Remember the photobooth listening sessions devised by the teacher, Jenna, at the beginning of this chapter (page 132)? After Jenna surveys families and connects with community partners, she learns that members of city council want to conduct town hall sessions to gather information from their constituents about marginalization related to housing, food insecurity, and transportation. Jenna launches the project and proposes to her students and established community partners that they work with the city council to showcase their curated video to a wider audience. They fervently agree and are able to extend their impact, putting students in the role of experts, uplifting hidden stories, and manifesting what's possible in a beloved community. This kind of beloved community is the realization of educators doing the inner work of unpacking biases and assumptions, and blurring the superficial boundaries between students, schools, and community.

Conclusion

Congratulations on starting or nurturing the work of unpacking your assumptions and biases to foster beloved community. You are building historical context for the project you are designing. You are seeing the community and your students as one and the same. This chapter also afforded you the tools for community outreach and ongoing communication with community partners. If you used this chapter as the guided planning tool it is intended to be, you have a community asset map to take into the next part of the project planner, liberatory learning and assessment pathways.

Key Takeaways and Reflection Questions

Consider this chapter's key takeaways and reflect on the following questions as you work to unpack biases and assumptions and uncover community assets through place-based learning. Use the Journey Log to further reflect, brainstorm, jot down ideas, make observations, or plan.

- Imagining equitable learning opportunities for students requires detecting implicit biases and unpacking assumptions about students, families, and communities.

- Historical contextualization is a necessary step in building community partnerships that are of all of the people involved and that draw on the identities and needs of the people, and in seeing the community not as separate from the lives of students and their education but as one and the same. This is what makes place-based learning potentially transformative.

- Place-based learning demands a much more nuanced and embedded relationship with community partners and necessitates different outreach and ongoing communication. Reciprocity in a community partnership ensures the relationship is mutually beneficial and respectful of what stakeholders bring to the project.

- As often as possible, build the community product, service, or action with the community partner.

- Where are you on your journey to unpack your assumptions about your students, their families, and potential community partners in order to build beloved community? What work do you need to do?

- How can you build historical context about the community you teach in and the students you serve?

- Who are the storytellers, the wisdom keepers, and the elders from whom you can learn? (Don't forget, they might be your students.)

- How can the partnerships you forge be transformative rather than transactional? What does practicing beloved community mean to you? What is your vision for beloved community?

Journey Log

Journey Log

Journey Log

CHAPTER 10

Follow Pathways to Liberatory and Decolonized Assessment Practices

There needs to be a lot more emphasis on what a child can do instead of what he cannot do.

—TEMPLE GRANDIN

ESSENTIAL QUESTION: How do we plan and implement equitable assessment practices?

Liberatory and decolonized assessment is an early step in decolonizing our entire curriculum and teaching to promote equitable practices. Formative assessments help move the work forward, creating a growth mindset that helps build a culture of feedback, revision, and reflection allowing students to produce high-quality work. Critical to liberatory assessment practices is the use of rubrics throughout a project. Doing so optimizes high-quality work and provides more meaningful and personalized feedback to students that acknowledges their skills, talents, and cultural backgrounds. This approach to assessment creates opportunities for students to become more reflective in their learning process.

In this chapter, we explore cutting-edge research on how to achieve equitable assessment with our students. We will explore what a decolonized and liberatory approach to assessment looks like in practice and provide tools to apply as you design a place-based journey. We introduce the second part of the place-based learning project-planning tool, *liberatory learning and assessment pathways*. This part of the planning tool asks you to begin with the end in mind—that is, with the community product (summative assessment), while also considering formative assessments and checkpoints along the way. In addition, the tool asks you to consider how you embed culture and scaffolds to support students. At the end of the chapter, you will have a completed project planner for your place-based journey with your students. The chapter also offers a chance to think further about its content through the Conclusion and Key Takeaways and Reflection Questions sections. It concludes with the Journey Log for writing down your thoughts and ideas.

What Are Liberatory and Decolonized Assessment Practices?

Liberatory assessment practices refer to educational assessment methods that prioritize empowering students and communities, promote equity and social justice, and undermine oppressive structures and power imbalances. They focus on students' strengths, interests, and cultural backgrounds, and encourage students to take an active role in their own learning and assessment process. Liberatory assessments aim to provide a meaningful, authentic, and relevant evaluation of student learning and growth, rather than simply testing for rote knowledge or conformity to predetermined standards.

The background of liberatory assessment practices stems from critiques of traditional forms of assessment that some see as oppressive and limiting to students' growth and development. Traditional assessments, such as standardized tests, have been criticized for perpetuating cultural biases, reinforcing inequalities, and narrowing the curriculum to focus solely on what can be tested (Rosales & Walker, 2021). In their *NEA Today* article "The Racist Beginnings of Standardized Testing," John Rosales and Tim Walker (2021) attest:

> Many communities [of color] have suffered the most from high-stakes testing. Since their inception almost a century ago, the tests have been instruments of racism and a biased system. Decades of research demonstrate that Black, Latin(o/a/x), and Native students, as well as students from some Asian groups, experience bias from standardized tests administered from early childhood through college.

In response to the limiting features of traditional assessment and testing, liberatory assessment practices emerged as an alternative approach, rooted in the principles of liberation pedagogy and critical education. In place-based learning, we shift away from traditional assessments that prioritize compliance and conformity, and toward forms of assessment that value students' experiences, perspectives, and agency. The aim is to create more equitable and just educational experiences for all students, particularly those who have been marginalized by traditional assessments.

To give an example of how traditional assessment may be limiting while liberatory assessment practices can offer more just and equitable learning experiences, let's consider a high school student named Tyler. Tyler is a bright and curious student who is on the autism spectrum. Tyler loves learning about science and technology, but despite a strong interest in these subjects, he struggles with traditional forms of assessment, such as multiple-choice tests and written essays. He finds it difficult to demonstrate his understanding of complex concepts in a way that aligns with his teachers' expectations.

Tyler's teachers are determined to accurately evaluate his learning and progress. Unfortunately, they rely heavily on standardized tests and other rigid forms of assessment that do not take into account Tyler's unique strengths and challenges. As a result, Tyler often feels frustrated and discouraged, and his test scores do not accurately reflect his knowledge and abilities.

One day, Tyler's new teacher, Mrs. Stills, introduces a different approach to assessment. She encourages Tyler to create a portfolio of his work, which includes projects and presentations he has created on his own time. She also incorporates self-reflection and performance-based tasks into her evaluations and considers Tyler's interests and background. With these new assessments, Tyler is able to showcase his knowledge and understanding in a way that feels more authentic and meaningful to him. He is no longer limited by traditional forms of evaluation and is able to demonstrate his true potential.

In the end, Tyler *and* Mrs. Stills learn that assessment can be a powerful tool for promoting learning and growth, but it is important to approach it in a way that is inclusive and equitable for all students, including those with autism. Mrs. Stills's new assessment practices are liberatory because they are built around Tyler's interests, perspectives, and personal experiences. They allow Tyler to feel valued and supported in his learning and give him the confidence to continue pursuing his passions.

Place-based learning is inherently liberatory because it is inclusive and honors each student. As Felicitas Fischer (2020), community coordinator for the Technology Access Foundation, which serves diverse communities, notes:

> Liberatory pedagogy flips the classroom on its head, treats students as co-creators of knowledge that learn alongside the teacher, and have a say in what they learn. By centering student voice and choice, students are liberated to lead their learning and make meaningful connections to the world around them. This helps develop a critical consciousness in which students are empowered to identify, question and solve relevant problems in society rather than passively absorb knowledge for no other reason than to be tested on.

Place-based learning is also an act of decolonization, and this act can be particularly important as it pertains to assessment practices and efforts to make those practices equitable for all students.

Table 10.1 (page 154) is our adapted version of the Emergence Collective's vision of what decolonized assessment practices might look like. The Emergence Collective works with a wide range of organizations to support organizational change. Their work is rooted in social justice and equity, and the collective is deeply committed to equity, justice, and collaboration.

Implementing authentic equitable assessment practices, such as those represented in table 10.1, moves us closer to providing opportunities for all students to succeed, not just in academics but in life skills. Such practices also provide opportunities for students to develop a sense of self and pride in their cultural traditions.

Asking ourselves the following questions is critical to equitable, decolonized assessment practices.

- Are our assessment practices culturally relevant?
- Do they value each student?
- Is there an opportunity for students to share their stories and their cultural identities?
- Are our assessment practices equitable?

These questions are so important because authentic assessments that build on cultural and social backgrounds value many different ways of knowing. The resulting practice allows you to build strong relationships with your students by providing opportunities for storytelling so that you can learn more about your students' backgrounds, cultural identities, and dreams and aspirations. To make sure your assessments are equitable, use multiple assessment types, provide options and choice for how students might demonstrate their learning, and ensure that content is accessible to all your learners.

TABLE 10.1: Decolonized Mindset and Assessment Practices

Colonized Mindset in Grades 4–12 Assessment	Decolonized Mindset in Grades 4–12 Assessment	Decolonized Assessment Practices
Focusing on achievement gaps	Focusing on opportunity gaps	Teachers provide scaffolds. Teachers provide timely, constructive feedback. Students track their own progress with student evidence trackers.
Teaching only a colonized perspective or teaching a single story; for example, teaching American history from a White perspective only, like the myth of Thanksgiving	Analyzing a variety of perspectives and exploring untold stories; using multiple perspectives and different primary sources when exploring historical events, such as looking at the gold rush from the perspectives of Indigenous peoples who occupied the land, Chinese immigrants, and African Americans	Teachers provide opportunities for students to reflect on their own biases, thinking, and actions. Teachers observe student interactions, looking for empathy and understanding of others. Teachers provide opportunities for students to learn about other cultures and worldviews. They also provide students opportunities to reflect on what they learned. Using sentence stems such as, "I used to think _____. Now I think _____," they guide students in reflections that provide assessment data about any shifts in thinking as a result of these explorations (thinking routine from Project Zero).
Using only Eurocentric texts, teaching history through a colonized lens, and focusing only on the dominant narrative	Engaging students of color with texts and literacies that reflect their racial identities, cultural practices, and social realities	Teachers foster student self-reflection on their own learning and progress. Students identify areas for improvement. Students engage in small-group discussions.
Using binary thinking in terms such as *either* and *or*	Using spectrum thinking in terms such as *both* and *and*	Teachers design interdisciplinary learning. Teachers use assessment for learning and growth rather than telling the student what is wrong with the work.
Approaching learning with fear of conflicting views	Approaching conflicting views as opportunities to share perspectives and deepen the learning rather than as something to be feared	Conflicts are used to foster reflection and self-awareness. Teachers set up timely feedback from peers, community partners, and themselves for revision opportunities.
Approaching learning with a need to be perfect	Approaching learning with aims for high-quality work rather than perfection	Teachers facilitate regular check-ins rather than waiting until the end of the project for feedback. Teachers guide students in using mistakes as a way to grow.
Valuing how much a student accomplishes over depth and quality of work	Valuing the quality of a student's work more than how much the student accomplished	Teachers provide multiple opportunities for revision. Students build and refine their community products around revisions based on community feedback.
Valuing students' right to remain in their comfort zones regarding their viewpoints	Seeing value in engaging in discussion and learning that may trigger discomfort through considering viewpoints different from one's own	Teachers acknowledge that learning new things or engaging in challenges might make students feel uncomfortable. Students use the realm of influence protocol from the National School Reform Faculty to look at what they are concerned about and what they have direct influence over.
Depending on the written word	Using multiple media to communicate ideas, research, and solutions	Teachers move away from written reports and presentation slides. Teachers provide multiple options for the community product. Students use a variety of inquiry methods (surveys, interviews, fieldwork, and so on) to support the creation of the community product.
Valuing speed and efficiency in learning	Understanding that comprehensive learning often takes time, and allowing students that time when possible	Teachers invest in relationship building with many community voices. Teachers create a realistic project timeline that allows for multiple revisions and opportunities for building knowledge, understanding, and life skills.

Source: Adapted from Beriont, 2020. Used with permission.

Ultimately, liberatory and decolonized assessment practices reveal learning and the possibility for learning rather than fixate on the achievement of a specific result. Educators Kelly Niccolls and Abby Benedetto (2023), in their blog for *Getting Smart*, work on ways "to reset the relationship with assessment by sharing Assessment as Revelation, not Destination framework." They discuss how a "destination" perspective to assessment is "a key barrier to more liberatory learning experiences." Niccolls and Benedetto ask, "*What if we shifted the mindset of assessment to experience it as a journey and revelation vs a destination?*" (emphasis original to source). That shift would be significant for the learning culture and learning experience for students. As a result of asking this question, Niccolls and Benedetto created a framework of revelatory assessment practices, shown in table 10.2, in support of liberatory pedagogy.

TABLE 10.2: Key Elements of Revelatory Assessment

Five Elements of Revelatory Assessment	Definition	What It Looks Like in Practice
Personal	There is a purposeful, meaningful, and authentic *why* to the assessment, designed by the learner, and an invitation to bring all the learner's rich identities into the moment.	Assessment goes beyond content and skills and is rooted in cultural identity.
Narrational	The assessment centers storytelling and other nonquantifiable methods as a way of knowing and being that is valued. Learners are the authors and narrators of their own stories of learning.	Students share their learning through storytelling and other ways of knowing such as art, dance, music, and so on.
Relational	The assessment design is rooted in sharing power to support meaningful exchanges of insight and learning between all those engaged in the learning and to reduce positionality.	This element values relationships built on trust. Students receive a variety of feedback from peers, community members, and experts.
Iterative	The assessment is built into a continuous cycle of learning that offers insight and celebrates the current milestone along a journey.	Formative assessments along the way celebrate and share a narrative about what students are learning throughout the place-based journey.
Reciprocal	The assessment is built on the importance of giving to and receiving from the community at large. The assessment asks the question, "What impact will students have on the collective wisdom, knowledge, and experience of those around them?"	Assessment in place-based learning is built on reciprocity with authentic community partnerships.

Source: adapted from Niccolls & Benedetto, 2023. Used with permission.

The framework shows the interconnectedness between teacher, students, and community and is rooted in place, offering a vision of what liberatory assessment practices in place-based learning might look like. While the authors define the key elements of revelatory assessment in the table, we have added what it might look like in practice.

Liberatory and decolonized assessment practices ask us to think about assessment as a revelation rather than a destination. This illustrates the interconnectedness between teacher, students, and community while rooted in place.

How Do I Implement Liberatory and Decolonized Assessment Practices?

At the most fundamental level, educators can implement liberatory and decolonized assessment practices by making mindset and habit changes in the classroom. These changes would include the following.

- Assessing with a deep understanding of who your students are
- Assessing with equity in mind
- Recognizing the difference between a grading orientation and learning orientation in assessment practices

Gaining a knowledge of your students and coming to respect and value their many stories is an important starting place in implementing liberatory and decolonized assessment practices. This is because it acknowledges student perspectives as important and works toward putting the power to self-define in students' hands. It also builds meaningful learning relationships, teacher to student and student to student. When getting to know your students, ask yourself the following as you think about who your students are and how their lives may have influenced them.

- What is their context, cultural background, community, student needs, and so on?
- What are their dreams, hopes, and fears?
- What are their cultural traditions and beliefs about themselves?
- What do they like to do outside of school?
- How do they learn best?
- What motivates them as a learner?
- What is their story?

Muhammad (2020a) suggests the related additional following questions to find out who your students are. You may ask these questions directly through one-to-one conferences or journal responses.

- "What's your name? What does it mean?"
- "What are your cultural identities?" For younger students, you might ask questions about their culture, cultural celebrations, language, food, and music.
- "What would your other teachers say about you?"
- "How are people like you depicted in society and the media?"
- "How might you describe your culture or ethnicity?"
- "How is science, mathematics, social studies, or language arts important in your culture or with regard to your ethnicity?"
- "Do you feel my teaching reflects your culture? If yes, how? If not, how could it be improved?"
- "If you could take me somewhere to help me understand your culture and your ethnicity, where would you take me?" (Muhammad, 2022a, p. 72)

Build on your process of getting to know students deeply by considering ways to engage students in storytelling about their own lives and lived experiences. One way to do this is by being vulnerable with your own stories. Dinah Becton-Consuegra (2019) points out in her blog:

> One of the prime launching points in building these relationships with our students is for adults to be able to tell our life stories. As a starting point, consider your purpose by reflecting privately on three key questions: Why are you an educator? What moment has defined your own why? What are you most passionate about?

Openness about who you are and what you care about in the world opens a door for students and creates a platform for them to tell their own stories with you and their classmates. A good friend and colleague of ours, Mike Kaechele, shared the *mini-selfie project* in a personal communication (June, 2021) with Micki as a way for educators to share their stories with their students and to give the students an opportunity to share theirs as well. To do the mini-selfie project, introduce the essential question, "Who am I?" Begin by sharing your story using Google Slides and selfies, photos, memes, and images. Include the origin of your name.

Explain to students that they will create their own digital stories about themselves. They can gather photos and take pictures of artifacts from home that they will use the next day to create their own stories about who they are. They can use photos, animation, sound, and print to convey their stories. Give them time to work on a thirty- or sixty-second presentation to share with the class. Prior to the presentations, students write the names of their peers. After each peer story, ask students to record two to three words about something they learned about their peers or something that stood out to them when they heard their peers' stories. You could also have students draw images or symbols to convey their thinking.

Micki likes to have students reflect about the danger of a single story by watching or reading the transcript of Chimamanda Ngozi Adichie's (2009) TED Talk and then discuss how people exist beyond single definitions. She furthers the discussion by drawing connections to the digital stories project the students did. The following questions can be used to guide such a discussion.

- ◆ What surprised you when hearing the stories of your peers?
- ◆ Why is it important to know other people's stories as they tell them?

Liberatory assessment asks us to reframe assessment through an equity lens. Respect for and knowledge of students in all their diversity of self, culture, and perspective are foundational for equitable assessment because providing opportunities for all students to succeed, not just in academics but in life, contributes to a sense of self and pride in their cultural traditions.

However, equitable assessment also requires that educators ensure students have access to the resources they need to learn at high levels. Lorrie Shepard (2021), in her blog post, "Ambitious Teaching and Equitable Assessment" for the American Federation of Teachers reminds us that "creating truly equitable and excellent educational opportunities means ensuring that each child has access to rigorous curricular resources and is supported to participate fully in instructional activities that enable deep learning." Creating equitable assessment in place-based learning asks us to ensure that all students have access to instructional activities, research strategies, content, and the right texts. Newsela (https://newsela.com) and CommonLit (www.commonlit.org) are two resources that provide free collections of articles and proper scaffolds to support equitable assessment.

When assessment is anchored in knowledge of and respect for all experiences and perspectives and students have fair access to the resources they need to learn, the concept of assessment becomes flexible, fluid, individualized, collaborative, organic, and present and future focused. This means that it focuses on change and evolution rather than on something static, and instead of a limiting designation becomes a pathway forward. In short, assessment becomes learning focused rather than grading focused.

A learning orientation puts students at the center, recognizes that growth is always possible, and taps into students' higher-level thinking skills. As educators strive toward equitable assessment practices in place-based learning, they need to use assessments that are appropriate to each student. These may vary from one student to the next, depending on the student's prior knowledge, cultural experience, and cognitive style. In a blog post for the Assessment Network, its founder Laura Greenstein (2021), who is also a professional development specialist specializing in assessment and a former classroom teacher, reminds us that:

> reframing assessment through a lens of fairness and equity means that every student has multiple and/or varied opportunities to show what they know, understand, and can do in response to visible learning intentions and well-defined and anticipated outcomes of learning.

Place-based learning provides the consummate opportunity to achieve this learning orientation. Formative assessments along the way help students to refine their efforts. On a visit we took to Leadership School in Albuquerque, New Mexico, one teacher likened the process of learning-oriented assessment with taking multiple bites out of an apple. The number of bites may be different from student to student, but the goal is the same: to create high-quality work. For example, if students are creating a final product for a client, it either works or doesn't. There's no option to accept a low grade. Revision is critical to place-based learning, and recognizing that leads to multiple attempts to create high-quality work.

In their book *The Landscape Model of Learning*, Jennifer Klein and Kapono Ciotti (2022) offer a helpful chart, adapted in table 10.3, for recognizing the difference between a grading orientation and a learning orientation in assessment practices.

TABLE 10.3: Grading Orientation Versus Learning Orientation

Grading Orientation Traits	Learning Orientation Traits
• Is teacher centered	• Is student centered
• Relies on extrinsic motivators	• Relies on intrinsic motivators
• Can favor compliance	• Favors metacognition
• Suggests lack of trust	• Suggests trust in learners
• Judges growth	• Sparks growth
• Calls for efficiency	• Calls for depth and complexity
• Emphasizes assessment *of* learning	• Encourages challenge
• Can dehumanize students	• Emphasizes evaluation for learning
	• Recognizes students' inherent humanity

Source: Adapted from Klein and Ciotti, 2022.

Now that you are prepared with a sense of everyday mindsets and behaviors to employ for liberatory and decolonized assessment, we will explore some specific, concrete strategies.

◆ **Use backward design:** Begin with the end in mind, prioritizing learning goals, rather than just the content to cover, to increase student choice and agency in the project.

◆ **Offer feedback:** Provide ongoing feedback throughout the project.

◆ **Move from feedback to feedforward:** Using feedforward rather than the more traditional language of feedback demonstrates that critiques and formative assessments help move the work forward.

◆ **Employ rubrics in service of high-quality work:** Rubrics provide specific and consistent feedback through peer review and self-assessment, which can improve students' metacognition at assessing their own and others' work.

These strategies, which we now describe in greater detail, clarify and further the fundamental, everyday mindset and behavior changes that support liberatory and decolonized assessment.

Use Backward Design

Backward design, from Grant Wiggins and Jay McTighe's (2011) *Understanding by Design* model, offers a framework to ensure that we first plan our assessments—including all the key teaching points and skills students need—as a guide to our instruction. This strategy requires beginning with the end in mind to inform your lessons, activities, and scaffolds. The process helps to ensure that teachers reach their instructional goals as they work toward the summative assessment. Courtney Brown (2021), senior professional development adviser for the Center for the Professional Education of Teachers, contends:

> In addition to planning for the summative assessment, we can also plan our formative assessments which will help us understand students' mastery of each discrete skill throughout our lessons. This will also create space to reteach concepts as needed, as well as ensure that we are offering students a range of possible opportunities to learn throughout [the project].

As we work backward from summative assessment, we can add formative assessments that move students closer to creating high-quality work.

Offer Feedback

Formative assessments are critical to place-based journeys because they provide real-time information about where students are with the content, the process, and what they are learning about themselves. According to the Lucas Education Research (n.d.) white paper:

> High-quality [project-based learning] depends on teachers using formative assessments both to drive student learning and in self-reflective ways to inform and improve their own instruction. In [project-based learning], strategically integrated assessments can provide a rich understanding of the student learning that takes place over time. (p. 18)

We want assessments to assess not only acquisition of knowledge but also the process of learning, students' interactions with place, and what they are learning about themselves and each other. Other skills we might assess include collaboration, critical and creative thinking, problem solving, and the understanding of multiple perspectives. A critical component of offering these exploratory forms of assessment is thoughtful feedback. Jorge Valenzuela (2022), in his blog post "Using Frequent Feedback Cycles to Guide Student Work" for Edutopia, explains that students "need feedback they understand and can readily act on along the continuum of the learning process.

They also need to be involved and invested in the feedback." Valenzuela also advises us to provide adequate time for students to complete their products. This provides time for students to create three to four drafts with feedback from peers, experts, community partners, and the teacher. Using critique protocols such as *I like*, *I wonder*, *glow and grows*, and a *tuning protocol* along the way allows students to receive high-quality feedback. Check out BetterLesson's (n.d.) "Giving and Receiving Peer Feedback" (https://teaching.betterlesson.com/strategy/511/giving-and-receiving-peer-feedback) for more information about different critique protocols.

Place-based learning asks students to create authentic, high-quality work that is meaningful to an authentic audience. As with anything of quality, first attempts are typically not our best, nor do most industries allow professionals to work in isolation without getting feedback from colleagues. If we apply these norms to education, then high-quality student work requires revision and reflection on the products and services students are creating and producing, with input from teachers, peers, experts, and community partners.

From a planning perspective, teachers need to build time into the project calendar for meaningful revision and reflection to take place. They also need to scaffold critiquing skills throughout the school year to set students up for success in their project work. Critiquing others is not a skill that comes naturally to many people, but it can be explicitly taught, and the benefit is evidenced in the work students produce. Infuse feedback and revision practices throughout your classroom practice, as they are critical to place-based learning.

For a practice to become a habit, the notion of critique, revision, and reflection should start early in the school year. Start simple, so the rationale is evident to students, then make it routine, so it's an expectation. By the time students need feedback and revision in their project work, they've already formed the habit. That said, the skills of giving and receiving feedback and incorporating that feedback into a project need to be explicitly, consistently, and patiently taught.

Move From Feedback to Feedforward

Language matters. If we shift the notion of feedback to feedforward, we remind ourselves that the work is not done and that there is always room for improvement. Feedforward is a response to student work that orients a forward-movement mindset by using language that focuses on ways to make the work better.

Jennifer Gonzalez (2018b) in her blog, *Cult of Pedagogy*, notes:

> there's a different way to give feedback that works a lot better, a way of flipping its focus from the past to the future. It's a concept called "feedforward," which was originally developed by a management expert named Marshall Goldsmith.

Using feedforward rather than the more traditional language of feedback demonstrates that critiques help move the work forward. This growth mindset helps to create a culture of revision and moves students to produce high-quality work. When you think about assessment in place-based learning, it needs to be student centered and transparent. You can use formative assessments at different project milestones. This provides a rich backdrop for students to reflect on their inquiry, ideation, and assessment of different solutions or actions. In this way, teachers, students, and community partners can use formative assessments to identify next steps. The community product is the summative assessment. Remember that the actual products students create will vary as a result of an open-ended essential question. When students share their final products with an authentic audience, it provides an opportunity for students to show what they know and why it matters to their public audience and stakeholders. In his article "How Does Assessment in PBL Differ From Traditional Classrooms," Paul Curtis (n.d.) of the New Tech Network reminds us:

> since our goal is to develop students' complex thinking, disciplinary literacy, and deeper learning skills, we need assessments that give us accurate information about student performance in these areas. While traditional assessments like quizzes, exit tickets, and problem sets often find a place in a PBL classroom, our primary measure of student learning comes from authentic project products and tasks. PBL tends to culminate in "performance assessments" like proposals, reports, presentations, and other products where students demonstrate their learning through tangible artifacts that can be assessed against clear and explicit criteria using a rubric or similar tool.

As we think about the community product, we want to use formative assessments as a guide to inform our next steps and move students toward creating high-quality work that makes a difference for others. Think back to chapter 2 (page 33). The daily P.I.N.s can fold into the formative assessment checkpoints you have planned out for the entire project, moving students to the final product and the summative assessments. There can be more than two formative assessment checkpoints, depending on the depth and breadth of content and ways of knowing included in the design. The formative assessment checkpoints are planned and can come in the form of feedback, reflections, and quizzes, to name a few.

After students participate in a critique protocol with their peers or with an outside expert or partner, have students turn in their revisions. You can use those revisions as a formative assessment. Students at this stage may also set goals for themselves as they progress toward their final product.

To start using feedforward in your classroom, stress that it is about the future. Rather than discussing what is wrong about the work, discuss what students can do differently moving forward. Ask students to continually reflect on what they are learning about themselves as learners. Feedforward is a way to do this because it is timely and individualized to meet each student where they are. Feedforward increases student agency by involving them in the process of setting goals for improving future work. Use feedforward to improve students' metacognition skills by providing opportunities for them to assess their own work and the work of others.

Employ Rubrics in Service of High-Quality Work

In this section, we demystify rubric development and describe ways to create rubrics that support liberatory and decolonized assessment practices. Erin had an opportunity to interview Dennie Palmer Wolf, principal researcher at arts consultancy WolfBrown (formerly of Harvard's Project Zero), on her advice for rubric development. The following summary of what she had to say transformed the way Erin thinks about and designs rubrics.

- Keep clarity about the difference between a higher-quality rubric and a higher number of criteria; three to five is an optimal number. The more elements you attempt to assess in a single piece of work, the more likely it becomes subjective. Keep it reasonable.
- Remember that rubrics are all about helping students move to a higher quality of work. (Quantitative items belong on a checklist, not on a qualitative rubric.)
- Use all levels in the rubric to describe rather than quantify growth. Each level of performance should paint a picture of incremental growth.

♦ Align rubric language with everything else that students are doing in their educational life, creating a common language and standard.

♦ Make rubrics understandable to students, parents, and community partners. (D. Palmer Wolf, personal communication, June 2003)

Still, Erin and Micki struggled with basic anatomy for a rubric, as well as with how time-consuming rubric development is. As such, they began by deciding the most important standards to assess—namely, the ones they were explicitly going to teach and assess throughout the project.

Erin and Micki decided in the criteria column of the rubric to identify the standard, then they turned that standard into a student-friendly learning target in the form of an *I can* statement in the *at standard* level of performance. Otherwise, they left the language of the standard unaltered. Next, they considered the verbs or language being used for the *at standard* level (pulled directly from the standard). For example, the *evaluate* and *support* claims are illustrated in figure 10.2.

How can we design solutions to the world's water crisis?				
Criteria	Goal Setting	Approaching Standard	At Standard	Above Standard
NGSS MS-LS2-5 Interdependent Relationships in Ecosystems			I can evaluate competing design solutions for maintaining biodiversity and ecosystem services (water purification systems, nutrient recycling, and so on).	
CCSS W.7.1 Argument writing			I can write arguments to support claims with clear reasons and relevant evidence.	

Source: Evans, Sanchez, & PBL Path, 2015. Used with permission.

FIGURE 10.2: At standard descriptor.

Visit **go.SolutionTree.com/instruction** for a free reproducible version of this figure.

Next, Erin and Micki referred to Bloom's taxonomy and identified the level for *at standard* (evaluate). To identify the *approaching standard* level, they referred to the level below *evaluate*, which in this case was *analyze*. They then considered appropriate verbs for approaching standard, basing selection on knowledge of their students. For example, students might not yet be evaluating competing design solutions (at standard), but they may be inventorying (making a list) of them (approaching standard).

Similarly, with argument writing, students relate claims before they can support claims with clear reasons and relevant evidence. Now that the descriptors for two levels of performance have been built out, a teacher using this rubric can introduce strategies and teach students how to progress from *inventory* to *evaluate* and from *relate* to *support*.

We know some students always perceive themselves as below standard, with no tangible evidence of what their next steps might be. Rather than discuss what is wrong with the work, Erin and Micki wanted to nurture a growth mindset. They replaced *below standard* with *goal setting* to help students identify next steps for improving the work, through a combination of self, peer, and teacher assessment. Similarly, for *above standard*, in order to remain focused on forward movement rather than an end point, they provided students with evidence as to why their work is above standard or asked them how they might push themselves beyond where they otherwise might go, therefore not limiting them to an *at standard* designation or to a predetermined, teacher-generated idea of above standard. You can change the terms for levels of performance to whatever you think will resonate with your students: *feedback*, *next steps*, *grows*, and so on.

In addition to giving the rubric a process focus and future focus, Erin and Micki recognized that there are many life skills that students can develop in a place-based journey, so they reserved a row for assessing a particular skill they wanted to emphasize throughout the project. For the project in the example shown in figure 10.3, they focused on the Alaska cultural standards. These standards were developed by the Alaska Department of Education and Early Development. They complement the content standards and provide guidance on how to engage students in learning through the local culture. Other options might include collaboration and critical thinking.

Criteria	Goal Setting	Approaching Standard	At Standard	Exceeding Standard
NGSS MS-LS2–5 Interdependent relationships in ecosystems		I can inventory competing design solutions for maintaining biodiversity and ecosystem services (water purification systems, nutrient recycling, and so on).	I can evaluate competing design solutions for maintaining biodiversity and ecosystem services (water purification systems, nutrient recycling, and so on).	
CCSS W.7.1 Argument writing		I can write arguments to relate claims with reasons and evidence.	I can write arguments to support claims with clear reasons and relevant evidence.	
Alaska Standards for Culturally Responsive Schools Traditional ways of knowing		I can compare solutions based on traditional ways of knowing.	I can generate solutions that are based on traditional ways of knowing.	

Source: Evans, Sanchez, & Path, 2015. Used with permission.

FIGURE 10.3: Skills criteria.

*Visit **go.SolutionTree.com/instruction** for a free reproducible version of this figure.*

Alternatives exist to shift the rubric even further from the traditional learning-as-end-goal form. In the following section, we explore several such alternatives.

The Medicine Wheel

The Medicine Wheel helps teachers to recognize Indigenous ways of knowing and values those ways in teaching and learning. Marcella LaFever (2016) shares her journey toward Indigenizing her classroom practices. In building her rubric, she moved from Bloom's taxonomy of learning domains to the use of the Medicine Wheel. She attests:

> The Medicine Wheel model is not the only cultural framework available to use and is not a model all Indigenous peoples will resonate with but because of its widespread use can be a helpful model for bridging non-Indigenous (teachers') understanding of Indigenous ways of knowing and being. (LaFever, 2016, p. 411)

In order to Indigenize learner outcomes, LaFever took a particularly close look at the spiritual domain of the Medicine Wheel when considering learner outcomes.

LaFever (2016) explains that her work "uses materials written by Indigenous scholars that contribute to an explanation of pedagogical philosophies and practices related to spiritual development and spiritual learning outcomes for a postsecondary learning context" (p. 413). This same practice can be adapted for students in grades 4–12. You will see similarities to the frameworks focused on social-emotional learning, which emphasize self-awareness, self-management, social awareness, relationship skills, and responsible decision making—all relevant skills for grades 4–12 students. You could select one of the criteria to add to your rubric as well.

Using the work of Indigenous scholars and their explanations of pedagogical philosophies on spiritual development and learning outcomes, LaFever (2016) distilled the following attributes.

- Honoring
- Attention to relationship
- Developing a sense of belonging
- Feeling empowered to pursue a unique path
- Developing self-knowledge of purpose

Table 10.4 shows how the sample verbs LaFever uses for learner outcome statements are applicable to a standards-based rubric.

Using this model shows an appreciation of a variety of approaches to assessment, expanding a worldview of what equitable assessment looks like in place-based learning.

As we think about assessment practices and skill development for students, note that the Medicine Wheel provides an opportunity to build in these critical life skills. While there is no definitive list of life skills, we consider the following to be especially important.

- Communication and interpersonal skills
- Decision-making and problem-solving skills
- Creative and critical thinking skills
- Self-awareness and empathy
- Assertiveness, equanimity, and self-control
- Resilience and ability to cope with problems (Skills You Need, n.d.)

TABLE 10.4: Sample Verbs and Progression for Creating Outcome Statements

Honoring	Valuing	Connecting	Empowering	Self-Actualizing
Definition Being conscious or aware of learning that is not based in material or physical things, and transcends narrow self-interest	**Definition** Building relationships that honor the importance, worth, or usefulness of qualities related to the human spirit	**Definition** Linking, building, and sustaining positive relationships with someone or something (such as community, culture, and so on)	**Definition** Providing and feeling supported by an environment that encourages strength and confidence, especially in controlling one's life and claiming one's rights	**Definition** Having the ability to honor and be honored as a unique individual within a group, in order for each member to become what each is meant to be
Sample verbs Consider Meditate on Be aware Seek Open Allow Listen Observe	**Sample verbs** Empathize Honor Acknowledge Balance Exemplify Serve Recognize Respect	**Sample verbs** Consult Work with Bond Support Relate to Respond Care for Cooperate Participate Provide Develop Build	**Sample verbs** Express Gain Speak out about Advocate Act on Defend Influence Engage in Reimagine Prepare Maintain	**Sample verbs** Become Self-define Use resources Create Progress Reinforce Remain Possess Sustain Dream Envision Guide

Source: Adapted from LaFever, 2016. Used with permission.

It's important that we dedicate a row on our rubrics to life skills, and that we intentionally teach that skill, provide opportunities for students to set goals, and give them time to reflect on the life skill.

The Single-Point Rubric

We find that single-point rubrics lend themselves well to place-based learning. This is because they break down the aspects of the project into categories and clarify for students what they need to accomplish in creating the final product.

A single-point rubric simplifies the learning path for students and ensures equity in assessment because the rubric is flexible and more accessible to all students. Single-point rubrics benefit students in multiple ways. They provide opportunities for personalized feedback based on the needs of each student. They are more approachable, especially to learners who have specific learning needs. They make the criteria clearer and are more supportive of the individual student's way of learning. And they encourage students to approach a project in creative and unique ways, illuminating their gifts and talents.

Danah Hashem, a reading and writing teacher who teaches tenth-grade world literature and Advanced Placement language, uses single-point rubrics to assess student learning. Hashem (2017) lists six reasons for using a single-point rubric.

1. It gives space to reflect on both strengths and weaknesses in student work. Each category invites teachers to meaningfully share with students what they did really well and where they might want to consider making some adjustments.

2. It doesn't place boundaries on student performance. The single-point rubric doesn't try to cover all the aspects of a project that could go well or poorly. It gives guidance and then allows students to approach the project in creative and unique ways. It helps steer students away from relying too much on teacher direction and encourages them to create their own ideas.

3. It works against students' tendency to rank themselves and to compare themselves to or compete with one another. Each student receives unique feedback that is specific to them and their work, but that can't be easily quantified.

4. It helps take student attention off the grade. The design of this rubric emphasizes descriptive, individualized feedback over the grade. Instead of focusing on teacher instruction in order to aim for a particular grade, students can immerse themselves in the experience of the assignment.

5. It creates more flexibility without sacrificing clarity. Students still receive clear explanations for the grades they earned, but there is much more room to account for a student taking a project in a direction that a holistic or analytic rubric didn't or couldn't account for.

6. It's simple! The single-point rubric has much less text than other rubric styles. The odds that our students will actually read the whole rubric, reflect on given feedback, and remember both are much higher.

Critical to equitable assessment is putting students at the center. Single-point rubrics allow educators to provide more meaningful and personalized feedback to students. Single-point rubrics establish student autonomy and ownership and remind us that assessment is not the destination. As Hashem (2017) says, "The ideology behind the single-point rubric inherently moves classroom grading away from quantifying and streamlining student work, shifting student and teacher focus in the direction of celebrating creativity and intellectual risk-taking."

Single-point rubrics can also be a useful tool for helping students to use assessment results and feedback to set their own goals. There is beauty in the simplicity of a single-point rubric as it provides a single set of criteria for producing high-quality work.

Figure 10.4 is an example of a single-point rubric Micki developed for a project on ancient civilizations for i2 Learning (https://i2learning.org). A single-point rubric like this uses just three levels of performance. Rather than *below*, *approaching*, *at standard*, and *above standard*, the performance criteria are designed to create a growth mindset and provide meaningful feedback.

The first column uses goal setting to identify next steps to meet the standard, and the third column describes the student's strengths and how they went beyond the assessed standards. You can also insert a life skill that you would like to be the focus of the project, such as collaboration, creativity, and so on. Note that the learning targets are identified and aligned with the C3 Framework for Social Studies State Standards and Massachusetts Curriculum Framework for ELA and Literacy.

In this example, the summative assessment is the final product, which is a museum installation. To emphasize place, students work with local museums to learn what curators do and how they create exhibits that teach, invoke emotion, and are provocative for the audience. Students are assessed on social studies and writing learning targets, along with criteria for an effective museum installation. Students create the artifacts highlighted in the museum installation throughout the duration of the project, basing the artifacts on new content and synthesizing what they learn.

Ancient Civilizations and Power Museum Rubric		
Goal Setting	**Criteria**	**Strengths**
	D2.Geo.6.6–8. I can create museum exhibits that explain the physical characteristics of Egypt and its relationship to culture.	
	D2.Geo.6.6–8. I can create a museum installation that identifies major features of ancient civilizations.	
	D2.SS.3b. I have included artifacts in the museum that tell a compelling story about ancient civilizations and power.	
	D2.SS.3b.Throughout the museum I can make clear connections and show evidence of the influence of ancient civilizations to the present day.	
	D2.Geo.6.6–8. I can create museum exhibits and text labels to explain how power was used by the pharaohs of ancient Egypt, in religion.	
	D2.Geo.6.6–8. I can categorize each artifact in appropriate categories related to ancient civilizations and the theme of power.	
Notes:		

Source: i2 Learning, n.d. Used with permission.

FIGURE 10.4: Ancient civilizations and power museum rubric.

*Visit **go.SolutionTree.com/instruction** for a free reproducible version of this figure.*

Students demonstrate their understanding of ancient civilizations, power dynamics, and the impact these ancient civilizations have on life today through the museum installation. The essential question is, How can we as museum curators create an interesting, engaging, and interactive exhibit to teach others about ancient civilizations, their power dynamics, and the impact they have on our world today?

Figure 10.5 (page 168) depicts a similar rubric, but is based on criteria used by museums in design and layout.

Throughout the project, students used the rubrics to assess their own work, reflect on their learning, and provide feedback to their peers. Community partners also used the rubrics to provide feedback to students. At the beginning of the project, students had an opportunity to unpack the rubrics to increase their understanding of what was being asked of them. The bottom row, titled *notes*, is where students can ask for specific feedback or you can add comments and resources to support them in their work. You can change the verbiage for any of the levels of performance any way you think would be most meaningful for your students, as shown in figure 10.6 (page 168).

Ancient Civilizations and Power Museum Rubric Museum Design and Layout		
Goal Setting	**Criteria**	**Strengths**
	I can arrange text and artifacts in a unified way in telling the story of power in ancient civilizations.	
	I can arrange the visual components to correlate with the museum labels.	
	I can create exhibits that invite exploration and interaction.	
	I can create a museum exhibit that has a pleasing appearance, with excellent use of color, signage, exhibit layout, and traffic flow.	
	I can create exhibits that are interesting to a variety of ages and experiences.	
Notes:		

Source: i2 Learning, n.d. Used with permission.

FIGURE 10.5: Ancient civilizations and power museum rubric—museum design and layout.

*Visit **go.SolutionTree.com/instruction** for a free reproducible version of this figure.*

Single-Point Rubric Possible Ways to Describe Levels of Performance		
Goal Setting	**Criteria**	**Strengths**
Areas for Improvement	Standards	Evidence of Exceeding Standards
Next Steps	Learning Targets	Beyond Expectations
Areas That Need Work	*I Can* Statements	Above and Beyond
Not Yet (evidence of how they are not reaching standard)	Learning Objectives	Evidence of Going Beyond
How You Can Strengthen Your Work	Cultural Competencies	Strong Aspects of Your Work
Feedback	Life Skills	Bright Spots

FIGURE 10.6: Possible words to describe levels of performance.

Rubrics Created With Students

Have you ever considered creating rubrics with your students? When students work with you to create a rubric, they gain a deeper understanding of what they're being assessed on. Educircles.org provides 21st century resources to K–12 teachers that empower students by creating a growth mindset. In their resource, "How to Co-Create Rubrics With Your Students," Educircles (2019) explains:

- Everyone in the class contributes some ideas—including the teacher.
- You're working together toward an end goal—creating an assessment rubric for a summative product.
- You work as a team to talk about key elements that you must include in your rubric.
- Through the discussion process, you realize that some ideas fit better than others.
- You go back and forth discussing with your students to create something that is more than the sum of its parts.
- Over time, you might tweak your rubric to make it even better and more accurate.

When you co-create rubrics, students become more invested in the process and the project. They have a much clearer idea of what is expected of them because they were part of the rubric-creating process. This is a highly reflective process, and students have a clearer idea of how to reach certain mileposts during a project.

Klein and Ciotti (2022) share a seven-step process for creating rubrics with students.

1. Students begin by brainstorming everything they are learning in a project, identifying the content and skills they find important to them. This may often evolve from the introduction of the essential question and listing everything they might need to know to answer the question.

2. The teacher facilitates a process to narrow the list down to what is most important in terms of content understanding and life skills, including collaboration, creativity, critical thinking, and so on. At this point, the teacher might introduce students to exemplars of high-quality work. For example, if students are creating a social media campaign to increase awareness around an issue or to call others to action, they might examine effective social media campaigns to identify criteria. "The argument underlying the use of rubrics and exemplars is that when they are used purposefully, they can help students understand the standard of work expected and as a result, students can work toward achieving the desired level of attainment" (Hawe & Dixon, & Hamilton, 2021). When students have a first draft, they can compare their work to the rubric and exemplars as they begin the revision process. However, there is also a caution to heed in using exemplars, such as when the product is so unique that it does not have an exemplar, or when teachers don't want to stifle student creativity with a model.

3. Using *affinity mapping* (a visual tool that helps organize ideas), the teacher may move students into small groups based on their interest in defining a given criterion. During this process, students consider the different levels of quality for this criterion.

4. Students share their quality levels with the class for feedback. The teacher could consider using a *feedback carousel protocol*, which is a way to get some quick feedback on each group's ideas. Visit www.schoolreforminitiative.org/download/the-feedback-carousel for more information on the feedback carousel protocol.

5. After the session, the teacher takes all of the ideas, makes any revisions, and drafts a rubric.

6. The teacher shares the draft, gets feedback from students, and clarifies some of the decisions made in the draft.

7. Students will use the final rubric for self-evaluation, for reflection, and to provide peers feedback on their works in progress.

No matter what format you use for developing your rubric, you want to introduce the rubric after you launch the project. It's good practice to have students unpack the rubric in class and even redefine the criteria in student-friendly language. You can divide students into groups and assign them one of the criteria to unpack. They can create a poster to teach others about what this would look like in practice and share with the class. This is a great time to provide any clarification or misunderstanding about the rubric criteria.

Rubrics are not designed to be used only after the final product is completed. Students can use them to self-assess their progress and what they are learning in terms of content and about themselves. Students can also use rubrics to provide feedback to peers, receive feedback from their community partners or experts, and for ongoing reflection opportunities. This use of rubrics requires us to build a culture of feedback, revision, and reflection. Klein and Ciotti (2022) point out:

> To be successful, educators will need to scaffold a classroom culture where honest feedback is good, a safe space where feedback is always growth-producing for the person who receives it. Educators should offer this feedback *just in time,* meaning it should happen right when the students need it most, usually critical points in the draft or prototype development process. (p. 166)

Liberatory assessment practices put a focus on students' strengths, interests, and cultural backgrounds, and encourage them to take an active role in their own learning and assessment process. Using culturally responsive formative assessments and rubrics ensures equity in the assessment process because they use an asset-based lens. They look at what a student can do and set goals that drive new learning.

Use the Place-Based Learning Path Planning Tool to Follow Liberatory Learning and Assessment Pathways

Part two of the planning tool asks educators to focus particularly on liberatory assessment practices, reminding us to include students as co-creators in the learning process and assessment of learning. Do so by beginning with the end—that is, with the community product (summative assessment) in mind. By filling in the supporting elements next, educators see what leads to the community product or products. The elements of this part of the tool are as follows.

- **Project title:** Create a title that will grab the attention of your students and your potential community partnerships.
- **Grade:** Identify your grade level or levels for which you're designing the project.
- **Estimated duration:** Use a calendar and work backward to determine the length of the project. Build in wiggle room, especially in the last two weeks, when students, with their community partner, are refining their culminating products and sharing more broadly.

- **Essential question:** Create an essential question that launches purpose-driven inquiry that promotes critical thinking and encourages students to explore diverse perspectives.

- **Project sketch:** Create your project sketch, which is the preliminary outline or plan for your project, including key goals, tasks, and timelines. The project sketch is intended to provide a high-level overview of the project and serve as a starting point for further development and refinement. Share the project sketch with others to give a sense of what this project is about.

- **Community product or products:** Create a product or products that demonstrate students' understanding and application of the learning goals, skills, and the complexity of the issue they are exploring. The product might be an action such as an awareness campaign, a solution to a local problem, an action plan for the betterment of the community, or a service to address a genuine need.

- **Ways of knowing:** Align your project to content standards while emphasizing (1) depth of understanding over content coverage, (2) comprehension of concepts and principles rather than knowledge of facts, and (3) the development of complex problem-solving and life skills rather than learning in isolation. Ensure your project encompasses facets of the local community and intersects with many learning disciplines so that you provide multiple paths for mastery of content standards, life skills, and different ways of knowing.

- **Journey checks and formative assessments:** Identify *journey checks* (checkpoints) and formative assessments to support students along the way to ensure high-quality work. This may include peer feedback opportunities, exit tickets, journal entries, critique protocols such as a gallery walk, a charrette, graphic organizers, note catchers, a summary of research, outlines, drafts, storytelling, narratives, reflections, and so on.

- **Culturally embedded teaching strategies for all learners:** Include strategies and scaffolds that represent the consideration and inclusion of students' community and cultures.

In the introduction (figure i.2, page 17) and throughout part I, we referenced Baton Rouge's Troubled Waters project. In figure 10.7 (pages 172–173), we revisit that scenario through part two of the planning tool, *liberatory learning and assessment pathways*. Take a look and consider this exemplar as you complete the planner for your project.

Next, we go into detail about how to fill out each section of the liberatory learning and assessment pathways part of the tool.

- **Project title:** When considering a title for the project, ask yourself, "Does this title evoke curiosity and excitement?"

- **Grade:** What grades does your project focus on? Is it possible to include other grades in the project in partnership with other teachers or schools?

- **Estimated duration:** What seems like a reasonable timeline for your project?

- **Essential question:** Does your essential question evoke deep thinking and inquiry?

- **Project sketch:** Does your project sketch provide an overview of the project that you can share with others?

- **Community product or products:** Do your culminating products demonstrate students' understanding of the content and the complexity of the issue?

Liberatory Learning and Assessment Pathways			
Project title: Baton Rouge's Troubled Waters **Grade:** 5–12 **Estimated duration:** Fifteen to thirty-five hours			
Essential question: How can we plan a public swimming pool that will honor the people and culture in our community?			
Project sketch: Baton Rouge's Troubled Waters project aims to address historical disparities in access to swimming pools within the Black community by planning a public swimming pool that honors local culture. Students will engage with community elders, landscape architects, and city council members to develop proposals for a sustainable and meaningful outdoor space. Through participatory design processes, research on community needs, and challenging stereotypes, students will create public awareness campaigns, proposals for legislation, and landscape architectural designs that promote social justice and inclusivity. By emphasizing storytelling, critical analysis of racism's impact, and building collaborative partnerships, students will not only learn about historical injustices but also develop essential skills in advocacy, communication, and cultural understanding.			
Community product or products *Presentations, performances, products, or services*	**Ways of knowing (in student-friendly language)** *Content and skills needed by students to successfully complete products*	**Journey checks and formative assessments** *To check for learning and ensure students are on track*	**Culturally embedded teaching strategies for all learners** *Provided by teacher, other students, experts; includes scaffolds, materials, lessons aligned to learning outcomes, and formative assessments*
Architectural designs for the pool and surrounding landscape	Design, technical, environmental, and social aspects of creating sustainable and meaningful outdoor spaces	1. Sketches and conceptual drawings 2. Site analysis 3. Design reviews 4. Models and renderings 5. Presentation preparation, rehearsal, and final sharing	☐ **Incorporating Cultural and Historical Significance:** Community leaders, historians, and local experts come to discuss and share the stories of how the Black community has been historically deprived of access to pools due to racism; students craft talking prompts for the experts and historians to share thoughts on the topic; students begin this exploration by viewing the documentary Baton Rouge's Troubled Waters (2008). ☐ **Participatory Design:** Students interview community members to actively engage them in the design and construction of the new swimming pool; students organize community meetings, workshops, and brainstorming sessions.
Social media and public awareness campaigns about landscape and pool designs that include the historical significance of the closing of swimming pools and the injustices these communities experienced	Goal setting, messaging, content creation, channel strategy, engagement and interaction, and evaluating or measuring campaign success	1. Audience analysis worksheet 2. Message development—developing and testing campaign messages 3. Social media metrics and analysis—tracking metrics and using the data to refine the campaign	☐ **Emphasizing the Power of Storytelling:** Students research and gather stories from the Black community about the impact of the historical closing of swimming pools. They can use these stories to create compelling social media content, such as video interviews, quotes, and personal narratives. By highlighting the stories of those affected by this injustice, students can raise awareness and create empathy toward the issue among the wider community. ☐ **Analyzing the Impact of Racism:** Students learn to critically analyze the historical context of racism that led to the closure of swimming pools in the Black community. They receive encouragement to research and explore the lasting impact of this injustice on the community's health, well-being, and access to

			recreational facilities. By educating the public on the negative impact of racism, students can challenge stereotypes and foster a more inclusive society. This lesson not only teaches students about social justice but also enhances their critical thinking and analytical skills.
Proposals to city council	Research and preparation, contacting the city clerk's office, drafting the proposal, reviewing, approval, and presenting the proposal to city council	1. Research 2. Proposal outlines, drafts, feedback, and revision along the way 3. Presentation preparation, rehearsal, and final sharing 4. Assessing stakeholder engagement strategies 5. City council procedure review worksheet	☐ **Understanding the City Council's Cultural Values:** It is important to research the city council's values, beliefs, and priorities to understand how to present the proposal effectively. For instance, if the city council values community engagement, the proposal should emphasize the involvement of the community in the project. Students can analyze city council meeting notes to determine how the council's values align to their project goals. ☐ **Researching Community Needs:** Students should be encouraged to research and understand the specific needs and challenges of the community in question. By doing so, students can identify how the proposed project aligns with community needs and present the proposal in a way that resonates with the community's values and goals.
	Unpacking and debunking the stereotypes associated with Black people and swimming capacities	1. Preassessment survey 2. Reflection journal responses to prompts like, "How has your understanding of Black people's swimming abilities changed through this unit?" or "What stereotypes or misconceptions did you hold before this unit, and how have they changed?" 3. Group discussions using prompts such as, "What are some stereotypes or misconceptions you have heard about Black people and swimming?" or "How do you think we can challenge these stereotypes?"	☐ **Challenge the Stereotypes:** Start by having an open discussion about stereotypes and how they can be harmful. Then, specifically address the stereotype that Black people are not good swimmers. Provide students with examples of Black people who are successful swimmers, such as Olympic gold medalist Simone Manuel. Discuss the reasons why this stereotype exists, and encourage students to think critically about why it is not true. ☐ **Provide Access and Opportunity:** Many Black people may not have had the opportunity to learn how to swim due to historical and ongoing systemic barriers, such as limited access to public swimming pools and swimming lessons. Educate students about these barriers and how they contribute to the perpetuation of the stereotype. Then, encourage them to take action by advocating for greater access to swim programs and resources in their communities. This could include organizing fundraisers to support swim programs, volunteering to teach swimming lessons, or advocating for policy changes that increase access to swimming facilities.

FIGURE 10.7: Baton Rouge's Troubled Waters project example—liberatory learning and assessment pathways.

Visit go.SolutionTree.com/instruction for a free reproducible version of this figure.

- **Ways of knowing:** Does your project allow for multiple ways of knowing as students explore the issue and corresponding learning goals?
- **Journey checks and formative assessment:** Have you built in timely checkpoints and formative assessments that tell how students are doing and inform your next teaching moves?
- **Culturally embedded teaching strategies for all learners:** Have you included culturally responsive instructional and literacy strategies and scaffolds that represent the consideration and inclusion of students' community and cultures?

Part two of the project planner, *liberatory learning and assessment pathways*, is a critical part of planning a place-based learning journey. Liberatory assessment practices remind us to include students as co-creators in the learning process and assessment of their own learning. These practices map out the assessment pathways to ensure that students move positively forward in the project while creating a safety net to ensure that students create high-quality work that they are proud of and willing to share beyond the classroom.

Conclusion

Decolonizing assessment is an early first step in decolonizing our entire curriculum and teaching practices. It provides the pathway to incorporating liberatory teaching practices in the design of a place-based learning project. The first steps toward personalizing learning and assessment for our students begin with storytelling. By engaging our students in storytelling, we provide them with the power to redefine themselves through their own narratives, not just the dominant narrative or someone else's narrative of them. This valuable information informs our own teaching and assessment practices so that all our students thrive. Using feedforward rather than feedback demonstrates that critiques and formative assessments help move the work forward. This growth mindset helps to create a culture of revision and reflection and moves students toward producing high-quality work. Using rubrics helps to optimize high-quality work by providing more meaningful and personalized feedback to students and creates opportunities to become more reflective in their learning process. Co-creating rubrics with students helps them to internalize the criteria they were involved in developing, making it more likely students will reach the highest level of quality in their feedback and work.

Part two of the planning tool, *liberatory learning and assessment pathways*, asks us to focus particularly on liberatory assessment practices and reminds us to include students as co-creators in the learning process and assessment of learning. This tool ensures that we consider ways to embed culture in teaching, learning, and assessment.

Key Takeaways and Reflection Questions

Consider this chapter's key takeaways and reflect on the following questions as you work to liberate and decolonize your assessment practices through place-based learning. Use the Journey Log to further reflect, brainstorm, jot down ideas, make observations, or plan.

- *Liberatory assessment practices* refer to educational assessment methods that prioritize empowering students and communities, promote equity and social justice, and undermine oppressive structures and power imbalances.

- Thinking about assessment as a revelation rather than a destination illustrates the interconnectedness between teacher, students, and community and is rooted in place.
- Culturally relevant performance assessments provide a critical space for students to reflect on and share their personal stories and their identities as learners.
- Formative assessments are critical to place-based journeys because they provide real-time information about where students are with the content, the process, and what they are learning about themselves.

- What strategies are you employing to know your students well in order to develop equitable assessments for place-based learning?
- How might you use storytelling as a way of getting to know your students and as an assessment practice?
- How might you go about decolonizing assessment practices in place-based learning?
- How might you use formative assessment and critique opportunities to ensure students are creating high-quality work?

Journey Log

Journey Log

Journey Log

CHAPTER 11

Plan Place-Based Learning Projects

*Planning is bringing the future into the present so that
you can do something about it right now.*

—ALAN LAKEIN

ESSENTIAL QUESTION: What do the design principles look like in practice?

In the dynamic landscape of experiential and immersive learning, the importance of effective planning cannot be overstated. It is within the planning phase that educators craft a road map for engaging students in authentic, real-world experiences, seamlessly integrating curriculum objectives with the unique attributes of a chosen location. This deliberate approach not only heightens student interest but also cultivates a profound understanding of the subject matter by placing it in a meaningful context.

This chapter delves into the meticulous planning process of place-based learning projects, emphasizing the pivotal role planning plays in creating enriching educational opportunities. As we explore completed planners, we unravel the intricacies involved in designing projects that not only captivate learners but also foster a deep connection with their surroundings, serving as the backbone for successful place-based learning initiatives.

Quality indicators emerge as guiding beacons throughout the planning process, offering educators a set of criteria to ensure the coherence and effectiveness of their projects. These indicators serve as a lens through which to assess the alignment of learning objectives, activities, and assessments, promoting a holistic and purposeful educational experience. Educators can use quality indicators to refine their planning strategies, guaranteeing that each element of the project contributes meaningfully to the overall learning journey.

In addition to quality indicators, a central theme within this chapter is the exploration of entry points into place-based learning projects. Identifying these entry points is a delicate art, requiring educators to consider the unique characteristics of both the learning objectives and the chosen environment. By skillfully pinpointing these entry points, educators can seamlessly integrate academic content with the surrounding context.

This chapter offers examples of completed planners. Through the examination of these examples, educators can find inspiration and guidance in crafting their own place-based learning initiatives. By gaining insights into successful projects, educators can adapt and refine their planning processes, ensuring that each project is a well-crafted, transformative learning experience for their students. The chapter offers a chance to think further about its content through the Conclusion and Key Takeaways and Reflection Questions sections. It concludes with the Journey Log for writing down your thoughts and ideas.

What Does a Completed Project Planner Look Like?

While the introduction (page 1) and chapter 10 (page 151) provided a glimpse into a completed planner with the example of Baton Rouge's Troubled Waters project, this section delves deeper, offering a more nuanced understanding of the intricate components that constitute a well-crafted place-based learning project. You will navigate through the specific elements, examining how learning objectives harmonize with the chosen location, how quality indicators guide the planning process, and how entry points seamlessly integrate academic content with the surrounding environment. By exploring these aspects in greater detail, this section aims to enrich the reader's comprehension of the thoughtful planning that underpins successful place-based learning projects.

We have always found it helpful to look at completed project planners to guide our own development of a place-based learning journey. As you examine the examples of completed planners in this chapter, think about how their design is influenced by who the students are and the places they live. Consider the elements of the plan that seem flexible to allow for purpose-driven inquiry and the elements that create a through line, or narrative, to help guide students in their exploration.

Look, too, for inspiration. These examples are not of your students or your community, but what in them is familiar? What sparks recognition? Take note of how the planner aligns to planning tools you currently use, and what may feel unfamiliar. Even the familiar could be sequenced differently than what you are used to. How does that land in the design? How does it change the emphasis?

Be aware of your reactions and opinions when surveying the completed planners for the first time, and then take a few moments to interrogate your reactions. For example, when Erin began teaching, she knew her principal expected her to begin every lesson plan with unit outcomes and daily learning targets derived directly from the standards, then move through the content and planning in a linear fashion. This method was tidy and fit with how she experienced school as a learner. Now, she pushes herself to instead prioritize her knowledge of students, moving it to the top of the planning process, recognizing that she is unlearning a long-ingrained habit that did not serve her or her students very well. Like Erin, discern how these sample planners coalesce with how you currently plan and then lean into what you believe will serve you and your students best.

It is valuable to point out that we don't call these planners *exemplars*. Planners are just that: a work in progress that prepares us for the complex work of facilitating learning experiences with our students. Therefore, you might notice that some of the principles stand forward more than others.

This may be by design, and it may be because it is hard to build every principle into every plan with the same level of detail. There will be variation. There is room for growth and evolution of any plan. We hope these plans both elucidate the path to designing a place-based journey and remind you to give yourselves grace as you design for equity. Following are the two completed planners.

- ◆ **Circles of Learning: The Legacy of Indian Boarding Schools:** This project explores historical injustices through the lens of Indian boarding schools and their continued impact on Native communities today, considering the toll of intergenerational trauma experienced by these communities

- ◆ **Voices of the Valley: What the Land Holds:** This project explores past and present social and environmental inequities that impact a community. Students examine these issues through a range of racial, cultural, sociopolitical, and generational perspectives.

We begin with the Circles of Learning example. Figure 11.1 (page 182) shows the community asset map for the project. Figure 11.2 (page 183) uses the Circles of Learning project to illustrate planning learning and assessment pathways. Next, we'll look at the Voices of the Valley example. Figure 11.3 (page 185) shows the community assessment map for the project. Figure 11.4 (page 187) gives an example of what the learning and assessment pathways would look like for the Voices of the Valley project.

As you reflect on the completed planners, you may have observed the deliberate alignment of learning objectives with the unique features of the chosen location. The importance of thoughtful entry points might have become apparent, as academic concepts seamlessly intertwined with the environment, providing a rich and engaging learning experience. As we navigate through the intricate details of these planners in the upcoming discussions, pay close attention to how each element contributes to the overall success of the project. Whether it's the intentional design of activities, the strategic use of assessments, or the purposeful engagement with the surrounding community, these planners exemplify the art of crafting immersive and impactful place-based learning experiences.

Community Asset Map for Circles of Learning: The Legacy of Indian Boarding Schools		
Who are my students? (What are their ways of knowing, their interests, their needs?)		
Most of my students live on the reservation and are culturally connected with their community. They are curious and very creative. Many have a visual learning style and also learn from modeling. As part of an oral tradition, they like storytelling. They prefer collaboration rather than working alone. They excel at place-based learning with its focus on culture and place. Most have been disengaged from school, especially those who attended the public school. Many are feeling more connected with the community now that they attend the tribal school. Many need support in research and inquiry methods, as well as scaffolds for reading informational text.		
What ways of knowing, issues, or infinite capacities am I trying to connect to the community?		
Revitalization of cultural traditions, connection with elders and contributions to their community. Practice compassion and empathy as they gather the oral histories of their elders.		
Who will be involved?	**How are they an asset? How will they be involved? How will we connect and reciprocate?**	**What learning will happen as a result of their involvement?**
Elders	Elders will discuss cultural traditions that were lost during the boarding school period and how the tribe is reviving some of these traditions. Elders will share stories from the past about Indian boarding schools. I envision teams of four students will be paired with an elder to gather their story.	Students will broaden their perspective about the impact of Indian boarding school experiences of the past to their community today. Students will understand the importance of reviving lost cultural traditions and recognize how these traditions create a sense of belonging and connectedness.
Tribal and community members	These partners will work with students to help them understand the norms for cultural sensitivity and empathy when interviewing tribal elders and identify elders willing to share their story. These partners will help students understand intergenerational trauma and its impact on their community today. This will increase respect for elders among students.	Students will learn appropriate interview skills for collecting oral histories.
Traditional storyteller	The storyteller will teach students the importance of Native storytelling. Students will learn specific Salish stories and learn how to tell them with the help of the storyteller. The storyteller will help students take their oral histories from the elders and weave them into a traditional Salish story. We will reciprocate by inviting him to the community event and provide him with a copy of the book.	Students will learn how storytelling in Native cultures is teaching. They will recognize that listeners must find in the story what they have learned. Students will learn how Native cultures have long passed down knowledge from generation to generation. Storytelling is a traditional method used to teach about cultural beliefs, values, customs, rituals, and history. Students will recognize the importance of teaching about this part of their history and what was lost and what needs to be regained. They will learn and practice storytelling using the voice, vocal and body expression, intonation, verbal imagery, facial animation, context, plot and character development, natural pacing of the telling, and careful, authentic recall of the story.
Cultural center creator	This partner will help students plan the community event and set up the space for an evening of storytelling and learning. By inviting non-Native community members to the event, they will see what a rich resource the center offers.	Students will learn the importance of what goes into creating a community event that will broaden non-Native and Native perspectives about the boarding school experience and its impact on their community today.
What is a potential community product, service, or call to action?		
Students will conduct a community event titled the "Legacy of Indian Boarding Schools." The event will be open to the public to teach others about the legacy of historical trauma as a result of the boarding school experience and its effect on their culture today. Students will synthesize their historical research and oral histories to publish a book (or digital format of their choosing) that they will share with community members. They will create a call to action to revive cultural traditions that were lost during this dark period.		

FIGURE 11.1: Circles of Learning: The Legacy of Indian Boarding Schools example—community asset map.

Learning and Assessment Pathways for Circles of Learning: The Legacy of Indian Boarding Schools			

Project title: Circles of Learning: The Legacy of Indian Boarding Schools **Grade:** 9–12 **Duration:** Four to six weeks

Essential question: How can we, as ambassadors of our tribe, use the Indian boarding school experience to positively impact Native and non-Native perceptions in our community?"

Project sketch (write idea of your project): Students will conduct research using primary and secondary sources on Indian boarding school experiences throughout the United States and Canada. Students will interview community members to learn the stories that have been passed down since the early 1930s of family members' experience in Indian boarding schools and learn about traditional storytelling. They will explore what cultural traditions were lost during that period and how the tribe is reviving some of these traditions. They will listen to archived oral histories and write narratives of these experiences as well as any oral histories conducted with tribal elders that they will then compile in a book. Students will synthesize their learning and create a community event to share the elders' stories using traditional Salish storytelling to teach others about the legacy of American Indian boarding schools.

Community products *Presentations, performances, products, or services*	Ways of knowing *Content and skills needed by students to successfully complete products*	Journey checks and formative assessments *To check for learning and ensure students are on track*	Culturally embedded teaching strategies for all learners *Strategies will be provided by teacher, other staff, and experts, and include scaffolds, materials, lessons aligned to learning outcomes and formative assessments*
Book of oral histories and research about the legacy of the Indian boarding schools and its continued impact on Native culture today	RI.11-12.1. I can cite strong and thorough evidence to support analysis of informational text, including determining where the text leaves matters uncertain.	1. Exit tickets 2. Journal entries 3. Socratic seminar	Through readings, text-based protocols, videos, and interviews with elders, students identify a historical aspect of the boarding school experience and its impact on traditional culture.
	RI.11-12.7. I can evaluate multiple sources of information presented in different media or formats to address a question or solve a problem.	• History Frame note-taking tool	Students will work in groups to share their History Frame note-taking tool for feedback on how they have organized their research.
	H.6-8.9. I can compare and contrast a primary and secondary source about the same topic.	• Summary of resources • Draft annotated bibliography • Research report outline	Tribal historian will work with students on assessing primary and secondary resources and determining their validity. Students will take a field trip to the cultural center to meet with curator and tribal elders about their research projects.
	W.11-12.5. I can produce clear and coherent writing appropriate to task, purpose, and audience. CC 6-12.W.5 Critical Thinking. I can revise inadequate drafts and explain why they will better meet evaluation criteria. Cultural standard: I can interact with elders in a loving and respectful way that demonstrates an appreciation of their role as culture bearers and educators in the community. Cultural standard: I can gather oral and written history information from the local community and provide an appropriate interpretation of its cultural meaning and significance.	• List of norms for oral history interviews • Draft oral history interview questions • List of team norms and roles • Transcription of oral history interview • Draft narrative outline (teacher, peers)	Students will receive lessons and take part in activities on traditional Salish storytelling and the role of storytelling in Native culture. A specific lesson will focus on norms for cultural sensitivity and empathy when interviewing tribal elders. Students will practice oral histories with a peer about their school experience. The class will co-construct team norms and group roles. Students will develop interview questions for the oral histories of tribal elders. Students will develop interviewing skills and empathy. Students will develop skills for using audio recording devices and transcribing oral history interviews. Students will establish and apply protocols for oral history storytelling skills. Students will develop collaboration and communication skills among each other, tribal elders, and tribal community members.

FIGURE 11.2: Circles of Learning: The Legacy of Indian Boarding Schools example—liberatory learning and assessment pathways.

continued →

Community products	Ways of knowing	Journey checks and formative assessments	Culturally embedded teaching strategies for all learners
	History GLE 4.2.2 I. I can provide evidence that explains how the Indian boarding school experience created a division in my community in the past and present day.	• Rubric jigsaw activity • Poster presentation • Expert feedback	Teacher will introduce critical thinking rubric by unpacking rubric vocabulary using a jigsaw, which students will apply to a non-content critical thinking activity. Students will create a poster presentation that provides evidence of how the Indian boarding school experience impacted the community (past and present).
	W.11–12.3. I can write narrative texts about real experiences of the Indian boarding school experience using well-chosen details and effective event sequences. W.11-12.5. I can use the writing process to focus on what is most significant for a specific purpose and audience. CC 6-12.W.7. I can ask follow-up questions that focus or broaden inquiry, as appropriate. W.9-10.3. I can write narratives to develop real experiences or events using effective technique, well-chosen details, and well-structured event sequences. I can identify the key elements of storytelling and its role in Native culture.	• Transcription of oral history interview • Draft narrative outline (teacher, peers) using key elements of traditional storytelling	Students will read a variety of oral history narratives and identify key elements for engaging the reader or listener. Teaching strategies will include the following. • Elements of storytelling lesson • Examination of oral history exemplars • Listening to NPR's StoryCorps program • Lesson on how oral history can nurture empathy and promote critical thinking
	SL.11-12.4. I can present information appropriate to purpose, audience, and task (conveying a clear and distinct perspective, such that listeners can follow the line of reasoning, alternative or opposing perspectives are addressed, and the organization, development, substance, and style).	• Draft narrative (peer, teacher, and expert feedback)	The class will hold a writers' workshop.
	I can find the dramatic moments of the oral histories to tell a compelling story. I can use storytelling to impact an audience.	• Draft storyboard • Practice presentation (peer, teacher, Salish storytellers)	
Community event	I can plan a community event that honors our cultural traditions.	• Agenda • Guest list • Speakers	Students will analyze effective community events. Students will interview curator and tribal planning committee to identify best practices to honor cultural traditions.
	I can reflect on the effectiveness of the community event.	• Oral or written reflections • Audience feedback form • Expert panel to provide feedback and listen to the reflections	Students will learn how to use storytelling to write or tell their reflection using elements of traditional Salish storytelling.

Community Asset Map		
Who are my students? (What are their ways of knowing, their interests, their needs?)		

Curious

Culturally connected

Love to talk and are not easily intimidated

Multigenerational households

Bi- and trilingual

One student's family owns two local businesses.

Three students have videography experience from working on the video yearbook.

Needs:

Many are reluctant to write things down; it's a struggle to get thoughts on paper.

Because many have demands on time after school, reading needs to happen in class.

Many have low i-Ready scores for reading informational text.

Some have not developed the habit of reflecting on process, content, context, or learning.

What ways of knowing, issues, or infinite capacities am I trying to connect to the community?		

Students' relationship to the land and the natural environment

Students' capacity for empathy and action (they care and they want to do something)

Who will be involved?	How are they an asset? How will they be involved? How will we connect and reciprocate?	What learning will happen as a result of their involvement?
Adams State University	This local university is a Hispanic-serving institution (HSI), so my students can work with college students who look like them, are just a few years older, and have a shared mission. After speaking to the instructor of the social science and filmmaking class, we envision each team of students from my class will be paired with a university student from her class to prepare for and conduct the interviews, as well as editing the documentaries. The instructor said she could commit to twelve hours of partnership support. We will reciprocate because our film festival will be a joint effort and the university students will get credit in their class as well.	Qualitative data collection Filmmaking processes Cross-cultural communication
Latino Community Center	We will work with our contact there to identify subjects who are willing to be interviewed, have the time to invest, and meet our criteria (to be decided by students and this partner). The interviewees share a culture with 97 percent of my students but are of different generations and, of course, life experiences. This partner will give us the generational diversity we need for this project. We will reciprocate by sharing copies of the documentaries with each person and with the center. We will also invite them to the film festival and provide food.	Habit of empathy Intergenerational communication Informational reading Informational writing Interviewing skills Research
Local VFW (Veterans of Foreign Wars)	We will work with our contact there to identify subjects who are willing to be interviewed, have the time to invest, and meet our criteria (to be decided by students and this partner). I think this connection is important to draw interview subjects from different racial and cultural groups representing the community. Our contact mentioned that the people we identify will need to be interviewed virtually and that they can set up a time and the technology for that to happen at the VFW. We will reciprocate by sharing copies of the documentaries with each person and with the VFW. We will also invite them to the film festival and provide food.	Habit of empathy Intergenerational communication Informational reading Informational writing Interviewing skills Research
What is a potential community product, service, or call to action?		

To film interviews with residents of our community and create short documentaries that uniquely answer the essential question, to showcase the documentaries, and then to create an online archive of those interviews, available to local educators and their students.

FIGURE 11.3: Voices of the Valley: What the Land Holds example—community asset map.

Learning and Assessment Pathways			
Project title: Voices of the Valley: What the Land Holds **Grade:** 9–12 **Estimated duration:** Thirty hours			
Essential question: How do the history and culture of our community members affect our relationship with the land on which we live?			
Project sketch (write idea of your project): Students will partner with local university students to examine the essential question both from a personal lens and as researchers gathering qualitative data to create mini-documentaries to shed light on social and environmental issues that impact their community. Students will interview members of the community from a range of racial, cultural, sociopolitical, and generational perspectives to inform their documentaries. Students will then host and showcase their documentaries in a film festival, as well as in an online archive.			
Community products *Presentations, performances, products, or services*	**Ways of knowing** *(in student-friendly language)* *Content standards, cultural standards, life and industry skills, partnership standards, and other skills needed by students to successfully create the product*	**Journey checks and formative assessments** *To check for learning and ensure students are on track*	**Culturally embedded teaching strategies for all learners** *Teacher, other staff, and experts provide strategies, including scaffolds, materials, lessons aligned to learning outcomes. and formative assessments*
Documentary film	Contextual background: • Geography • Topography • History of area, including Native peoples, immigration, migration, historical events, and geologic events • Current issues of land use by different groups Determine the central ideas or information of a primary and secondary source Interviewing skills Research Qualitative data collection	Contextual research using history frames and social science notebook Individual contribution to visual timeline of community events Feedback, revision, and reflection tools and processes Gallery walk protocol for interview question review Fishbowl practice interviews Empathy reflection post-interviews Message, mean, matter protocol with storyboards Peer feedback cycle with reflection Community partner feedback cycle with reflection	1. Neighborhood walk with university students, ending at Latino Community Center, focused on the community's relationship to the land 2. Co-creation of inquiry questions, with an open sort of questions (sorting questions with no predetermined categories or outcomes) 3. Lesson and activity on students' relationship to the land 4. Team formation based on interest, skills (possessed and needed), time commitment, relationships, and support 5. Creation of team working agreements (based on individual need and collective commitment) 6. Creation of contracts (with focus on equity and accountability) 7. Lesson on trauma-sensitive practices and trauma triggers 8. Student-driven lessons on contextual background, with readings at Lexile levels that reflect zone of proximal development 9. Subject and content research, scaffolding with visible thinking routines **Purpose-driven inquiry strategies:** Throughout the project, students build a timeline of community events through prior knowledge, research, and interviews. They add and adjust as they uncover new information and new questions arise. Students watch segments of sample documentaries and examine them for structure and objective, building their documentary schema over time.
	Intergenerational communication Informational reading Informational writing	Building interview subject criteria Interview prep (questions, subject research, practicing) Interviews	1. Students build criteria for selecting interview subjects and share with Latino Community Center and VFW 2. Students practice interviewing skills in low-stakes ways (with peers and a family member)

		Video transcriptions Second interviews for clarification	3. Tech lesson on tips and tricks of video transcribing 4. Logistics, including preparing for the big day and setting "field work" norms; how bilingual students will be an asset; how university students will support
	Storytelling Integrate visual information with other information in print and digital texts Make strategic use of digital media	Finding the "story" within the qualitative data Capturing B-roll Video storyboarding Written video outline Video editing	1. Reviewing transcriptions and addressing what makes a story and how it answers the essential question 2. Activity: What if there are follow-up questions? 3. Student-led video editing lesson from students with editing experience, with the help of university students 4. Story in Three Images activity; storyboarding 5. Teams brainstorm what other research they need to gather and what B-roll they'll need to capture 6. Work time to gather B-roll 7. Share sample documentary outlines and create one outline per team 8. Documentary creation, critique, and revision
Film festival	Persuasive writing Understand how to create a budget and adjust it as needed Reciprocity Honoring elders Present information, findings, and supporting evidence	Marketing strategies and budgeting notes with reflection on why they used the particular notetaking strategy they did (from menu of options) Invitation flyer design with peer feedback Budget proposal (formative) Community partner feedback form (create from rubric criteria) Handwritten thank you cards with videos for gift bags Film festival reflection on process and learning	A local business owner (who is a student's uncle) talks to students about marketing strategies and budgeting. Students participate in reciprocity activity and brainstorming. Students create film festival budget. Students meet with principal and view facilities. Each student designs either a festival flyer or an invitation with documentary QR code and is responsible for sharing with interviewee and three to five guests. Students prepare logistics, including roles and responsibilities, gift bag assembly and distribution, and so on. Film festival day!
Online archive	Studying and analyzing thoughts, feelings, and actions in an effort to improve Making work public for the benefit of the community Narrative writing	Artist's statement and personal reflections on the essential question, either in writing or on video, to accompany the documentary	Students draft writing, with differentiation for process and environment. Students write read-alouds as critique and revise. Students take part in lab with university partner. Class holds second round of peer and teacher critique. University partner provides feedback using Like, Wonder, Have stems. Class publishes the archive with university partner.

FIGURE 11.4: Voices of the Valley: What the Land Holds example—liberatory learning and assessment pathways.

How Do I Lift Up the Design Principles in Project Design?

As you consider different place-based learning journey ideas, you will want to be intentional about how each of the place-based learning design principles is evident in your projects. Identifying where the design principles live in your place-based learning experience is an important component of planning. What follows is an example of narrative planning for a project called *the Empathy Museum*, in which we highlight each of the place-based learning design principles.

The Empathy Museum

The Empathy Museum project is designed for middle grades to high school students. Essential questions for the project could include the following.

- How can we create an empathy museum that highlights stories from our community to increase understanding and empathy for each other?
- How can we share these stories in a way that reveals the past, illuminates the present, and informs the future?

Project sketch: The Empathy Museum is dedicated to helping us look at the world through other people's eyes. With a focus on storytelling and dialogue, the museum explores how empathy can not only transform our personal relationships, but also help tackle global challenges such as conflict and social injustice.

Stories have a transformative power to allow us to see the world in a different way than we do if we just encounter it on our own. Stories are an entry point to understanding a different experience of the world. In this project, students will create their own pop-up participatory empathy museum using story, art, and music based on the work of Clare Patey, an award-winning artist and curator and founder of the Empathy Museum, to illuminate the different voices within communities, thereby increasing understanding of each other.

Elevate ways of knowing: This project opens up many opportunities for students' ways of knowing to shine bright across content areas. Here is an initial brainstorm based on knowledge of the participating students.

- English language arts: storytelling, oral histories, narrative writing, explanatory writing
- Social studies: historical perspective of the community, social-emotional learning, empathy, critical and creative thinking, collaboration, and cultural norms and standards

Embed culture in teaching and learning: This project honors the beliefs and values of the community through the power of storytelling. Storytelling makes space for stories that might not be heard and provides a platform for individuals and communities that don't feel connected to the more dominant established narratives to speak up and share their own personal experiences. This project encourages a process for all stories to be heard to develop empathy and understanding for each other.

Build authentic community partnerships: There are several potential partnerships schools might establish with this project. These include a local museum and curator, community organizations that represent different cultures within the community, and community members willing to share their stories, art, or music.

Facilitate purpose-driven inquiry: The project will launch with students viewing the Empathy Museum's exhibit *A Mile in My Shoes* on the museum's website (www.empathymuseum.com /a-mile-in-my-shoes). Give students time to explore the Empathy Museum's site to learn more about their exhibits. Ask students to reflect on Barack Obama's quote, "The biggest deficit that we have in our society and in the world right now is an empathy deficit. We are in great need of people being able to stand in somebody else's shoes and see the world through their eyes" (Goodreads, n.d.). Conduct a chalk talk in which students respond to Obama's quote. *Chalk talk* is a silent way to reflect and generate ideas about a topic. To conduct a chalk talk, put the words *empathy deficit* in a circle on a large sheet of paper, chalkboard, or whiteboard. Provide students with chalk or markers to write down their ideas and make connections to other students' ideas by drawing a line and making a comment (National School Reform Faculty, 2014).

Introduce the idea of a journey journal and have students write about their understanding of empathy. Using primary and secondary sources, students will learn about the history of their community by uncovering the many assets and challenges faced over time. This inquiry into orientation in place and time might include personal histories, stories, and journeys of community members. Students might inquire into discoveries, explorations, and migrations of community members and consider the relationships between and the interconnectedness of individuals and community, from local and global perspectives. Through inquiry, students will look at different participatory museum installations and decide on their own unique approach to creating an empathy museum for their community.

Engage in feedback, revision, and reflection: Students will receive feedback from their community partnerships, the individuals they interview, and their peers as they design their installation. Students will have multiple opportunities for revision based on the feedback they receive. Galley walks, charrettes, and additional critique protocols can maximize the quality of feedback. Students will keep a journey journal as they explore what empathy means to them, how they recognize empathy, and ways they can practice empathy daily.

Empower student ownership: Students will have opportunities to express voice and choice by selecting which historical context or period of community history they focus on, what resources they will use, who they interview, and how they conduct the interview. How they wish to display stories from their community is also up to them. For example, it could be a written narrative, art, music, a podcast, or another form.

Create community product: For this project, the community project is a pop-up participatory empathy museum installation that students share with the community. Elements of the community product include the following.

- Journey journal on empathy
- Storyboard sketch, draft of installation and interpretive signs, and final installation
- Museum plan or layout
- Museum signage and interpretive display panels
- Participant feedback survey

In addition to creating a narrative artifact to aid your own sense of intentionality in including the design principles in a project, figure 11.5 (page 190) offers another way you can capture how each of the principles will live in your project.

Narrative planning forms, like the Empathy Museum, play a crucial role in deepening our understanding of place-based learning projects. While the project-planning tools provide a structured framework for organizing objectives and activities, narratives serve as dynamic companions, offering a vivid depiction of how these design principles unfold in real-world contexts. The principles come to life during various stages of the project, offering educators valuable insights during planning, implementation, and reflection. They act as bridges between the theoretical framework

Project idea:		
Essential question:		
Project sketch:		
Design principle	**What it looks like in the project**	**Possible learning activities**
Elevate ways of knowing		
Facilitate purpose-driven inquiry		
Build authentic community partnerships		
Empower student ownership		
Engage in feedback, revision, and reflection		
Co-create an authentic community product		
Embed culture in teaching and learning		

FIGURE 11.5: Capturing the project idea sketch and design principles.

*Visit **go.SolutionTree.com/instruction** for a free reproducible version of this figure.*

and the lived experience, enriching the planning process by providing a nuanced perspective on the interplay between learning goals and the unique characteristics of the chosen environment. When used in tandem with the project-planning tool, these narratives create a harmonious synergy that elevates the overall quality and impact of place-based learning initiatives.

Quality Indicators for Project Planning

Another supporting tool to use with the project-planning tool are the *quality indicators*, which are a means of reflection and assessment for place-based design. Meant to be used first as you plan, the quality indicators act as a guide to ensure inclusion of each of the seven design principles in a meaningful and robust manner, and as a check for equity in the plan. They are then used to gauge progress during implementation, and finally to reflect on a project at its conclusion.

As with a first foray into any new pedagogy, expect that there will be aspects of project design that are stronger, that more clearly stand out as a distinguishing marker, and that reflect other aspects of the design that are present but not as pronounced. Use the quality indicators to reflect on where you notice this. Ask whether there is something you can bolster or whether a less pronounced aspect of a design principle is a result of the way you see the project naturally unfolding, remembering that the design principles are not an exact measurement or formula. The quality indicators also give you an opportunity to set goals or write a short to-do list in the *path to higher quality* section (under each indicator), keeping in mind all projects have their strengths and areas for growth as you reflect and refine. Figure 11.6 provides an example of using quality indicators. As a reminder, each section of the quality indicators corresponds to one of the seven design principles.

Quality Indicators	
Design Principle	**Quality Indicator**
Elevate ways of knowing	• My project design is aligned to Common Core State Standards, or state standards and cultural standards (for example, utilizing the expertise of elders, integrating home language, using cultural methodology, using traditional settings such as camps, cultural centers, and sacred sites for experiential learning). • My project design requires me to partner with students, their families, and the community to weave cultural identity with content knowledge and skills. • My project design includes opportunities to teach skills such as critical thinking, empathy, cultural competence, emotional competence, creativity, and collaboration. • My project design immerses students in cultural understandings like community participation, storytelling, honoring, developing spiritual consciousness, mentoring, helping and healing, learning songs, and taking cultural journeys. • My project design requires me to learn from my students.
Path to higher quality (How do I get there?)	
Example: Create a skills inventory in home language to ascertain how families can contribute to this, and future projects. Ask tribal elder to do storytelling on water-related story and also ask if they could read second drafts of students' water cycle stories. Build in a lesson and activity on empathy and environmental stewardship.	
Build authentic community partnerships	• My project design requires that students learn, collaborate, problem solve, and receive feedback from experts, mentors, elders or organizations within their community or region. • In this project, the community provides the context for learning, student work focuses on community needs and interests, and community members serve as resources and partners in every aspect of teaching and learning. • I have considered both learning outcomes and partners' needs. • I have a plan for effective collaboration and will, together with students and the community partner, come up with a measurement for success.
Path to higher quality (How do I get there?)	

Embed culture in teaching and learning	• The cultures represented in my classroom are present in the project I have designed because I have constructed ways to explore the following questions:
	  ◦ "Who are my students?"
	  ◦ "Where is my community, and what cultures are represented?"
	  ◦ "How did cultures represented in my classroom learn traditionally?"
	  ◦ "Whose voice may not be at the table?"
	  ◦ "Whose table is it, anyway?"
	• I have built a classroom climate that honors the beliefs and values of cultures represented in the community. I leverage the cultural ways of knowing represented in the community and utilize culturally responsive teaching strategies.
	• I work to decolonize my curricula by diversifying materials and content, designing projects that address power and social justice, designing assessments that allow students to demonstrate mastery in diverse ways, and involving students in the creation of knowledge, content, curriculum, and project design.
	• My project design uses culturally responsive teaching strategies to reach all students.

Path to higher quality (How do I get there?)	

FIGURE 11.6: Example for using the quality indicators.   continued →

Visit go.SolutionTree.com/instruction for a free reproducible version of this figure.

Design Principle	Quality Indicator
Facilitate purpose-driven inquiry	• My project design shifts the focus from coverage of content to uncovering knowledge, skills, processes, information, and perspectives. • My project design allows for students to drive the inquiry. • My project design goes beyond research and includes inquiry such as interviewing, consulting experts, conducting surveys, field studies, focus groups, and data collection. • My project design is flexible, allowing me to pivot to provide just-in-time resources. • Specific learning tasks and activities support and scaffold student-centered learning. • I have drafted a strong essential question that will harness students' inquiry and aligns with what I want students to know and be able to do, as demonstrated by the community product. • My project plan includes a routine for students to process each day's work, incorporate the day's work into the larger project picture, and revisit the essential question.
Path to higher quality (How do I get there?)	
Empower student ownership	• My project design includes ways to explicitly teach self-management skills. • I have taken into consideration both my own and students' project efficacy when creating this project design. • My project design includes opportunities for students to take small, manageable risks that lead to growth and project efficacy. • The self-management skills I will teach in my project are based on data I collected (self-assessments, skills inventories, and so on) to identify areas of growth. • My project design personalizes the project based on a calculated balance of freedom and structure, putting in place appropriate scaffolds and removing them as students gain efficacy. • I have examined my own attitudes and beliefs, and what has influenced these beliefs, about my students' ability to self-manage. This is reflected in my project design.
Path to higher quality (How do I get there?)	
Co-create an authentic community product	• The products in my project design are embedded to assess students' understanding of content, concepts, skills, and cultural knowledge. • My project design includes community partners who will increase the quality and authenticity of student work, lending purpose to the products students create. • I have built in deliverables and formative assessments along the way to make sure students stay on target and strive toward creating quality work. • My project design includes individual products and ways to assess individual students' understanding of content and concepts, both formatively and summatively. • I have built in processes that engage the voices of all students and community partners in forming next steps (and, in many cases, deciding on the end product).
Path to higher quality (How do I get there?)	
Engage in feedback, revision, and reflection	• My project plan or calendar has time built in for meaningful revision and reflection to take place. • I will explicitly teach the skill of critique, with opportunities for practice and actionable feedback, using protocols and processes. This is evident in my project design. • I have identified the enduring understandings of my content, and will use those as the basis of lesson planning and formative assessment. • My project design shows how community partners will contribute to the feedback and revision loop, and how the feedback from community partners falls within their purview and my learning goals. • My project design offers ample opportunities for students and myself to reflect on their learning, the project process, and next steps.
Path to higher quality (How do I get there?)	

Reflecting on the indicators individually is a solid place to start, but think also about reviewing the quality indicators with a peer, both to model making your work public and to share your enthusiasm for the work. It can be helpful to talk through the story of your project, having a colleague listen, and then reiterate what they have heard. We'll continue to discuss ways to make the quality indicators and the other tools a part of your professional practice in part III (page 201), but for now, think of the quality indicators as the field guide to place-based design, meant to assure you that your plan is maturing.

How Do I Find Entry Points to Designing a Place-Based Learning Journey?

As you begin searching for authentic place-based learning journeys within your community, it is helpful to capture what you and your students notice as assets such as human, cultural, social, political, and geographical, and challenges or issues within your community. This can begin with a class discussion, a chalk talk activity, a community walk, story mapping as we discussed in chapter 3 (page 49), or using local newspapers to identify possible opportunities for journeys. Erin searches for possibilities with her students by creating a *wonder wall*, a place for students to share wonderings about things they notice in their community on an ongoing basis. The things they notice and wonder about might be generated by current events, by things happening at school, or by conversations from home. It is easy to refer to the wonder wall when thinking about possibilities for new project designs. Figure 11.7 depicts an example of a wonder wall.

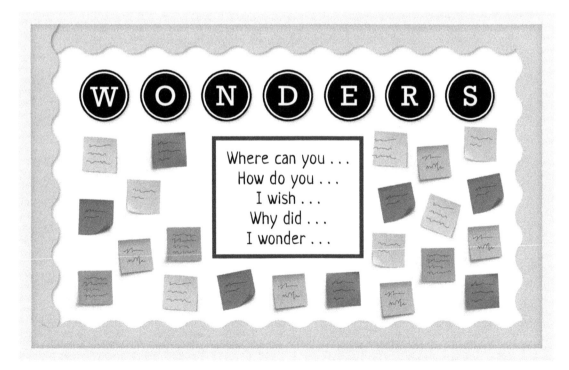

FIGURE 11.7: Wonder wall example.

When considering liberatory practices and decolonizing curricula, there are key topics that you can leverage to connect students to place in a variety of ways. Developing a wonder wall can often lead students to these key topics. We have also compiled a list of key topics described in the following section for you to consider as you plan your place-based learning experiences with your students. For each of the following key topics, we recommend the three following elements.

1. A set of potential place-based explorations called a *launchpad*, which can be an action to take or a piece of information or data that warrants further inquiry

2. Potential observations and statements to explore called *notices*

3. Potential questions called *wonderings*

You and your students may engage in these actions while simultaneously making connections to the topics contextualized within your community. The launchpads can become entry points for place-based learning projects. By including students in this process of noticing and wondering, you incorporate design principles into the process. In this case, you empower student ownership and facilitate purpose-driven inquiry.

- ◆ **TOPIC: Current inequities**
  - **Launchpad:** Watch local news stations and read local newspapers to document how crimes are reported.
  - **Notice:** How are crimes are reported on the news in your community?
  - **Wonder:** Why have nearly half of those killed by police been Black or Latinx, and why are officers rarely held accountable?

  - **Launchpad:** Observe patterns in the verbiage used to describe Black and White survivors of Hurricane Katrina as they were searching for supplies in the wake of hurricane destruction.
  - **Notice:** Fewer than half of White victims, but more than three-quarters of Black victims, believe that Hurricane Katrina highlighted persisting problems of racial inequality.
  - **Wonder:** What are the barriers that make it more difficult for some to access disaster aid? How do the impacts of such barriers play out in other communities after a natural disaster?

  - **Launchpad:** The Flint, Michigan, lead-contaminated drinking water crisis is perhaps one of the most vivid examples of health inequalities in the United States. Since 2014, Flint citizens—among the poorest in America and mostly African American—had complained that their tap water was foul and discolored. But city, state, and federal officials took no action. In March 2016, an independent task force found fault at every level of government, including falsifying water-quality results, allowing the people of Flint to continue to be exposed to water well above the federally allowed lead levels.
  - **Notice:** Who is getting sick in your community, how are they cared for, and what health inequalities are evident in your community? How are historical and contemporary injustices addressed?
  - **Wonder:** How can we ensure health equity for all? How might we overcome economic, social, and other barriers to health and health care?

  - **Launchpad:** Survey those who are experiencing food insecurity or are houseless to find out what resources are available for them in your community.

- **Notice:** Who is experiencing food insecurity and inequality of access to healthy food—which communities are most impacted by food insecurity?
- **Wonder:** What can be done to increase access for those who are experiencing food insecurity and inequality of access to healthy food?

- **Launchpad:** Explore the cities with the worst income inequality, such as New York City, Miami, San Francisco, New Orleans, Atlanta, or Washington, DC.
- **Notice:** What these communities have in common and what historical factors and demographic trends are apparent.
- **Wonder:** Why is income inequality at its highest in seventy-five years?

- **TOPIC: Ageism**
  - **Launchpad:** Look into *The View* cohost Joy Behar's reactions to criticism that at age eighty, she should retire, and her defense of President Joe Biden.
  - **Notice:** What role do media and advertising play in promoting negative or positive attitudes toward aging in our community?
  - **Wonder:** What are some common stereotypes about aging that you have seen or heard?

- **TOPIC: Sexism**
  - **Launchpad:** Women and girls represent half of the world's population and half of its potential. But gender inequality persists everywhere, impacting social progress. On average, women in the labor market still earn 23 percent less than men globally, and women spend about three times as many hours in unpaid domestic and care work as men.
  - **Notice:** Notice where textbooks, resources, and literature used with students address the historical and current fight for gender equality.
  - **Wonder:** What does feminism look like in the 21st century? Who decides? What role has your community played in the history of gender equality?

- **TOPIC: LGBTQ+ biases**
  - **Launchpad:** Over one hundred bills attacking transgender people have been introduced in state legislatures since 2020, according to the American Civil Liberties Union.
  - **Notice:** How do attitudes toward LGBTQ+ youth impact your school community?
  - **Wonder:** How do LGBTQ+ youth in your community locate resources to deal with discrimination and hate crimes, and gain access to mental and physical health practitioners?

- **TOPIC: Historical injustices**
  - **Launchpad:** Whitney Plantation educates the public about the history and legacies of slavery in the United States.
  - **Notice:** How does the legacy of slavery continue to impact your community today?
  - **Wonder:** What can be done to dismantle current structures of racism and oppression?

- **Launchpad:** Indigenous peoples in the United States have lost 99 percent of the land they occupied. Consider forced migration events, such as the Trail of Tears and the Dawes Act of 1887. Indigenous peoples were often forcibly relocated to land that settlers considered less valuable, and those lands are more at risk from climate change hazards today.
- **Notice:** Find out who has been removed or excluded from the land you occupy.
- **Wonder:** What was the justification? Explore past and current exclusion of communities of color.

- **Launchpad:** During World War II, the United States forcibly relocated and incarcerated at least 125,284 people of Japanese descent, many of whom were American citizens, in seventy-five identified incarceration sites.
- **Notice:** Where has exclusion happened in your community? Where does it continue to happen?
- **Wonder:** Explore the long-term impact of incarceration on Japanese American citizens, past and present. Could something like this happen again? How did they resist while incarcerated? Consider resistance movements from the Japanese internment era to modern BIPOC justice movements and activism today. Note: the Wing Luke Museum in Seattle, Washington, has some great educator resources on this topic.

- **TOPIC: Community celebrations and traditions**
  - **Launchpad:** Mardi Gras Indians, who celebrate the relationship between enslaved Africans and Native Americans, pay homage to the Indigenous Peoples of New Orleans for their support in escaping slavery and accepting them into their community.
  - **Notice:** What is being celebrated (culture, heroes, and so on) in your community?
  - **Wonder:** How might these celebrations create coalitions for change or for celebrating the assets of the community?

- **TOPIC: Environmental concerns**
  - **Launchpad:** Consider Cancer Alley in Louisiana as a case study in which the Environmental Protection Agency cites how regulators have neglected Black residents' concern about toxic industrial air pollution.
  - **Notice:** Explore environmental racism in your community and the level of awareness and response.
  - **Wonder:** Who is most impacted, and why?

  - **Launchpad:** Explore the two dams removed from the State of Washington's Elwha River through efforts spearheaded by the Lower Elwha Klallam Tribe that resulted in salmon and watershed restoration. Explore regional and local watershed restoration.
  - **Notice:** How do humans impact local watersheds?
  - **Wonder:** How might local ecosystems be preserved and protected?

- **TOPIC: Changemakers**
  - **Launchpad:** Explore the Ashoka organization's website (www.ashoka.org/en-us) to learn about what they do. Read or watch some of the young changemakers' stories (www.ashoka.org/en-us/collection/stories-early-changemaking) on the site.

- **Notice:** What is Ashoka trying to change, and what strategies does it use to create positive change?
- **Wonder:** What is something you would like to change in your community?

- **Launchpad:** Check out Good Good Good's article "8 Kids Making a Difference & Changing the World (2023)" (www.goodgoodgood.co/articles/kids-changing-the -world). Have students analyze the strategies each of these changemakers used to create change.
- **Notice:** Who are the changemakers in your community?
- **Wonder:** Who do the changemakers impact? Who is listening to them? Who isn't?

- **Launchpad:** Explore stories about the Parkland shooting activists and how their hope lives on. Analyze what they did, how effective their strategies were, and what impact they had regarding issues such as new gun control laws passed in all fifty states, the March for Our Lives movement, and so on.
- **Notice:** What impact have the Parkland activists had on gun reform?
- **Wonder:** How might you start a youth political movement against gun violence?

Asking students to notice and wonder about issues and challenges in their own community is an effective way for designing place-based journeys drawing on student interests and passions. If you teach a specific subject matter such as social studies or history, you can guide students to notice and wonder using historical thinking concepts like the following.

- Establish *historical significance*
- Use *primary source evidence*
- Identify *continuity and change*
- Analyze *cause and consequence*
- Take *historical perspectives*
- Understand the *ethical dimension* of historical interpretations (The Historical Thinking Project, n.d.)

If your subject matter is science, perhaps the focus will be on scientific observations students find in their community. For example, they may begin studying human impacts on the environment within your community, such as a polluted waterway, with an observation (notice) and asking a question (wonder).

Guiding and encouraging students to get curious, and giving them the experience to draw from, lays the groundwork for designing a place-based learning journey grounded in your content area and student interests. It's a great way to launch purpose-driven inquiry. This process also increases student ownership and provides a framework for critique, revision, and reflection.

Conclusion

Reviewing the completed planners provided in this chapter may spark ideas for your own project design that connects to your context, place, and content. We provide a variety of project examples showing how to lift up the design principles by illustrating how each principle is addressed in planning. It is important to note that perhaps not all projects will elevate each design principle in the same way. Some may play a more important role based on the needs of your students and your context.

Use the quality indicators as you plan to assess progress during implementation, and finally to reflect on a project at its conclusion. You can use the quality indicators as a tool to ensure inclusion of each of the seven design principles in a meaningful and robust manner, and as a check for equity in the plan.

The wonder wall creates a place for students to share wonderings about things they notice in their community on an ongoing basis, building the foundation for future project ideas. We conclude this chapter with possible entry points for project ideas that you can contextualize to your community to ignite ideas for future place-based learning journeys with your students.

Key Takeaways and Reflection Questions

Consider this chapter's key takeaways and reflect on the following questions as you work to plan your place-based learning projects. Use the Journey Log to further reflect, brainstorm, jot down ideas, make observations, or plan.

- ◆ Be intentional about the incorporation of the place-based design principles; it is helpful to think through how they will be embedded in your project design.
- ◆ As you begin searching for authentic place-based learning journeys within your community, capture what you and your students notice and wonder about in terms of assets and challenges within your community.
- ◆ Use the quality indicators as a means of reflection and assessment when designing place-based learning projects.
- ◆ Use the entry points to consider ideas for a place-based journey, engaging students in what they notice and wonder about within their community and place.

- ◆ What do you know about your students' and community's cultural assets that could help you make the project culturally embedded?
- ◆ Consider your content standards and community partner. Are there other product options that are needed?
- ◆ How will you initially engage students in the purpose of the project? What will really connect with your students to launch the project?
- ◆ What are the formative assessments that you will use to move *your* students toward producing high-quality work for the community product or products?

Journey Log

Journey Log

PART III

Support and Sustain Place-Based Learning Implementation With an Equity Lens

As teachers, we know we have an impact on students that can last a lifetime and can change the trajectory of individual lives. This is a weight and a privilege. It is why we strive to get better at our teaching year after year and why trying something different is not done on a whim. As you embark on, or enrich, your existing place-based learning practice, we want you to do it in a supportive ecosystem, where the culture, structures, and leadership work in tandem to sustain place-based learning so that all students can be empowered and experience the power of place.

School leaders, part III directly involves you too. We want place-based learning to be the norm on campuses. For that to be possible, there needs to be an appraisal of current conditions and an embrace of new processes and structures that will bolster this liberating methodology.

Part III examines what processes and structures educators need to have, build, or dismantle to support and sustain equitable place-based learning. This work can be done in isolation, as is the case for many teachers who feel alone in their place-based learning journey, but it shouldn't be. Teachers, in partnership with their school leadership team, and in some instances with students, families, and community partners, are the sustaining force behind any school change initiative. Once you witness the full force of a place-based practice, you will want it to spread. Part III will give you the assets and understandings to do so.

CHAPTER 12

Sustain Place-Based Learning Through the Practitioner's Round

Good ideas are not adopted automatically. They must be driven into practice with courageous patience.

—HYMAN RICKOVER

ESSENTIAL QUESTION: How does a cycle of practice lead to place-based learning sustainability and more significant student outcomes?

The *practitioner's round* is a tool we've invented to illustrate the typical sequential steps of the path on a place-based learning journey. The practitioner's round also makes it clear that projects develop in iterative stages and often branch off into new projects or are revised and recycled for another group of students to make their own. This iterative, sometimes surprising, development of a place-based learning journey plays an important role in the sustainability of place-based learning.

In this chapter, we take you and your stakeholders step by step through the practitioner's round to leverage learning structures and protocols. The round begins with tuning a project before it goes live in the classroom. Next, in the middle of the project, you will help students revise their work toward a beautiful community product. Finally, the round ends with reflective protocols to engage you, your students, and community partners. We spotlight the iterative pattern of projects, improving them with each round. We also shed light on leader moves that parallel each step on the path. The chapter offers a chance to think further about its content through the Conclusion and Key Takeaways and Reflection Questions sections. It concludes with the Journey Log for writing down your thoughts and ideas.

What Is the Practitioner's Round?

Although each project is unique, with students and community partners creating diverse place-based landscapes, projects tend to follow a predictable path; they have a first step and a concluding step. This concept of cycles and iterations should be familiar, as teachers are used to refining strategies and skills from week to week and year to year, discarding what doesn't work for students and bettering what proves effective.

The practitioner's round, however, provides more than the familiarity of regular practice. It is meant to assist in guiding teachers, coaches, and leaders through professional practices at each stage of the project process to ensure place-based learning is prioritized and sustainable. It is useful because its use of vetted protocols helps prevent teachers from feeling like they are left alone after the initial planning. With an emphasis on equity at every step, from trailhead to summit, the tool offers guidance. See figure 12.1 for a visual example of the practitioner's round tool.

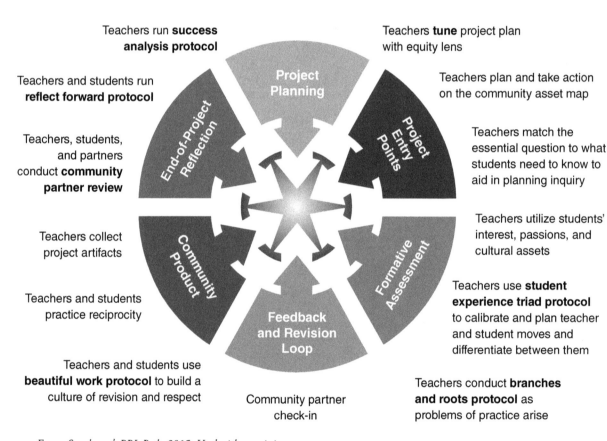

Evans, Sanchez, & PBL Path, 2015. Used with permission.

FIGURE 12.1: Practitioner's round tool.

The project steps make up the inner circle and commonly begin at the top with project planning, moving clockwise. Anywhere you start on the practitioner's round is the right place, as long as you do indeed start. Along the outer edge of the graphic, moving in conjunction with the project steps, are teacher actions, accompanied by the protocols that make the practitioner's round a tool for professional development.

You may have any number of reasons for wanting to pursue place-based learning. Maybe you already have experience with project-based learning and you want to deepen your practice. Maybe you want to build a stronger connection with the community, or perhaps you want place-based project ideas or inspiration, or to deepen your equity stance. Whatever your reasons, it is important to note that the practitioner's round is what connects the *design* of place-based projects to the *practice* of making the pedagogy live in your classroom permanently.

Too often, projects happen once or twice during the school year, with varying degrees of success, usually determined by the teacher in relation to student engagement and performance using traditional assessment metrics. The bulk of school days is taught in the manner we've grown accustomed to and, most likely, experienced as learners ourselves. In order for place-based learning to be the norm, we instead want to see continuous cycles of projects and project refinement happening, with teachers clearly seeing how place-based learning is the primary medium of knowledge and skills students learn each school year. This isn't a small ask, nor is the process of taking this on a quick one, or even one that you have control over in its entirety. Later, we discuss what is within a teacher's realm of influence (page 236), but the practitioner's round gives you something you do—indeed, have influence on—in order to change your practice in meaningful, personal ways.

In her article "The Power of Protocols for Equity," Hammond (2020) discusses a rationale for the use of protocols with students:

> I suggest that a good starting point for facilitating deeper, more equitable discussions is to use structured protocols. . . . The overly structured nature of protocols might seem counterintuitive to the goal of encouraging a free-flowing discussion that welcomes all students. In reality, it is just the opposite. Protocols create ways into the discussion for students typically left out.

The same is true for adult learners. Traditional professional development is often dominated by people in leadership positions or trainers from outside the learning community, who, in the name of expediency, fail to share power with teachers and ask instead for compliance as they lecture with text-heavy slide decks. For lasting change to happen, for a movement toward student-centered practice and place-based learning, teachers need to be trusted to lead their own professional learning (even in addition to excellent outside development that may be egalitarian and nontraditional). Employing protocols placed at strategic points throughout a place-based project is a solid first step.

How Do I Use the Protocols in the Practitioner's Round?

When we work with teachers and school leaders to systematize the practitioner's round, we start with what the teacher is ready for, whether they are on a place-based journey or teaching another way. We encourage teacher ownership of the tool, with leadership leveraging the time and resources to make it happen. If you look at the practitioner's round, read about the protocols, and think, "I'd love to reflect more deeply with my students on the last unit I taught," then begin with the reflect forward protocol. If a colleague told you about a recent project and you'd like to know more about how to do something similar with your students, request a meeting with the teacher and a few other staff members and run a success analysis protocol. As stated earlier, there is no right way to begin the practitioner's round. The more you explore it and condition yourself to the protocols, the more it will help you on your place-based journey.

Here are a few ways to use the practitioner's round.

- ◆ Read this book with a small team of teachers who are committed to supporting each other through the practitioner's round.

- ◆ Ask your school coach to conduct a coaching cycle with you using the practitioner's round as the tool.

- ◆ Use your social networks to introduce the practitioner's round to teachers from other schools who may be interested in running the protocols with you.

- ◆ Ask your administrator to support you with leadership moves aligned to the practitioner's round. We supply examples of these leadership moves in recurring instances, titled *Callouts From Practitioner's Round, Leader Actions*, in figures 12.3 (page 209), 12.10 (page 219), and 12.12 (page 222).

- ◆ Start small, knowing that even if you can only manage to conduct a few of the protocols and processes in the practitioner's round during your first cycle, you are embracing the practice and moving forward.

Note that the nature of protocols in the practitioner's round is collaborative and includes time to think, listen, examine, prepare, and contribute with parity. This is empowering to teachers and, ultimately, to students.

The protocols in the practitioner's round are as follows.

- ◆ **Protocol 1, *the tuning:*** This protocol is instrumental in putting that final polish on a place-based learning plan before it unfolds in the classroom.

- ◆ **Protocol 2, *student experience triad:*** This protocol allows us to share power with students in a project and hear from them, through the data we collect, about the experiences they are having with the project.

- ◆ **Protocol 3, *branches and roots:*** When we encounter obstacles in a place-based learning journey, this protocol helps us examine the issue from multiple perspectives to uncover the root causes.

- ◆ **Protocol 4, *beautiful work:*** This protocol involves students, teachers, and, ideally, community partners in looking at a draft of a community product to get timely, actionable feedback.

- ◆ **Protocol 5, *community partner review:*** This protocol, which can be run asynchronously, is a way for students and community partners to reflect on the project experience by creatively expressing their takeaways through visual art and creative writing.

- ◆ **Protocol 6, *success analysis:*** This protocol engages colleagues in appreciative inquiry around the reasons behind successes related to place-based learning implementation to inform future practice.

- ◆ **Protocol 7, *reflect forward:*** This protocol asks students to individually and then collectively reflect on their project experience and give valuable advice for future place-based journeys.

If protocols are a new practice for you, keep these strategies in mind.

- ◆ Be patient. Sit with the discomfort that may come from using an unfamiliar structure.

- ◆ Notice how the setup of the protocol impacts the outcome. What did you accomplish?

- ◆ Debrief the process. How did you feel during the protocol? What steps were more comfortable, and where were you pushed outside of your typical modes of communication?

◆ Do you see transfer of this protocol to the classroom? How could you use this, or a similar process, with students?

A common adage in professional development circles is *the power is in the protocol*. When teams of educators or students experience protocols, those that adhere most closely to them have the most significant outcomes.

Protocol 1: The Tuning

There are times when being a teacher can feel especially isolating. During Erin's first few years of teaching, planning a project that was going to engage her students, harness their ways of knowing, and invite the community to partner with her students was not only a tall order, but it also felt unscalable and lonely. You may be familiar with Erin's sense of aloneness. She wondered, "Do all my colleagues experience this? Are they all sitting alone in their poorly lit classrooms on a Friday night, wondering if their project designs are going to be laughed at by their students?" Then Erin took a position at a small neighborhood school just south of Seattle, where the principal and place-based learning coach had a unique ask of teachers. Before they could kick off a project with students, teachers had to assemble two colleagues, a student from another class, and the coach for twenty-five minutes in the staff room to fine-tune the unvetted plan using a tuning protocol. (This tuning protocol was originally developed in 1992 by the Coalition of Essential Schools, then adapted by and housed with the National School Reform Faculty.)

Participating in this group tuning was an expectation of every teacher on campus. Plans that had formerly lived only in teachers' heads or had been written out in the loosest ways saw the light of day, and in the hands of colleagues became stronger and more tenable. The whole team at PBL Path has since used a version of the original tuning protocol with thousands of teachers across the world and couldn't conceive of a practitioner's round without it. Simple, fast, and powerful, the tuning is an indispensable tool for project planning. Figure 12.2 (page 208) demonstrates the steps of the protocol.

Leaders, you can encourage and then engrain the use of the practitioner's round with teachers by taking action on the things uniquely within your control and influence. The first Callouts From Practitioner's Round, Leader Actions feature in figure 12.3 (page 209) aligns protocols to the project-planning step on the project path.

At the conclusion of a tuning, we routinely hear teachers say they felt validated in their work. They looked at their plan with a new perspective and felt much more confident about beginning the project in the classroom with their students. Validation, perspective, and confidence—just a few of the potential benefits of this protocol.

Protocol 2: The Student Experience Triad

Once the inquiry process begins in earnest and students are beginning to ask and answer questions in the project, educators start collecting formative data to assist them in the following.

◆ Calibrating and planning teacher and student moves

◆ Responding to that data by thinking about how the information informs what comes next

◆ Differentiating so that all students can access the content the project demands and thrive in acquiring and using the skills they gain

Tuning for a Place-Based Journey	

Time: Twenty-five minutes per project plan

Number of participants: Minimum of four

Roles:

- **Timekeeper:** Helps the team adhere to the protocol time and structure, and also participates
- **Norms observer:** Observes and reminds participants to adhere to the agreed-on norms for collaboration, and also participates

Preparation:

- The presenting teacher shares the project-planning tool with the team prior to the protocol, giving enough time for review and sufficient detail for deep examination.
- The presenting teacher locates a quiet space where everyone can be easily heard during the protocol, ensures team members have writing supplies, and provides blank copies of the quality indicators (chapter 11, page 179).

Time	Protocol Steps
Four minutes	**Set or restate norms.** During this collaborative time, each person shares what they need from the team.
Four minutes	**Review.** Using the quality indicators as an evaluative reference tool, and with an eye toward equity, participants silently review the project-planning tool documents, formulating their clarifying questions and feedback.
Four minutes	**Present.** The presenting teacher talks the group through the project using whatever structure they think will convey the significant points of the plan.
Two minutes	**Clarify.** Participants ask clarifying questions of the presenter (for example, "What is the estimated timeline for the project?" or, "What community partners are involved?").
Six minutes	**Gather feedback.** The presenting teacher turns away from the group, still listening and taking notes on what they hear, but no longer participating in the conversation. Participants share feedback on the plan, using the sentence starters, "I appreciate _____" and "I wonder _____," drawing language for their feedback from the quality indicators.
Two minutes	**Reflect.** The presenter rejoins the group and reflects on what they have heard that has pushed their thinking.
Two minutes	**Share.** Everyone shares (a resource, an idea, a connection).
One minute	**Do a norms check.** The norms observer reports on how well the team adhered to the agreed-on norms for collaboration and shares any areas for improvement.

Protocol Debrief: Time permitting, or asked the first time a group uses a tuning. The debrief is intended to be done collectively, with some questions directed toward the presenter and some toward all participants.

- How did it feel to bring a piece of work to the group for tuning? How was the experience of presenting? (Presenter)
- How was the experience of separating from the group and listening silently? (Presenter)
- Was the outcome of this protocol different from other attempts to improve the work? How? (Presenter)
- How did the experience feel from your perspective? Was it equitable? Was it culturally responsive? What adaptations would you make? (All)
- Could you see other applications for this protocol? (All)

Source: National School Reform Faculty, 2015. Used with permission.

FIGURE 12.2: Tuning for a place-based journey.

Project Stage	Callouts From Practitioner's Round, Leader Actions
Project Planning	Leadership provides a mechanism for teachers to collaborate, such as common planning, professional learning communities (PLCs), dedicated professional development on place-based learning, and so on.
	Leadership creates a schoolwide place-based learning calendar to track projects.

FIGURE 12.3: Leader actions during the project planning step of the practitioner's round.

Leading educators and authors Shane Safir and Jamila Dugan (2021), in their book *Street Data*, say, "It's time to repurpose data from a tool for accountability and oppression to a tool for learning and transformation" (p. 53). These authors believe collecting and prioritizing data on the student experience models decolonized assessment practices, sharing power with students by elevating their voices in the classroom and using those contributions to lead instruction. Safir and Dugan call this *street data*, or data directly from the experiences of students.

In designing this second protocol in the practitioner's round, we leaned upon Safir and Dugan's (2021) work, asking teachers to think about how students are moving through the project. Which elements of the project process or content are students excelling at? Which elements of the project process or content are students struggling with? What are you curious about? Consider, too, the relationship you have built with your students. In order to collect data on the student experience and conduct the protocol, a high level of trust, respect, and transparency is requisite.

In the first quarter of the project, collect a robust sampling of data on how your students are experiencing the place-based learning journey you've taken them on. There's no need to examine it yet; that is what the protocol is for, but you should share with your students the purpose for which you are collecting it. Sources of data to collect might include the following.

- ◆ **Journal entries:** Entries might be about the project process, project ideation, reflections, or notes about the community product, for example.
- ◆ **Flip video reflections:** Use Flip or a similar video tool to elicit responses to prompts you provide related to their project work, content, and skill building.
- ◆ **Focus group transcripts:** Meet with small groups of students, ask questions about their project experience, and then either transcribe the recording or compile the notes. With this process, participants should review and clear the transcript, so they feel their voices are accurately captured.
- ◆ **Advisory circle takeaways:** Advisory circles, homeroom, community circles, crew, and other similar school structures can be used to collect data in writing or from verbal interactions. Again, seek permission from students to use information collected during this time.
- ◆ **Identity maps:** These can be a written or visual representation students create to show the connection, or lack thereof, between their ways of knowing and being and sense of belongingness, and the project you are asking them to engage with.
- ◆ **Interviews:** One-to-one interviews, with a set of questions provided to students in advance, could involve teachers interviewing students, students interviewing one another, or community partners interviewing students.

Once you have collected enough data on the student experience, and from a wide swath of students that is amply representative of all, it is time to call the triad together. Solicit the help of a trusted colleague, one who is an adept listener and who also has a history of pushing your thinking and challenging you. Reach out to a student who has a strong relationship with their peers and a sense of student sentiment in the school. Select a time and a place and convene your triad. Figure 12.4 demonstrates how to interact with the data.

The Student Experience Triad	
Time: Thirty minutes **Roles:** • Journey teacher: The teacher who is running a place-based learning journey, who collected data and called the triad together. • Thought partners: One trusted colleague who is an adept listener. One student who has a sense of student sentiment. Decide who will keep time. **Preparation:** Journey teacher provides a way for the triad to access the data, either in print or digitally, with all identifying information removed. Thought partners may want to review the data in advance to prepare additional probing questions.	

Time	Protocol Steps
Five minutes	**Contextualize:** Journey teacher shares a brief overview of the place-based learning journey and the learning experiences that have taken place thus far, as well as any prompts and context for the sources of data collected.
Three minutes	**Predict:** With an ear tuned to biases and assumptions, the journey teacher shares what they predict the data will tell them and why they believe this to be true. Thought partners hold the journey teacher accountable for using asset-based language and challenging/uncovering biases and assumptions. "I predict the data will show . . . because . . ."
Five to seven minutes	**Review:** Journey teacher and thought partners independently review data. Thought partners use this time to formulate probing questions for the journey teacher, which they will ask in the *reflect* step.
Five minutes	**Describe and synthesize:** Journey teacher describes what they *feel* as a result of reviewing the data. They are not expected to judge or explain their feelings, only to acknowledge them. Then, the journey teacher can synthesize the data, using the prompt, "What the data told me was . . ." The journey teacher can share trends and patterns, as well.
Two minutes	**Empathize:** Take a learner stance and do a culture check, ensuring that White supremacist cultural norms (perfectionism, defensiveness, either-or thinking, sense of urgency) are not sneaking in to the process before moving to the next step.
Five minutes	**Reflect:** Thought partners ask probing questions of the journey teacher. The journey teacher listens and makes note of questions that push their thinking. *Questions are not answered.* **Keep in mind, probing questions:** • Don't place blame on anyone • Allow for multiple responses

	• Help create a paradigm shift • Empower the person with the idea or dilemma to solve their own problem • Avoid yes or no responses • Elicit a slow, thoughtful response • Move thinking from reaction to reflection • Encourage multiple perspectives **Possible questions to ask:** • What do these data reveal about the experiences of our learners? • Where is the greatest opportunity? • What will help us learn more? • What would have to change in order for _____? • What would it look like if _____? • What is your hunch about _____? • What is the connection between _____ and _____? • What if the opposite were true? What might happen? • How might your assumptions about _____ influence how you are thinking about _____ ? • What does success look like? Whose version of success is it? • What are you learning from this that you want to remember in the future? • Is this the right work for kids? Would they agree? • What surprised you? Why? • How have students been failed in this project? • Who has been left out, and how? • What are the unmet needs that may impact learning? • What steps or actions might come next?
Three minutes	**Act:** Journey teacher shares questions that pushed their thinking. Then, the journey teacher shares 1–3 actions they are considering, using the prompt, "As a result of the student data and your probing questions, I plan to try, incorporate, improve, collect, ask, or do _____" Take a final minute to express gratitude for the process and one another!

FIGURE 12.4: The student experience triad.

Collecting and interacting with data on student experiences of place-based journeys opens the door to a teacher's ability to make agile adjustments to project design and implementation that can have a dramatic effect on the course of a project. Possible actions resulting from the examination of data on the student experience include the following.

◆ Co-editing the essential question with students, colleagues, or both

◆ Refinement of inquiry questions

◆ Additional scaffolds, minilessons, or resources to support all students

◆ Additional time to practice new content and skills in a low-stakes way

◆ Refinement of standards taught and assessed through the project

◆ Refinement of the rubric or other measurements for success

- Classroom culture building
- Modified interaction between students and community partner
- Varied or different opportunities for collaboration or teaming
- New or modified ideas for community products

Protocol 3: Branches and Roots

In our work with teachers, we often find that it is the middle of a project that teachers are especially concerned about getting "just right," and it is this middle portion that is, by nature of any inquiry process, the most ambiguous. We know how we want to begin a project, we know what we want students to learn and be able to contribute to the world and community by the end of the project; it's everything in between that gets a bit fuzzy.

That ambiguity can breed unhelpful behaviors in students (apathy, lack of productivity, frustration, loss of interest) and, for teachers, a tendency to fall back into familiar patterns of instruction that don't always serve students well but maintain order. What we want to do instead is harness the potential of this middle phase in a project to more meticulously examine the root causes of the outward manifestations we see in the classroom so that we can learn to empathize to understand before taking action. What is it about the classroom culture we have created that is causing the behaviors we are seeing? What is it about the place-based learning experience we are in the midst of that results in what we are witnessing?

The *branches and roots* protocol shown in figure 12.5 is simple in design and deep in payoff. Any or all of the steps outlined in the figure can also be done as prework, so a small team of stakeholders have time to consider before coming together. Pay special attention to the third step, identify the outward manifestations of this dilemma. As you do so, maintain an asset-based lens as you consider possible root causes and factors that contribute to the external behaviors you are noticing. These dilemmas could, with the further examination required through this protocol, point to an issue with the project design, school or classroom culture, or something outside your purview. Set aside your own perceptions and consider your students' feelings, constraints, questions, struggles, and investment before sharing your interpretation of the root causes and factors. Acknowledge, also, that you may be wrong, but that, collectively, with your colleagues, your odds of finding a solution are much better.

Figure 12.6 (page 214) gives an example of what the work of this protocol may look like when captured on a whiteboard or chart paper poster.

The branches and roots protocol is the antithesis of the trap of assumptions and quick conclusions we get mired in when we work fast and in isolation. When we're able to freeze the experience we are having and seek help in looking more closely, we can come to more subtle, thoughtful actions that better our projects and our teaching practice.

Branches and Roots Protocol	
Time: Twenty-five minutes	
Roles:	
• **Timekeeper:** Helps the team adhere to the protocol time and structure, and also participates	
• **Norms observer:** Observes and reminds participants to adhere to the agreed-on norms for collaboration, and also participates	
Preparation:	
• Draw the tree image on chart paper or whiteboard (see examples)	
• Have chart or dry-erase markers available for each participant	

TIME	PROTOCOL STEPS
Three minutes	**Set or restate norms:** To ensure collaboration, each person shares what they need from the team.
Three minutes	**Name the dilemma (the visible problem):** This represents the *branch* within the protocol. Any team member can do this, but the person who called the meeting usually names the dilemma. (For example, "Students think their first drafts of the community art installation are good enough. They don't want to revise.")
Four minutes	**Identify the outward manifestations of this dilemma:** This represents the *leaves* within the protocol. Everyone shares aloud and writes on the tree graphic. Participants share what they see and hear, taking the full time allotted, even if there are moments of silence. (For example, participants report that students say, "It's good enough," that they goof off during feedback sessions, and that they get easily frustrated and shut down.)
Six minutes	**Using an asset-based mindset, think of the causes or factors leading to this implementation dilemma:** This represents the *roots* within the protocol. Everyone shares aloud and writes on the tree graphic, taking the full time allotted, even if there are moments of silence. (For example, participants may list that there are not enough steps to create community product or that the steps are confusing, that feedback on the process is unclear, that the scope of project could be too big, or that the school does not have a widespread culture of revision.)
Five minutes	**Name actions you can take to impact this implementation dilemma:** This represents the *trunk* within the protocol. Participants consider their realm of control and influence. Everyone shares aloud and writes on the tree graphic. (For example, participants may suggest involving the community partner in this step of the project to hold students accountable, breaking tasks into more clear and manageable steps, or modeling and scaffolding the feedback process.)
Four minutes	**Discuss:** What will you try first? Next? How will you know if your actions have the desired impact?

FIGURE 12.5: Branches and roots protocol.

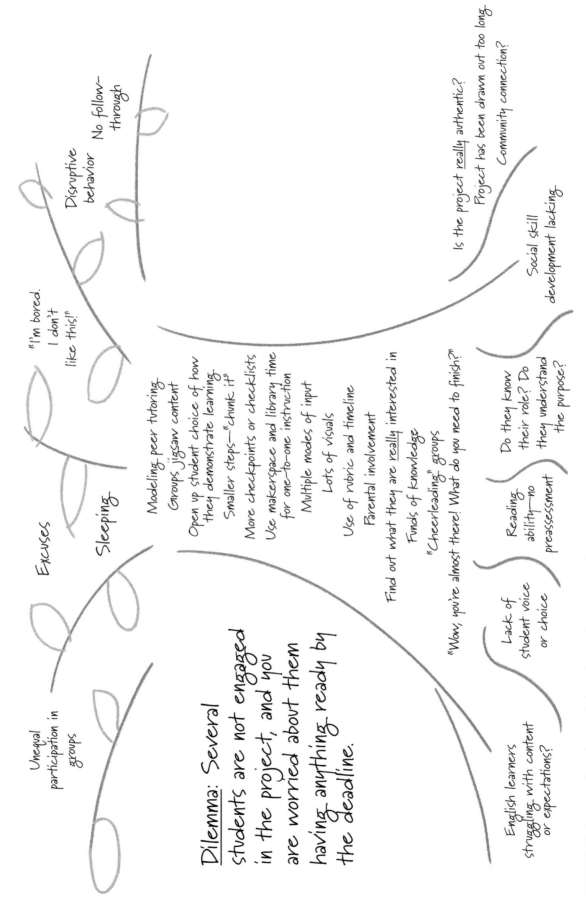

FIGURE 12.6: Image-based example branches and roots protocol.

Protocol 4: Beautiful Work

Young and adult learners alike benefit from a structure when giving and receiving feedback. It need not be overly complex—a defined process and a few sentence starters will work nicely. The beautiful work protocol is that straightforward. Students examine their peers' work, share in writing what is strong (the "wow" prompt), and share verbally their suggestions to make it better (the "what if" prompt), building on one another's suggestions.

We named the *beautiful work protocol* in admiration for Ron Berger's (2003) seminal leadership in helping educators create a culture of critique and revision in the classroom, and his belief in the aesthetic nature of all endeavors taken with purpose and care. This protocol embodies Goldsmith's (n.d.) feedforward process of critiquing with a future focus. This student-facing protocol sits between the feedback and revision and community product steps in the practitioner's round, and we assume that by the time educators use this protocol, several assessment practices have already come into play. These might include formative assessment with the use of a rubric or other measurement for success, and practice giving and receiving feedback. Essentially, if you are scaffolding the skill of critique with your students, you would use this protocol once they've developed some proficiency. Our assumptions about the protocol are as follows.

- The measurement for success is developed and refined with all stakeholders.
- The measurement for success allows students to develop mastery in diverse ways.
- The measurement for success allows students to demonstrate their growth in content, concepts, skills, and cultural knowledge.
- The measurement for success is oriented toward learning, as opposed to grading, as outlined in Klein and Ciotti's (2022) learning orientation traits.

We also assume that by this point in the project journey, students have practiced critique and revision in scaffolded and low-stakes ways, through common starter critiques like *gallery walks* and *praise-question-polish* (PQP) protocols, in which students use these prompts to leave critical and positive feedback, as well as probing questions. Keep in mind that students need feedback they can understand, act on, and are invested in. Those providing the critique will have practiced using the rubric or other measurement for success to ensure they are giving "kind, specific, and helpful" feedback, as described in Berger and colleagues' (2014) peer critique guidelines (p. 171). When students arrive at the beautiful work protocol, they should have a second or third draft of their community product (or component of it) to share. Figure 12.7 (page 216) provides an example of the beautiful work protocol.

Following the protocol, students need time to reflect on and incorporate the feedback they received into their summative product. That incorporation will likely need scaffolding as well. Teaching a process for sorting and weighing the "what ifs" and deciding what changes will benefit the community product will require instruction and coaching from the teacher.

Beautiful Work Protocol

Time: Fifteen minutes per presenting student (can be spread out over multiple days)

Number of participants: Groups of four representing students plus community partners and teacher, if possible

Roles:
- **Timekeeper:** Helps the team adhere to the protocol time and structure, and also participates; alternatively, the teacher can act in this role to model for the whole class
- **Norms observer:** Observes and reminds participants to adhere to the agreed-on norms for collaboration, and also participates

Preparation:
- Have each student bring a draft of their final product (if the product is a presentation, student plans to share five minutes of the presentation with the team).
- Find a quiet space where everyone can be easily heard.
- Bring something to write with and on.
- Print copies of the rubric or other measurement for success (or have available digitally).
- Prepare a poster or write on the whiteboard these prompts: "Wow," "What if . . . ?" and "Yes, and what if . . . ?"
- Bring sticky notes.

TIME	PROTOCOL STEPS
Five minutes	**Review:** Participants review a draft of summative work (or listen to presentation).
Two minutes	**Prepare:** Participants devise kind, specific, and helpful feedback using the rubric or other measurement for success for language choices. They write "Wow" feedback on sticky notes but will give "What if . . . ?" feedback verbally.
One1 minute	**Pass:** "Wow" feedback to the presenter will be read later.
Six minutes	**Share:** The first person shares "What if . . . ?" feedback aloud. The next person says "Yes, and what if . . . ?" Participants resist the urge to answer the questions, which are meant to probe the presenter's thinking. Presenter remains silent, listening and taking notes.
One minute	**Take action:** Presenter shares one action they will take as a result of the feedback they have received.
Repeat fifteen-minute round as needed.	

FIGURE 12.7: Beautiful work protocol.

Be sure to remind presenters to read their *wow* feedback as an affirmation of all the beautiful work they've done thus far!

Protocol 5: Community Partner Review

Working together with a community partner to create a beautiful end product changes people. Charity's former student walked the grounds of Whitney Plantation and then took action to sway hearts and minds, and changed through the course of that project. The community members who were interviewed for Baton Rouge's Troubled Waters project were changed by the deep empathy and curiosity expressed by students. Each project has the potential to be transformative for all involved, so how do you curate those transformations? How do you record that shared experience?

This protocol attempts to do just that, albeit in a simplified way that honors the time community partners have already devoted to the work and the reality that every project must come to an eventual end. In the life of a classroom teacher, we're usually overlapping projects and additional content, wrapping one up as another begins. Before that happens, we encourage you to secure the stories of impact in a *community partner review*, which calls on students and community partners to creatively express their takeaways through visual or tactile representation and creative writing, making this step not only effective but also fun!

This process can take place asynchronously. That is, you can send the community partner review electronically for community partners to complete at their convenience (accompanied by a personal note from students if desired) and to students to complete in class. The teacher should model the process of completing the student portion and show a sample of what's possible (with the inclusion of realia, sketches, artifacts, and more). Of course, it is ideal if the review can be done at the last meeting of community partners and students, but no matter the locale, the process of creatively contemplating and actualizing on paper what the partnership has meant is a must-do reflective step. Figure 12.8 provides an example of a community partner review protocol.

Community Partner Review
Task one—Impact in three images: Think about the project we have been working on together. Think about the partnerships we have built. Close your eyes, take a few deep breaths, and let the words racing around in your brain (or your internal narrator) be replaced by images. What images come to mind when you think of this project and this community partnership? The images may be related to content knowledge you gained or shared, cultural knowledge or understanding, relationships you built, the project process, or something else. Use the following to find or create three images that tell a story of your project experience or the impact it has had. *(You may take photographs, find images online, use objects, or use another artistic medium to complete this task. Don't let the space limit you.)*
Task two—Contemplating the shift: Think about the essential question that you have attempted to answer through this project. Students, think about the questions you initially had when you first saw the essential question. Community partners, think about your role in helping to answer the essential question. What did you think at the outset of the project—about the task, the product, the partnership, one another, the possible outcome? What do you think now? How has your thinking, feeling, and understanding shifted as a result of this project? Record your reflection in the following spaces using the suggested prompts (but don't be limited by them). You can write several statements, or a longer narrative. You can write free verse or haiku—whatever captures "the shift."
"I used to think _____." "Now I think _____."
Task three—Leave a legacy: In the following space, record anything you would like students, community partners, or teachers participating in future iterations of this project to know. You could also express this with photos from the project, student work, results, news coverage from the project, and so on.
Task four—Make your thoughts public: If you are able to meet together, form small groups of three to six people and allot a time for each person to share whatever parts of the community partner review they would like, ensuring parity in the discussion. The teacher conducts a whole group debrief, if appropriate.

FIGURE 12.8: Community partner review.

Visit go.SolutionTree.com/instruction for a free reproducible version of this figure.

Figure 12.9 returns us to leader actions for the practitioner's round, this time focusing on the project's entry points, formative assessment, feedback and revision, and community product steps.

Project Stage	Callouts From Practitioner's Round, Leader Actions
Project Entry Points	Leadership promotes the visibility of the essential question in the classroom. Leadership models the use of essential questions during professional development.
Formative Assessment	Leadership communicates place-based learning basics to families (through a newsletter, open house, exhibition, or other means) in their home language. Leadership provides timely satellite (aggregate) data (i-Ready, MAP, NWEA) and map (disaggregate, classroom, or student) data (rubric scores, report cards) to teachers to assist in project implementation and differentiation.
Feedback and Revision Loop	Leadership promotes and models personalized learning teacher and leadership mindset, where teachers are encouraged to take risks and revise their work, with support.
Community Product	Leadership creates and promotes the use of a community partner database to track community interactions as place-based learning grows.

FIGURE 12.9: Leader actions during the entry points, formative assessment, feedback and revision, and community product steps of the practitioner's round.

Before you slip into the next project or unit of study, before the next most urgent thing pops up on the school calendar, take time to complete the community partner review, cementing the learning and honoring the partnerships that have been forged.

Protocol 6: Analyze the Successes

Often, we use protocols to analyze problems of practice; in other words, we rely on protocols when things fall apart. We learn much from these protocols that often results in solutions and ideas to move our practice forward. However, Elena Aguilar (2018), coach and author of *Onward: Cultivating Emotional Resilience in Educators*, reminds us of what we need to keep in mind when implementing new pedagogy. Aguilar writes:

> Most simply said, here's what it comes down to when we want to make change: we can focus on what isn't working and do less of it, or we can focus on what is working and do more of that. (p. 176)

What we love about the *success analysis protocol*, developed by Daniel Baron (n.d.), codirector of the National School Reform Faculty, is that it moves us from problem-centered thinking to a strengths-based approach. The success analysis protocol engages colleagues in appreciative inquiry about the reasons implementing place-based learning succeeded. This protocol helps us to better understand the circumstances and actions linked to success. By sharing these successes, we can apply this understanding to future practice.

You can use the success analysis protocol in whole-staff professional development, so each group can see the successes of the other groups. You can also use it with a small-group, grade-level team, project team, or other collaborative team meeting. You can shorten or modify the protocol as needed.

Consider using this protocol at the end of the project as a postproject reflection focused on success. It gives participants an opportunity to celebrate successes in community.

Figure 12.10 is our adaptation of this protocol to share successes aligned with the seven design principles of place-based learning.

Success Analysis Protocol	
Time: Twenty-five minutes per round	

Number of participants: Groups of three presenting teachers

Roles:

- **Timekeeper:** Helps the team adhere to the protocol time and structure, and also participates.
- **Norms observer:** Observes and reminds participants to adhere to the agreed-on norms for collaboration, and also participates.
- **Facilitator:** Helps the group stay focused on how the practice or strategy described by the presenter was successful in realizing one of the seven design principles. The facilitator is a full participant in this protocol.
- **Scribe:** Notes specific descriptors from the presenter's story and participants' reflection. Creates charts for use in the debrief or gallery walk to analyze the practice or strategy and consider future project development.

Preparation:

- Bring a journal for reflection and a copy of the quality indicators.

TIME	PROTOCOL STEPS
Five minutes	**Choose:** Select a best practice or strategy used in your project that was highly successful in implementing one of the design principles. Reflect on what made this practice or strategy so successful. Write a short description that describes the specifics of the success.
Three minutes	**Describe:** The presenter describes the success. In groups of three, one person shares their best practice or strategy while the rest of the group takes notes. The scribe notes specific descriptors from the presenter's story and participants' reflection on chart paper.
Three minutes	**Group:** The other group members ask clarifying questions about the details of the best practice or strategy.
Five minutes	**Group asks:** Group members ask questions that help the presenter reflect on the success and uncover reasons for it. The presenter answers the questions, but there isn't any back-and-forth discussion. Some examples of questions include: • Why do you think _____? • What was different about _____? • Why did you decide _____?
Three minutes	**Group reflects:** The group discusses what they heard the presenter describing, reflects on the success story, and offers additional insights and analyses of the success. **Note:** Presenter does not participate in this part of the discussion but does take notes.

FIGURE 12.10: Success analysis protocol.   continued →

TIME	PROTOCOL STEPS
Five minutes	**Presenter reflects:** The presenter reflects on the group's discussion of what made this learning experience so successful. The group then discusses briefly ways they can apply what they have learned to all of their work.
One minute	**Appreciate:** Participants take a moment to appreciate the good work of their colleague.
Repeat rounds as needed.	
Fifteen minutes	**Whole group gallery walk (optional):** All groups post the description of the successes so that participants benefit from the experiences of others.
Five minutes	**Debrief:** Participants debrief the protocol as a whole group. Some examples of questions include: • What worked well? • How might we apply what we learned to strengthen one or more of the design principles in future project development?

Source: Adapted from National School Reform Faculty, n.d. Used with permission.

The success analysis is such a joyful way to collect the best of the work teachers so tirelessly do and make meaning of it for future use. You could also tuck away the notes from your analysis and pull them out on an especially challenging day as a motivator to keep moving forward.

Protocol 7: Reflect With a Future Focus

In tandem with reflecting with colleagues on the successes of a project, debriefing the student experience gives us indispensable data on our own practice and insight into how the project landed with our end users: our students. There are numerous ways to go about reflecting on a project with students, from surveys to video journals to whole-class discussions. We have created the *reflect forward* protocol knowing that there is a legion of options but few that help students make meaning *and* shape the future of a project, while reflecting with their peers in real time. This protocol aids students in building a visual representation of the progression of their thinking from the beginning of the project to the end, with an eye toward individual and collective growth, as well as future iterations of the project. Figure 12.11 illustrates how the reflect forward protocol is not only a tool to support teacher planning, but is also another way to build student agency in their learning and make them partners in every step of the project.

Reflect Forward Protocol

Time: Sixty minutes

Roles:

• **Timekeeper:** Helps the team adhere to the protocol time and structure, and also participates

• **Norms observer:** Observes and reminds participants to adhere to the agreed-on norms for collaboration, and also participates

Preparation:

• Hang seven pieces of chart paper horizontally at eye level along one or two walls in your classroom or hallway.

• Label the charts as follows, from left to right, with the question at the top.

    1. What were you most nervous or excited about when the project began?

2. As the project progressed, what surprised you about what you were learning?

3. How do you feel this project tapped into your strengths and interests? How did it push you?

4. How did working with our community partner(s) impact the project?

5. What did you learn through the creation of the community product?

6. What do you know now about the way you learn best that you didn't know at the beginning of the project?

7. What advice would you give to your teacher and students doing this project in the future?

- On each of the seven posters, add these two subheadings below the questions: "Reflections," directly under the prompt, and "Moving Forward and Suggestions," written midway on the poster.
- Have chart markers and at least ten sticky notes available for each student.

TIME	PROTOCOL STEPS
Three minutes	Teacher sets or restates class-created norms for collaboration.
One minute	Teacher explains that the protocol will help students collaboratively reflect on their project experience, from beginning to end, while also thinking about what could make the project (and all projects) better next time.
Ten minutes	Students silently look at the questions on the chart paper and record reflections on sticky notes. They then post their sticky notes in the "Reflections" section of the appropriate poster. *(Teacher or facilitator can decide if they would like to team students and have them rotate to each poster in sync or if students complete this step independently. Including their name on the sticky notes is also at the teacher's discretion.)*
Twenty-one minutes (Seven rounds of three minutes each)	Students form seven groups of equal numbers, and the facilitator conducts seven rounds, with students beginning at their assigned poster and rotating clockwise. (For example, group seven would start at the last poster, "What advice would you give to your teacher and students doing this project in the future?," and would then move to the first poster, "What were you most nervous or excited about when the project began?") Students discuss and write their top responses in the "Moving Forward and Suggestions" section of the poster. As groups rotate and this section of each poster fills up, students can annotate with a + or ! next to contributions the group agrees with.
Ten minutes	Once each group returns to their original poster, they should: - Read and do an open sort of the reflections, categorizing by common features - Read and discuss the "Moving Forward and Suggestions" responses, circling or highlighting themes and patterns - Be prepared to share out a synthesis of the "Reflections" responses and themes and patterns from the "Moving Forward and Suggestions" responses
Fourteen minutes	Each group selects at least two members to share the responsibility of sharing out with the whole class. Beginning with the first poster, each group shares a synthesis of the reflections and themes and patterns from "Moving Forward and Suggestions." Teacher scribes or records.
One minute	Each student shares a last word that summarizes the way they feel about the project now that it is complete. The sharing continues until everyone has spoken.
	At the completion of the protocol, if possible, the teacher should share what they scribed so everyone can benefit from the synthesized reflective timeline.

FIGURE 12.11: Reflect forward protocol.

Figure 12.12 is the last callout box of leader actions to take during the practitioner's round.

Project Stage	Callouts From Practitioner's Round, Leader Actions
End-of-Project Reflection	Leadership celebrates project successes by: • Documenting the project process • Making student work visible • Promoting and sharing place-based learning with all stakeholders

FIGURE 12.12: Leader actions during the end-of-project reflection step of the practitioner's round.

The reflect forward protocol gives students a lasting visual representation of their learning, as well as an opportunity to collectively make meaning of all that has transpired.

Conclusion

As with all of the tools we share, we encourage you to make the practitioner's round your own, customizing it to your unique context. Think about how the culture, structures, and routines distinct to your school could optimize the tool. For example, an advisory structure might be the perfect vehicle to collect data on the student experience more than just once during a project cycle. An International Baccalaureate (IB) school could use the round to inform semiannual inquiry unit development. In the midst of arguably the busiest profession on the planet, the practitioner's round is there for teachers as a map, a touchpoint, and an assurance that there is a plan for each place-based learning experience, and that even if not everything on the round is accomplished during every project cycle, there is meaning and growth in the journey.

Key Takeaways and Reflection Questions

Consider this chapter's key takeaways and reflect on the following questions as you consider and implement protocols in the practitioner's round. Use the Journey Log to further reflect, brainstorm, jot down ideas, make observations, or plan.

- ◆ The practitioner's round guides teachers, coaches, and leaders through professional practices at each stage of the project process, with a goal to prioritize and sustain place-based learning.
- ◆ Teachers need to be trusted to control the means and methods of their own professional learning, and employing protocols at strategic points throughout a place-based project is a solid first step.
- ◆ Even if a teacher can only manage to conduct a few of the protocols and processes in the practitioner's round during their first cycle, this should be celebrated, as they are embracing the practice and moving forward.
- ◆ Leaders can bolster place-based learning with vital moves at each step in the project process using the practitioner's round as a guide.

- Who or what has been instrumental to your growth as an educator?
- What would you like to do more of in your professional practice? What would you like to do less of?
- What role do your students play in your growth as an educator?
- What aspects of the practitioner's round show up in your answers to the preceding questions? What would you like to try? Who can be your ally?

Journey Log

Journey Log

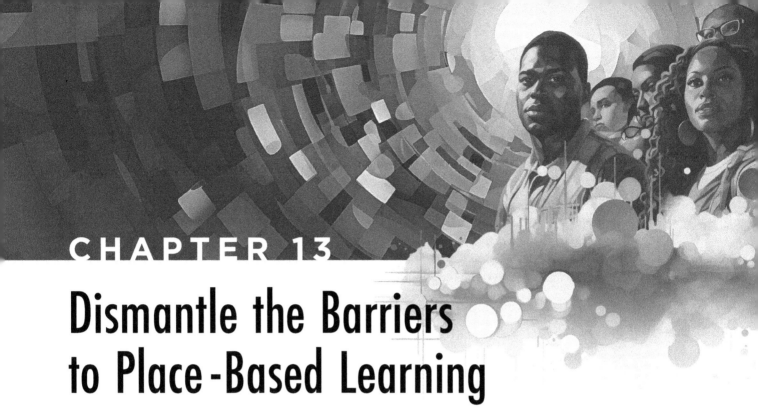

CHAPTER 13

Dismantle the Barriers to Place-Based Learning

Love recognizes no barriers. It jumps hurdles, leaps fences, penetrates walls to arrive at its destination full of hope.

—MAYA ANGELOU

ESSENTIAL QUESTION: What internal and external work is necessary to create a fertile landscape for place-based learning to grow?

Those of us who have worked in schools, whether in the classroom or in building leadership, know that it is hard to move a mountain but not impossible. When we see what sparks curiosity in a previously withdrawn student or what gets a struggling reader to turn the next page, educators will move mountains one boulder at a time to drive a pass through what can seem impassable to those outside the system. All the while, the mountain is doing its darnedest to maintain itself. This metaphor may feel oppressive, but it is meant instead to acknowledge that paving the way to create a fertile landscape for place-based learning to grow is not simple or small, but that every educator has seen something work for their students and then made sure that the larger school, district, or state system allowed them to do more of that thing. Place-based learning is worthy of mountain-moving.

In this chapter, we show you where to begin to move those mountains and what tools to pick up to first do the inner work of recognizing your own influence and shifting your mindset. Then we look outward to examine how you can make time for place-based learning, how community partners can become your best allies and assets, and how you can do place-based learning on a budget. With your colleagues, you will set a vision for equity that will mark your course and give you the power to collect and tell your school's story, articulating why place-based learning and amplifying the voices of students, colleagues, and partners are often drowned out of the school change discussion. The chapter offers a chance to think further about its content through the Conclusion and Key Takeaways and Reflection Questions sections. It concludes with the Journey Log for writing down your thoughts and ideas.

Where Does the Work of Dismantling Barriers to Place-Based Learning Start?

In 2018, Lindsay Unified School District in Tulare County, California, and Summit Public Schools in Redwood City, California, partnered with Transcend Education, an organization that innovates with schools, to design the *student impact framework*, a model of how teacher mindsets impact student learning. We've been fans of Transcend Education for some time and found this series of tools to be especially helpful at refining and naming how teachers think about themselves, their students, and the practice of learning, and how those thoughts influence the totality of the learning environment. A portion of the framework, the *educator personalized learning mindsets* shown in table 13.1, offers an "articulation of capacities and mindsets needed to implement new personalized learning practices, and confidence that the changes [teachers] are making will positively impact outcomes for students" (Lindsay Unified School District, Summit Public Schools, & Transcend, Inc., 2018, p. 3).

As you read over the mindsets, check in with yourself about what rings true and what may feel like a stretch for you at this particular time. Get curious about why that might be, and what and who are affected by your mindset.

TABLE 13.1: Educator Personalized Learning Mindsets

Mindsets About Learners and Learning	Mindsets About Myself and My Role
• Every student can achieve at the highest levels. • Students learn best as active participants in the process of acquiring knowledge. • Every student is unique in key ways (strengths, needs, interests, identities, and life context). "One size fits all" fits no one. • Positive relationships are foundational to a student's sense of safety, belonging, and willingness to challenge themselves. • Students must be equipped to be lifelong learners, armed with the skills and habits to keep learning and growing as they face new contexts in and beyond their school. • Students' investment in their learning is the shared responsibility of educators and students.	• I am responsible for my students' outcomes. • I deeply understand each student's strengths, needs, and interests to effectively customize their learning. • I collaborate with peers to customize learning and understand the whole student. • I am aware of my cultural biases and foster belonging for all students. • I continuously seek feedback, iterate, and improve my own skills as an educator. • I am committed to overcoming challenges and persevering to create an excellent personalized learning environment for all students.

We share these mindsets with you for a dual purpose. First, we share them because these mindsets reflect the asset lens we've affirmed through our design principles for place-based learning. Second, we want you to notice something as you review these mindsets: there is much in the role of teacher that is beyond the teacher's realms of control or influence. Most of us do not control the master schedule or have influence over curriculum adoption, mandated testing, or district initiatives. What we do have control of are our beliefs and our mindsets about teaching and learning, and how those manifest for the students we serve. The work of dismantling barriers to place-based learning starts with defining what we do have control or influence over in our roles as teachers and using those realms of control and influence to impact outcomes for students.

If you were to articulate your own mindsets about learners and about learning, and about yourself and your role as a teacher, what would they be? Take a few minutes to consider this question and then engage in the following activity that was originally developed by Stephen Covey in his 1989 book *The 7 Habits of Highly Effective People*, later adapted for schools by Daniel Baron (n.d.) of the National School Reform Faculty, then adapted again by PBL Path for our purposes. Use the diagram in figure 13.1, which we call the *realms diagram*, as you complete the three steps of the activity.

1. On a sheet of paper or in a journal, draw the concentric circles as shown in figure 13.1 and label them *control, influence*, and *concern*, accordingly. Conjure the *yeah, buts* that creep into your mind when you think about implementing or expanding place-based learning in your school, voices in your mind perhaps saying, "Yeah, but how will I get permission to take students off campus?" Fill the outer edges of the paper with all the concerns you have.

2. Then think about how you have influence over some of your concerns. The influence could be using your voice at a staff meeting, writing a proposal to district leadership to amend a rule or requirement, or arranging for a community partner to come on campus for a first meet and greet. Draw a line from the concern to a spot in the influence realm and, using *I can* statements, write down what sway you have. Also, take note of where you don't have influence and be OK with that.

3. Now that you are aware of your influence, think of what you have control over, as it relates to your concerns. Write this down in the inner circle. Reflect on your attitudes and beliefs about what you can control and what you cannot. Is your perceived control, or lack thereof, positional? Does it stem from a stock story you've been told about your race or other identity marker? Does it serve you or hinder you? Does it serve your students or hold them back? How could you view the realm of control with more objectivity? When you are ready, we encourage you to come up with one to two commitments, or action items, that you have direct control over or influence on. Write them in the inner circle using *I will* statements.

CONCERN

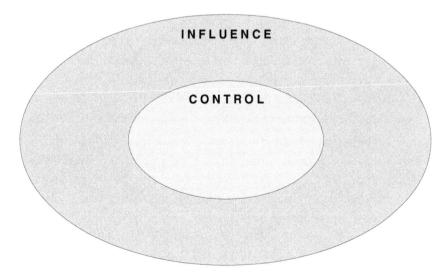

FIGURE 13.1: Template for realms diagram.

Visit go.SolutionTree.com/instruction for a free reproducible version of this figure.

This activity might be just the thing needed as you enter into conversation with colleagues or school leadership about the real and perceived barriers to seeding and sustaining place-based learning in schools. As we engage in this chapter, return to your realms diagram. See if there are additions in the forms of new commitments you can make to the influence and control realms. See figure 13.2 for a completed example of the realms protocol Erin used with coaches in a discussion about teacher reluctance to embrace project-based learning.

Now that we've discussed how the work of dismantling barriers to place-based learning starts with leveraging the realm of control you do have, we will discuss specific actions you can take to exert influence.

How Do I Dismantle Barriers to Place-Based Learning?

Taking a leap of faith and making a change in classroom practice, whether it is deemed necessary by school leadership or an individual teacher, requires courage—tremendous courage. In the words of Emily Leibtag, chief programs and partnerships officer for Education Reimagined, author, and all around learner-centered guru, "There is very little change capacity in schools, districts or state offices. It is tough to balance improvement and innovation simultaneously. Schools simply were not designed to innovate" (Vander Ark, 2017).

A constant push for improvement, a push that tells teachers and students to aim for perfection, that tells them there is one right way to achieve, and that perpetuates a constant sense of urgency is White supremacy, baked into the system of education since its inception. As Tema Okun (2021), author of *White Supremacy Culture*, says:

> White supremacy is a project of colonization—a project of "appropriating a place or domain for one's use" (according to the Oxford Dictionary). White supremacy colonizes our minds, our bodies, our psyches, our spirits, our emotions . . . as well as the land and the water and the sky and the air we breathe. White supremacy tells us who has value, who doesn't, what has value, what doesn't in ways that reinforce a racial hierarchy of power and control that dis-eases and destroys all it touches.

Although each school has its own distinct culture and may be populated by predominantly Black and Brown students, White supremacy exists within the larger system of schooling in the United States, and by its very design was meant to exclude students of color and maintain a racial hierarchy (Okun, 2021).

The legacy of White supremacy is what we're up against every time we labor to know our students deeply, share power with them and their families, listen to their stories, and build a classroom practice that centers their ways of knowing and being. So why take on such a monumental task? As Cristina Rivera Chapman (2021) of the Earthseed Land Collective says, "Because the end game of dismantling white supremacy is getting free together. We all get to swim" (Okun, 2021).

Remember, we are only asking you to break down the barriers that are within your realms of control and influence, and to hold the commitments that you set in the previous section. We've been preparing you to do just those things throughout this text. Now, we'll address some of the most commonly cited barriers to place-based learning implementation in traditional school settings, such as time constraints and fear of losing time to a project, inflexible master schedules, and the difficulty with organizing the logistics of student and community partnerships. Here are some specific actions you can take to address these barriers.

- **Lose time's hold on projects:** We share suggestions, considerations, concerns, and solutions to *right size* any project, given your individual context.

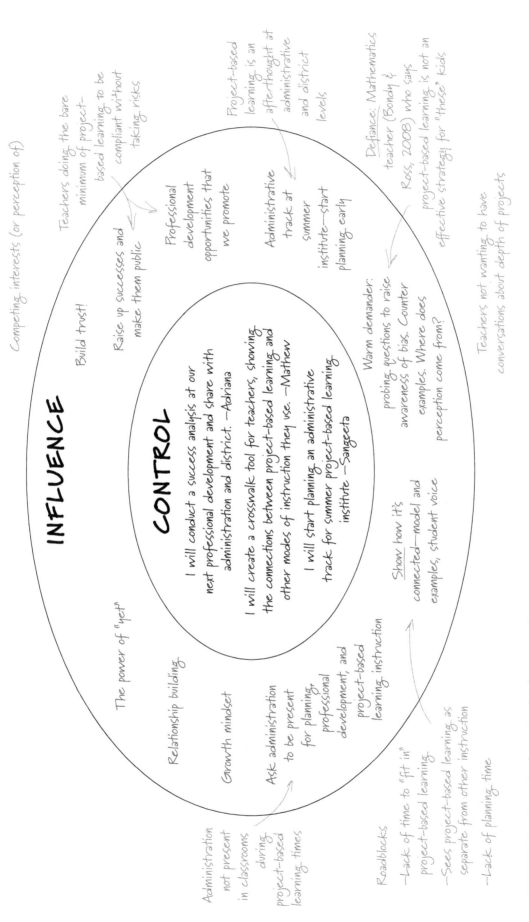

FIGURE 13.2: Example of completed realms protocol.

- **Stop serving the master schedule:** Find out the connection between place-based learning and the school schedule.
- **Make an ideal schedule for place-based learning:** Explore what's possible, examine your school schedule, and do what you can within your current structure to advocate for more autonomy.
- **Organize the logistics of school and community partnerships:** Get granular about how to make the most of community outreach, how to prepare for field experiences, and how to manage student and partner expectations.

Lose Time's Hold on Projects

Let us start by saying, "We hear you." The three of us have sat with countless teachers looking for a way to insert a meaningfully designed learning experience into the rigid scope and sequence of 180-plus school days, and we have compassion and respect enough not to pretend that place-based learning is an expedient endeavor. John Larmer (2015), project-based learning authority, discusses the benefits and challenges of place-based learning in a feature for Edutopia:

> It is true that projects take time, but it is time well spent. A project is not meant to "cover" a long list of standards, but to teach selected important standards in greater depth. The key is to design a project well, so it aligns with standards, and manage it well, so time is used efficiently. Not all projects need to take months to complete—some can be only two weeks long. And a teacher does not have to go all-PBL, all the time—even one or two projects a year is better than none. Some teachers are concerned that planning a project takes too much time. PBL does require significant advance preparation, but planning projects gets easier the more you do it. You can also save planning time by collaborating with other teachers, sharing projects, adapting projects from other sources, and running the same project again in later years.

The project planner discussed throughout part II (page 113) gives license to dream big and plan big. Now we ask you to look at that plan and scale, based on student-driven factors such as the following.

- How well you've prepared students for the content and concepts you'll teach and assess through the project
- Students' familiarity with the project process, including with the skills of feedback, revision, and reflection
- How well you know your students and can use that knowledge to shape the project
- Site-dictated factors like how often, and for what length of time, you see your students and can maintain engagement in the project
- The amount of time you typically spend teaching and assessing the standards you've aligned to your project
- The support you will receive from school leadership to co-define what *success* in the project looks like

As you gauge these factors, size the project so that you aren't scaling back so much that you lose the integrity of your design, and you are not falling too far forward that you lose balance and misplace the *joy* of engaging in place-based learning.

Figure 13.3 provides guidance on some of the time-related questions of concern we hear in our coaching work.

Concern		Right-Sized Solution
"What if we can't work on the project every day?"	→	Just like in our personal projects outside of school (for example, planting a backyard garden), some days and weeks you will devote more time to it, sometimes less. You will no doubt be teaching other content in tandem with the project, managing time with the community partner, and teaching skills in low-stakes ways. Striving for a neat and tidy calendar will only bring you disappointment. One rule of thumb: there should be a touchpoint at least once a week, with a refocus on the essential question. For longer-term projects (six weeks or more), you may need reengagement activities at key points throughout the project to record new questions that arise and reignite excitement for the project.
"What if the project extends beyond the end date I've set?"	→	This is typical for teachers and students new to place-based learning and should be expected. Build in two to five *cushion* hours at the end of your project calendar for those unexpected issues and opportunities that arise. As you become more adept at planning projects and your students become more skilled, independent, and interdependent learners, your project calendar will be more accurate. Another aspect of project design that is refined with time is choosing the number of standards to teach and assess within the timeline you've set. This is finessed as you improve your ability to preassess and visualize the whole of the project during the planning phase. Cutting back, adding, shifting, and clustering standards is nuanced.
"What if teams are not collaborating effectively?"	→	Collaboration is one of the most, if not *the* most, time-consuming elements of place-based learning. The keys to sizing the time it takes to collaborate are: 1. Teach collaboration all year, not just when it comes to project work. 2. Co-establish norms and routines with your students for teamwork at the onset of the project. 3. Co-create learning agreements with your students as well as ways to hold each other accountable. 4. Have teams of students create team contracts and adhere to them. 5. Have record-keeping systems for students. 6. Use task logs during work time, and build students' stamina for work time slowly. 7. These structures may take time initially but will save time overall. 8. Examine your project plan and determine where it is necessary to have a team component and what can be done individually but with plenty of collaboration.
"What if colleagues are ahead of me in the pacing guide or curriculum?"	→	Employ ways to measure the nondominant knowledge and skills your students are gaining through the project (using tools like journaling, collecting samples of student work, and recording your findings from protocols in the practitioner's round). Use these as confirmation that the time you are spending on the project has value beyond the pacing guide or curriculum. If it is still troubling you, ask yourself, "Is competition with my peers a White-dominant culture trait I want to uphold?" Our hunch is that the answer is "no."
"What if the community product doesn't measure the standards I aligned to the project? I've wasted all that time!"	→	The liberatory learning and assessment pathway in our project-planning tool is designed to catch a potential misalignment of content and product before you enter the project. However, when products are co-created with a community partner, there is room for it to stray from the original intent. Keeping the essential question at the forefront when planning with the community partner is critical, as the question corrals ideas and suggestions, always bringing us back to the intended learning goal. If you catch the misalignment too late, don't be disheartened. We've yet to come across a community product that didn't teach to standard, even if it wasn't the standards originally intended. Review your standards again. • Are there standards that align better, even if they're meant to be taught at another time of the year? • Are there standards from another discipline that can be pulled in (with the help of that content teacher)? • Are there minor alterations students can make to the end product to create better alignment? • Is there a supplemental product or assessment that could assess the intended content?

FIGURE 13.3: Right-sized solutions to concerns about time.

We want to be honest with you. Projects take time. Students are not productive all the time. Community partners are busy and unpredictable. Students come to understandings at different paces. Prototypes fail. The adage goes, "Plans are worthless; planning is everything," and for a methodology where the initial planning is extensive, the plan, adapt, plan, adapt nature of place-based learning can feel like a betrayal. In reality, it is the way the world outside of the walls of school operates. It is the way the communities in which our students reside work. By mimicking that pliancy in our planning and project implementation, we are teaching our students (and they are teaching us) boundary intelligence and tenacity.

Stop Serving the ~~Master~~ Schedule

A question we hear more often than we would like in our work with educators is, How do I do projects in a forty-five-minute period with a student load of 150? The answer is, in a limited capacity. Constraints like a six- to seven-period day with multiple preps, where it is a challenge just to learn students' names, let alone connect with families and reach out the community, create an impediment to place-based learning. A response to a packed schedule like this can be to do place-based learning in small, slow, sure steps, securing your footing. First, introduce essential questions into current units. Next, plan a five-hour inquiry unit with one or two classes, then expand that size unit to all classes. Finally, design a real-world problem to investigate, working your way up to a place-based project with a conservative scope and a realistic community product. While it does no good to ignore the restrictions of a schedule, doing so doesn't need to completely curb one's ability to innovate.

While the fixed nature of many school schedules often requires diligence to accommodate the flexible nature of place-based learning, it is also noteworthy that many schools have made major shifts toward block scheduling, common planning time for teachers, cohort models for students (at least at the middle school level), and standards- or competency-based grading, and it is just as important to leverage these options. Conversations that at one time were only happening at outlier schools are now part of mainstream dialogue happening with building and district leadership. There are varied tools and supports for schools ready to refashion their schedules.

Emily Leibtag and Mary Ryerse, writing for the Getting Smart website's series *Scheduling for Learning, Not Convenience*, say:

> In our increasingly project-based world, there is a greater degree of recognition that content isn't learned or consumed in isolation. Ideally, learning is interdisciplinary and connected. Time constraints and stringent schedules can get in the way when thinking about how to create innovative ideas and divergent thinking. The Carnegie Unit, while still in full-force in many institutions, is starting to hold less and less weight and the focus is more on competencies. (Vander Ark, 2017)

Leibtag and Ryerse go on to name four characteristics of effective schedules, which we have synthesized as the following.

1. **Work sessions:** Extended time for students to work on transdisciplinary projects
2. **Less rigidity:** Classes bleed into each other based on student inquiry, and the bell doesn't rule the day
3. **Time for multiuse spaces:** For students to create community products, they need flexible access to different types of spaces such as makerspaces, labs, shops, and kitchens
4. **Advisory:** A time devoted to relationships where all students are known well by at least one adult

These four characteristics, when leveraged for place-based learning, allow students to work in an environment that respects their developmental needs (to be known well, to have personal and shared space, to work to a satisfactory conclusion) and communicates to them that they deserve the same respect granted to adults when they work on a complex task. We want our schedule to communicate to students that we're preparing them to enter the professional world.

Another support, Education Resource Strategies (ERS, n.d.), empowers "school system leaders to make transformative shifts in resources, structures, and practices so that all students—especially those with the greatest learning needs and those furthest from opportunity—attend a school where they can learn and thrive." ERS has a do-it-yourself school design hub to assist schools ready for a more student-centered schedule. In their publication *Designing Schools That Work*, ERS authors Karen Hawley Miles, Kristen Ferris, and Genevieve Quist Green (2017) name the successes they've seen:

> Critically, high-performing schools also build schoolwide systems that support more targeted and flexible use of the resources that support differentiated and individualized instruction: people, time, programs, and technology. This means tailoring schedules, class sizes, teacher loads, and technology use to the specific needs of individual students, content areas, and lesson types. For example, writing teachers might have student loads of 60 versus the school average of 90 so they can provide meaningful and applicable feedback several times a week. Students studying key subjects in important transition grades, such as Algebra I in 9th grade, might be given additional time in the master schedule, smaller group sizes, and/or access to the school's most expert teachers. Biology students may have extended time blocks each week to enable hands-on lab work. (p. 10)

If you are a teacher reading this, you may feel helpless to make changes as substantive as scheduling. Even building leaders might not be in charge of scheduling. Instead, scheduling is often the purview of school counselors or district personnel who feel they must, given real constraints, work the schedule like a mathematical formula, devoid of humanity. But we know school schedules influence transportation, staffing configurations, state and federal funding, and more. What a teacher can do is advocate for themselves and their peers (through their union, school board, or within the school). Teachers can share what they are hearing from their students and families, centering the humanity of schooling. Read on for examples of how scheduling can be done differently, and what you can do to further progress.

Make an Ideal Schedule for Place-Based Learning

In the introduction (page 1), Erin writes about starting her teaching career at Minnesota New Country School, a self-directed, place-based learning school. The grades 6–12 schedule at MNCS hasn't changed in thirty years. The day begins with advisory, followed by the morning project block. Next comes lunch and sustained silent reading. The afternoon consists of a second project block, and the day concludes in advisory. Mathematics work groups are interspersed during project blocks. That's it.

At ACE (Architecture, Construction, and Engineering) Leadership High School in Albuquerque, New Mexico, students don't sign up for courses. Instead, they sign up for projects, each of which is born from a genuine need expressed by a community partner. The schedule, similar to MNCS's, includes advisory, morning project, afternoon project, and a second advisory. (We're sure they eat lunch at some point.) One example of a project at ACE that addressed standards in all core subjects was the designing and building of kiosks and bridges for the Silvery Minnow Refugium for the U.S. Fish and Wildlife Service that was the first outdoor classroom of its kind when it opened in

2013. This project was possible because the schedule at ACE Leadership High School put project learning first and built the infrastructure around it.

There are place-based schools that operate on maritime vessels and study the hidden lives of octopuses, schools that run Socratic seminars on mountain peaks, and schools where student exhibitions take place on light rail trains speeding across the city. What all these schools have in common, primarily, is autonomy—that is, the freedom to build infrastructure, create staffing models, and design learning programs liberated from the system that most teachers and students are mired in. While this is a good thing, in and of itself, it's not so good if you don't happen to have the level of autonomy that these schools do. However, there is still much good news to share, because there is really no such thing as an ideal place-based learning schedule.

We have seen place-based learning happening at a Los Angeles high school of three thousand students, at a comprehensive middle school in eastern Washington trying an academy approach (groups of students moving as a cohort, with teachers devoted to that smaller load of students), and at a turnaround elementary school in New Orleans. Not only have we, the authors, taught in highly autonomous environments, but we have also taught under inflexible schedules and did the best we could to bring place-based learning to students in small but meaningful ways. Table 13.2 presents some strategies to bring place-based learning into your practice, no matter the level of autonomy, based on our insights from teaching in a variety of different learning environments.

There are avenues of place-based learning to pursue, even in schools with limited teacher autonomy. Do what you can to bring the power of place-based learning to your students. Deliberate, also, on your realm of influence when it comes to scheduling. Is there a way to influence the subject with school leadership? Do you have a receptive ally in the administration? Pose the following questions, first to yourself, then take it beyond yourself and speak truth to power.

- Does your schedule center students?
- Does your schedule care for the adults on campus?
- Is your schedule inclusive of families?
- Does your schedule prioritize the process of learning over production and urgency?
- Does your schedule invite the community to be a partner in the learning process?
- Are your school's mission and vision evidenced in the school schedule? How would you explain the connection (or disconnection)?

If you answered no to any of these questions, it is time for a reckoning. Advocate by speaking up consistently (and repeatedly, if necessary) about the importance of creating infrastructure that is conducive to place-based learning. Keep in mind the words of the brilliant Toni Morrison (2015): "There is no time for despair, no place for self-pity, no need for silence, no room for fear. We speak, we write, we do language. That is how civilizations heal."

Organize the Logistics of Student and Community Partnerships

Recall that we considered the role of community partnerships in place-based learning in chapter 3 (page 49) when we established the authentic community partnerships and community product design principles. We also explored community partnerships in part II (page 113) when we determined a path to make community partners an essential element of the project plan. At this stage, you have knowledge of the process of building partnerships, a community asset map, and samples and tools for reaching out to potential partners. Yet, our hunch is that there are logistic

TABLE 13.2: A Step for Every Schedule

If your school's schedule is . . .	Try . . .
Rigid *(Six- or seven-period day, lack of common planning, one-hundred-plus student load)*	• Partnering with another discipline-alike teacher (or grade-level teacher who has the same planning period as you) to plan a mini-project to run simultaneously in each of your classes, using a pre- and postprotocol from the practitioner's round to reflect • Nudging your discipline or grade-level team to plan a community-building project to start the school year with the goal of having each teacher complete the community asset map (from the project-planning tool) for at least one class • Involving one community partner in a project or unit of study, possibly inviting them in during one class period and recording the session so all your other classes can benefit
Permeable *(Block schedule, common planning, cohorts, less-than-ninety student load)*	In addition to place-based learning happening at least a few times a year for *every* student, try: • Planning a project with one core teacher and one elective teacher so students begin to see the interconnectedness of the content • Collecting and curating student work into portfolios to showcase at an exhibition or celebration of learning, including work that is not yet part of a project, and inviting community members to the event • Setting a goal of connecting with at least one community partner at each grade level or cohort to establish a lasting relationship to tap into for projects
Versatile *(Project-focused schedule, cohorts of students and teachers, elective teachers push in to projects, small student load)*	In addition to the place-based learning happening throughout the school for *every* student, try: • Asking students at the beginning of the school year to ideate on ways they can impact their community, allowing them to be part of the project mapping process, then letting students take the lead to connect with potential community partners • Asking yourself and your colleagues how the learning environment could be more authentic and more representative of your students and their lives outside of school; keep working to make it a reality • Bringing families into the role of advisers, learning designers, experts, and mentors

components to community partnerships that may still be unclear. In the following, we list some of those components of community partnerships that tend to present hurdles.

◆ **Initial contact:** Identifying and reaching out to potential community partners, preparing students for the first contact, and understanding the logistics that make for a successful partnership

◆ **Transportation:** Planning for and navigating the requirements of getting students to and from endeavors in the community

◆ **Field trips:** Putting a place-based spin on traditional field trips and opening the doors to additional ways to connect students with their community

◆ **Money:** Funding a place-based learning journey not needing to be a barrier

◆ **Student behavior:** Managing expectations with student and community partner preparation

While we focus on how to address hurdles related to forming and maintain community partnerships in this chapter, we also think it is important to tell you that you can learn much from developing these partnerships and refining, with your students and partners, as your place-based learning capacity increases. Now let's examine those hurdles or barriers and confront them so we can create actions and then get past them.

Initial Contact

If you are relatively new to identifying and reaching out to potential community partners, the task can appear daunting. No one wants to spend their lunch break cold-calling local organizations and industry professionals to ask them to care about our students as much as we do. Let's instead start with what we are comfortable with, what is closer to the connections we already have and make, and hear from people who do the work of connecting schools and communities really well.

Oregon-based nonprofit SOLVE (www.solveoregon.org) aimed to build a legacy of stewardship through environmental action and put this mission into practice for more than fifty years. In the following list, we paraphrase recommendations (originally written by Susan Abravanel) for initiating partnerships (SOLVE, 2006).

- Before approaching a partner, research that partner—know their mission, goals, and so on.
- Welcome the community partner into the project planning process. Consider a face-to-face planning meeting with the partner.
- Be clear about your goals and expectations for the partnership. What will you provide the organization, and what will they provide you?
- Prior to beginning the partnership, clarify what specific elements must be included in it—for instance, whether students will be on site or working in a different location.
- Consider your partner as an academic resource, one that may be able to help you make good academic connections.
- Be organized and give your partner time to build a schedule that includes you.
- Be clear about what each person's role will be, especially as those roles pertain to leadership. For instance, will students lead a particular component of the project, or will the partner?
- Be clear in communication about what work students may or may not do, your limitations on scheduling, and any possible barriers to access that students might face.
- Since organizations are usually used to working with adult volunteers, communicate with them who will be responsible for and supervising your students.
- Be clear in any phone messages you leave with the organization to avoid any unnecessary back-and-forth.
- Always respond in a timely fashion when contacted by a community partner, arrive on time, and stay for time you committed to. Be sensitive to their time investments in your project.
- If a nonprofit organization says they cannot accommodate you, ask them if they know of another that can.
- Provide an adequate number of adults to supervise the students. Seek the partner's guidance on an ideal supervisor-student ratio as well as adhering to your school's protocols.
- Offer the partner activities through which to reflect on the partnership process throughout.

Transportation

Public transportation to and from community partners may work well for older students in most urban and suburban areas (and it is common for urban districts to provide students with bus passes), but for students in elementary and middle grades, transportation needs to be arranged through the proper channels (school administration) well in advance. For this reason, the option of partnering with businesses and organizations within walking distance to the school, especially for a first project, is appealing. This can ease the tension of making transportation arrangements. It is also possible to work with a community organization that transports residents by van and enter into a van-sharing agreement. They may be able to accommodate small groups of students on a consistent basis. Erin's students got a ride to a neighboring town once a week on a van primarily used to transport older community members on errands. Administration or the transportation department will need to initiate such arrangements to meet safety and legal requirements, but if your school is moving to place-based learning, you will need to examine transportation options beyond what is currently in place.

Field Trips

When it comes to taking students off campus, safety is the supreme goal and should take precedence over any inconvenience to adults, like carrying around twenty-five to seventy-five pieces of paper with medical and allergy information while trudging across the city. But if we can find equally safe ways to get students beyond the school building and lessen the burden on teachers, even better. For this reason, you might consider the following.

- Plan field experiences close to home. Walking is always going to be easier than arranging transportation, and if you do need wheels to get to a close spot, a quick trip will optimize your time on site.

- Go digital. There are a surplus of companies that digitize the permission slip process, even sending the paperwork to families' phones to e-sign. Check out Linq and signNow. You could even have your students do the research and put together an infographic to share with school administration.

- Swap the same old predictable annual field trip for place-based learning field study. If every fourth grader has been going to the natural history museum for the last thirty years, talk to your administrators early about using those funds for a trip (or two) to a site that aligns to a project you are planning. Or, consider ways to make a more meaningful partnership with the history museum.

- Bring the experts to you. As much as we would like to have students out in the community, it isn't realistic to do so as often as we need it to happen in place-based learning. As a solution, make the school a community center of sorts and welcome partners to campus. Work to devise a simple sign-in process that is safe and fast, assuring everyone that you will be present with guests at all times.

Money

Lack of money for place-based learning is a perceived hurdle, but we assure you it can be done without additional funds. Each of the authors has taught in environments that provided no additional stipends for place-based journeys. That said, as with everything in life and in teaching, additional funds allow for more opportunities. Supplies, field experiences, texts, online subscriptions, software, equipment—when you plan a project, you manage the tension of limiting yourself to a realistic budget and giving your students what will allow them the best experience. We have a few suggestions that we have personally used to ease that tension.

- Seek free resources. Don't be afraid to ask if businesses and organizations have surpluses of materials or funds—everything from gift cards to scraps for your makerspace.

- Ask businesses to match funds, empowering students to create, produce, or use their skills to raise money.

- Write grants. Teachers are master grant writers, and some even enjoy it. Who is that person on your campus who always knows about grant opportunities? Who has been awarded a grant that could give you some tips? How can your students help?

- Make time a resource. Can you and your students volunteer time in return for a new community partner? Time is valuable, and the investment you make can pay dividends in your next project.

- Designate a space in your classroom or school as a makerspace. Help students send out a communication blast, asking other students, faculty, and families for supplies to slowly, over time, build a supply surplus for you and your students to get creative with.

Student Behavior

Damage to property, endangerment to human lives, mass suspensions—it is easy to get over-whelmed thinking about what can go wrong during a field experience or even when students interact with community partners on campus. The worst-case-scenario switch gets flipped. As with nearly all manifestations of negative behavior, relationships and preparation are our greatest resources.

Set realistic expectations with the partner, as mentioned in the recommendations from SOLVE (2006). Remind them that young people are *trying on* adult roles but haven't grown enough devel-opmentally for those roles to quite fit yet. There are also cultural nuances that will come into play during interactions. Co-creating and sharing norms that include checking biases and respecting cultural differences should happen well in advance of the first meeting.

With your students, practice probable situations they will encounter, using scenarios and role play. For example, the community partner might assume students have experience or background infor-mation that they do not and misinterpret their role. Students will need to practice how to politely advocate for themselves. This need is as true for seniors in high school as it is for upper elementary students. The time for practice gives students permission to be vulnerable, ask questions of you they wouldn't dare ask a community partner, and know that it is OK to be nervous and unsure.

With solid relationships and a little preparation, your worst-case scenarios will remain unrealized.

Reflect now on the hurdles. Based on your experience and the suggestions we have given, what are one or two actions you can take to erode these barriers? It is not possible to anticipate all of the nuances and surprises that a project brings, but your forethought will add to the potency of the overall project. It was our intent, through this section on the logistics of community partner-ships, to fortify you with additional fuel to journey into place-based learning with confidence.

Establish a Schoolwide Focus on Race and Equity Through Place-Based Learning

The barriers to place-based learning that we have previously broken down are the obvious ones, the ones we talk about in the staff room or assure families that we have considered in the newslet-ters we send home. This next demand arises from a barrier that doesn't get talked about enough:

the barrier of racial inequity. This barrier is hidden in school discipline practices, in our aversion to failure, and in our isolation from the communities in which our schools sit. In order to dismantle this historically entrenched hurdle, we must curate a schoolwide focus on race and equity.

Our definition of place-based learning asks individuals, leaders, and the school community to focus on race and equity. It lives in our design principles, our project designs, and our assessment practices. As such, it is important to think about your school's theory of action for equity work and how it relates to place-based learning implementation.

When race and equity are brought into the light, are prioritized, and are talked about in breakrooms and newsletters with the same fervor as other aspects of schooling, it affects far more than just the classrooms where place-based learning is happening. As Jennifer Kuhr Butterfoss (2021) writes, "When school leaders make equity an explicit and visible priority, it permeates throughout the school culture and offers a clear path forward toward hope, healing, and transformational results for the student learning experience."

However, it is not just the school leaders who can promote an equity-centered approach; it takes everyone—teachers, families, and community. Place-based learning is the perfect place to start your school's journey with an equity focus. Through its very nature, it asks us to understand the community from which our students come. Through story mapping and asset mapping, we learn the history of the community, and we understand what is located in the community, such as grocery stores, parks and playgrounds, public transit, and so on. Through community mapping, we can locate the places community members, families, and students gather, like restaurants, churches, community centers such as the Boys and Girls Club, sports fields, and so on. Place-based learning asks that we embed culture into all our project designs, decolonize the curriculum, utilize liberatory literacy practices, and incorporate equitable assessment practices. Place-based learning is the starting point for beginning schoolwide equity work.

Use Storytelling to Sustain Place-Based Learning

Anytime you are implementing a new initiative, a good place to start is through storytelling. This is equally true for implementing and sustaining schoolwide place-based learning. This pedagogy may be new for teachers, students, families, and community members, and it is important they understand and help create your school's mission and vision around place-based learning. When teachers, students, families, and the community understand the power behind place-based learning, they more easily get behind this initiative, so we recommend bringing place-based learning to life through story.

Storytelling provides all stakeholders with a voice. It can be an effective way of breaking through perceived barriers and hurdles. It allows for a safe place to share fears as well as excitement around the possibilities of place-based learning. In the blog post "The Power of Stories," Project Zero (2019b) contends, "Stories can help individuals adopt new ideas by aiding them in overcoming personal barriers to change, while also acting as a social 'contagion' that allows the idea to spread rapidly between individuals." The Project Zero writers go on to say:

> People are not passive recipients of change—to adopt a new idea, individuals need to overcome various emotional and rational barriers. While both barriers are important, stories are an especially effective communicative form for helping individuals overcome emotional barriers like fear and/or a general discomfort with change.

Writer and botanist Susan J. Tweit (2009) reminds us:

> Stories nurture our connection to place and to each other. They show us where we have been and where we can go. They remind us of how to be human, how to live alongside the other lives that animate this planet. When we lose stories, our understanding of the world is less rich, less true.

In "Using Story to Change Systems," Ella Saltmarshe (2018) identifies the following three qualities of story and narrative to sustain change efforts.

1. **Story as light:** "Story helps illuminate the past, present, and future, thus lighting up the paths of change."
2. **Story as glue:** "Story is also a tool for building community through empathy and coherence. It enables people to connect across differences and to generate narratives that hold together groups, organizations, and movements."
3. **Story as web:** "We can use story to reauthor the web of narratives we live in. Specifically, we can use it to:
   - Change the personal narratives we have about our lives.
   - Change the cultural narratives that frame the issues we advocate for.
   - Change the mythic narratives that influence our worldview." (Saltmarshe, 2018, p. 2)

Storytelling helps to make sense of the past (what strategies or initiatives have worked and what have not). Our journey of where we have come from and where we are going helps us to understand the present and provides the impetus to create a new future around teaching and learning.

It is interesting to note that when a person tells a story, the same regions of the brain are activated both in the storyteller and in the listeners (Zak, 2013). Bonnie Leedy (2019), CEO for School Webmasters, introduces us to the notion that stories help create connections and relationships between people and affirms that storytelling is a powerful way to build trust and build physical connections:

> Stories have the unique ability to create connections between us and others. When we hear a well-told story, our brains mirror that of the storyteller. Our brains react as if we are experiencing this story ourselves because it puts us inside the story. Our empathetic nature and our shared emotions create a connection through the story.

As such, storytelling makes space for stories that might not be heard, providing a platform for individuals who don't feel connected to the more dominant established narratives to participate in the larger conversation and share their own personal experiences. Listening and collecting stories can liberate people and allow them to count themselves as part of their community and its history.

To begin building a culture of story gathering and storytelling in your school community, you might begin with using writing prompts to initiate the sharing of personal stories among staff and students. Shane Safir (2015), a brilliant coach, facilitator, and author, focuses her work on the use of storytelling as a way to transform schools. She asks us to reflect on the following questions:

> Who are you as an educator, and who do you aspire to be? What pivotal moments have shaped your journey? Reflecting on, writing down (in visual or written form), and sharing your story with students and colleagues will help you to model social-emotional intelligence. Through your vulnerability, you will invite other people's stories into the learning community. (Safir, 2015)

While storytelling is a powerful way to build community and relationships, it can also make individuals vulnerable. For this reason, it is important to establish community agreements (by which we create and honor parameters for how we want to relate to one another) in order to build trust and transparency. The National Equity Project (n.d.) stresses that:

> Developing community agreements is a powerful strategy for coalescing a group into a team. The process of constructing agreements is often more important than the product. Agreements come from a consensus-driven process to identify what every person in the group needs from each other and commits to each other to feel safe, supported, open and trusting. As such, they provide a common framework for how people aspire to work and be together as they take transformational action.

The National Equity Project's webpage "Developing Community Agreements" (www .nationalequityproject.org/tools/developing-community-agreements) provides more information on developing and using community agreements.

Some points to include on community agreements might include the following.

- Stay engaged by listening fully.
- As the listener, do not give comments, provide feedback, or interrupt with your story.
- Assume best intentions.
- Maintain double confidentiality so that the storyteller knows their story is safe within the group.

Teams are encouraged to add to the agreements. These agreements should be referred to on a regular basis and added to as trust is established.

To get started in sharing personal stories, consider some of the following writing prompts.

1. Think about a person who has helped you get where you are today—a guide, mentor, or advocate who has been important and has made a positive impact on your life.
   - How did this person change your personal narrative so that you were able to move forward in positive and meaningful ways?
2. Think about your most powerful learning experience. What were the factors that made it so powerful? How does this story impact your teaching or leadership today? How does it inform your place-based practice?
3. Write about your class, ethnicity, gender, sexual orientation, religion, size, age, and ability backgrounds.
   - What has been difficult coming from your background?
   - What are sources of strength coming from your background?
   - How might your social identity show up in your leadership or teaching? Your interactions with others (both positive and negative)? Your expectations of others (both positive and negative)?
4. What people have had a significant impact on your life, and why?
5. What hardships have you faced and overcome? How can others learn from those experiences?
6. Is there a story that someone else shared with you that made a difference in your life and stuck with you over time?

To build a culture around storytelling, start staff meetings with one of the writing prompts. Provide two to three minutes to freewrite and four minutes to share out. You can create established learning groups of three or more pairs and mix and match as appropriate. As trust is built, begin sharing prompts around place-based learning as a way to share successes and challenges.

It is also important to build a culture of storytelling and active listening in your classroom as well. This sets up an environment in which students feel comfortable sharing their own personal stories, especially their unheard stories. Sharing individual stories is a first step in creating a culture of trust. Sharing and crafting stories helps to share and strengthen the purpose and importance of place-based learning for all stakeholders, including students.

These stories help inform next steps, celebrate successes, and share the challenges that arise with implementing a new pedagogy. Stories situate us between the past and the future. When a collective narrative is built around place-based learning and the values and experiences of those involved in the experience, it's much easier for people to connect to it and feel a sense of ownership. Crafting a shared narrative allows teams to identify clear roles for working together as they implement school wide place-based learning. When educators can see how their role fits with the roles of others within the bigger story of place-based learning, it creates a team culture of interdependence and accountability. Capturing these stories begins to paint a picture of your school's learning story around place-based learning that can be shared with families and community members.

The following are possible writing prompts to find your school's place-based learning stories.

- Write about a time during project implementation in which one particular design principle really stood out.
- Share a story about a success in addressing equitable assessment during the project.
- Share a story where students were highly engaged in purpose-driven inquiry.
- Share a story about a community partnership and reciprocity.
- Describe a student success within the project process.
- Describe a teacher's success in place-based learning implementation.
- Think about the school's goals and values around place-based learning implementation. Describe a time where you saw this value manifested by a student, teacher, or community member.

Once storytelling becomes part of the school culture, you can begin to curate the stories of your students and teachers about their place-based learning experiences. As you curate, consider how you will share your place-based learning story with families and the community. In her blog post "How to Tell Your School's Story," Leedy (2019) stresses the power of student's stories around place-based learning:

> Consider using students as authors. A good segment on writing nonfiction narrative can produce a talented crop of writers for your storytelling school (and provide the students with their first crack at publication). Students are also great resources for discovering great story ideas that support your school's mission and goals. They are privy to experiences your staff might not know about but support your storytelling purposes.

School leaders and teachers can capture your student stories about their experiences with place-based learning through reflection journals and interviews that are written into a narrative to be shared.

In addition to making sure educators and students are involved in the storytelling of place-based learning, it is important that families and communities be part of the story as we introduce place-based learning. When students, families, and communities are deeply involved in the learning story of place-based learning implementation, they can create solutions that address their own unique needs. Students, families, and community members need the opportunity for meaningful engagement to name the challenges associated with place-based learning and collaborate with devising solutions and refining strategies throughout the year. Invite family members to share stories about their children's experiences with place-based learning. Likewise, ask community partners to share their stories about the students they worked with and their successes and challenges throughout the partnership.

For successful implementation of place-based learning, all members of the community must be represented. Consider how to create meaningful opportunities for shared storytelling, perhaps making this sharing a year-end reflection or a way to start off the school year. Sharing stories about place-based learning from teachers, students, family members, and community partnerships is critical in sharing your school's place-based journey. The stories you gather (through surveys, quotes, and interviews, for example) can be shared in your school communications, as website content, or in social media campaigns. These stories can engage families in what is going on at school around place-based learning implementation. Because of the community nature of place-based learning, these stories can also connect community members to the school community and forge new community partnerships.

Figure 13.4 demonstrates a number of ways school leaders can build a storytelling culture and curate their school story.

Using	Use a narrative format to draft opening remarks for staff, parent, and community meetings.
Writing	Write regular newsletters, bulletins, blog posts, and website updates that tell your school's evolving story around place-based learning.
Designing	Design adult learning experiences that promote story sharing around place-based learning implementation.
Sharing	Share student stories and experiences with place-based learning with the greater community.

FIGURE 13.4: Curate your school story.

In addition, make time for annual team retreats away from the school building, if possible. Retreats offer a powerful opportunity to share personal narratives and develop a forward-moving organizational narrative around place-based learning implementation. Engage in a listening campaign with students, colleagues, families, and community members throughout the school year. Invite people to share their experiences, hopes, and challenges with you. Be a listener. Practice strategic vulnerability by sharing pieces of your story that humanize you and express your core values as an educator (Safir, 2015).

Respecting the power of story will help you to create the conditions for implementing and sustaining place-based learning. These stories build a place-based learning culture and a foundational component for successful place-based learning. In previous chapters, we have discussed the collaborative and relational aspect of place-based learning, which is magnified through storytelling, supporting a culture where relationships can thrive and all voices are heard.

Conclusion

In this chapter we looked at specific ways to dismantle the barriers to place-based learning. This begins with doing the inner work, focusing on what we can control and influence and naming perceived barriers that may be holding us back from implementing place-based learning in our classroom and as a whole school. We considered some of the barriers such as time, scheduling, and working with community partners. We explored mindsets we have about our learners and mindsets we have about ourselves and our roles. We explored the power of storytelling in sustaining place-based learning and as a tool to give all stakeholders voice. Storytelling creates the opportunity for those not part of the dominant narrative to share their stories and perspectives. Curating your school's story informs others about your journey and highlights both the successes and challenges when practicing place-based learning.

Key Takeaways and Reflection Questions

Consider this chapter's key takeaways and reflect on the following questions as you work to dismantle barriers to place-based learning. Use the Journey Log to further reflect, brainstorm, jot down ideas, make observations, or plan.

Examining your realms of influence and control assists you in breaking down the barriers that are within those realms, and holding the commitments that you set.

- Finding "right size" solutions to common concerns about the time it takes to do place-based learning can help you move forward when you encounter challenges.

- Although there is no such thing as an ideal place-based schedule, there are factors and considerations that create space to do the practice more in depth. Studying the tools and examples shared in this chapter will guide you to do what you can to bring the power of place-based learning to your campus.

- Creating a story gathering and storytelling culture builds trust and relationships and informs others about your school's place-based learning journey. You can begin this process using writing prompts during school meetings and in your classrooms, to capture your students' stories and those of your community partners.

- Examining where our realm of influence and control lie can give us the insight and will to overcome common obstacles when implementing place-based learning.

- Look back on the essential question for this chapter: *What internal and external work is necessary to create a fertile landscape for place-based learning to grow?* What have you discovered about the work to be done? What mindset shifts have you made or will you make as a result of this exploration?

- Look back on the realms activity you completed (page 229). Are there adjustments you need to make based on what you have learned or actions you have taken? How will you hold the commitments you have set? What additional commitment might you make?

- What bridges did you build to alleviate the stress of common barriers to place-based learning implementation? What barriers remain? How do you view them?

- How might you promote a story gathering and storytelling culture in your classroom, within your school, and with your community partners?

- What writing prompts might you use to capture your students' experiences during a place-based learning journey?

Journey Log

Journey Log

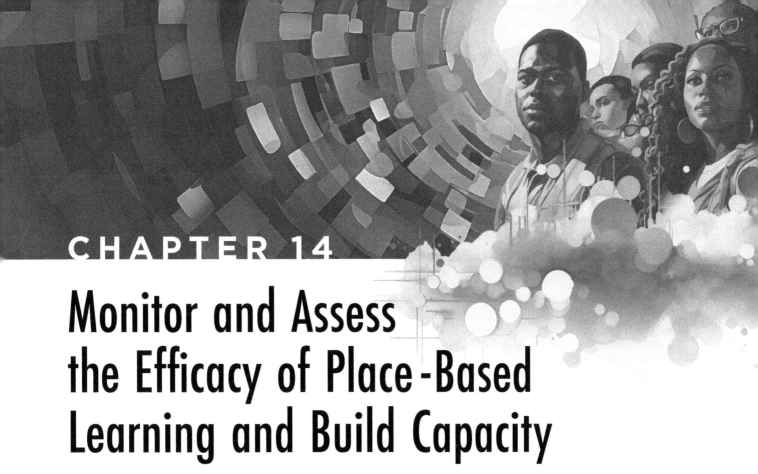

CHAPTER 14

Monitor and Assess the Efficacy of Place-Based Learning and Build Capacity

To succeed in life, you must build the CAPACITY to go through failure and the RESISTANCE from allowing that failure go through you.

— AWOLUMATE SAMUEL

ESSENTIAL QUESTION: Does your organization reflect what you believe about teaching and learning? How does this impact learning?

When it comes to place-based learning, it's important to consider not just what is taught, but also how it is taught. One aspect of this is the alignment between a classroom's values and its practices. So, ask yourself, "Does my school (leaders) or classroom (teachers) reflect what I believe? And how does this impact learning?"

In this chapter, we will explore these questions and the importance of assessing the effectiveness of educational practices that aim to foster place-based learning and build capacity. This chapter emphasizes the importance of sustaining place-based learning by fostering a culture that supports ongoing teacher professional development, integrating local knowledge, and scaling the approach across the curriculum. Leaders play a critical role in embodying place-based learning principles within the community and modeling inquiry-based and collaborative learning. Their multifaceted responsibilities include setting the vision, providing resources, and fostering continuous improvement. We discuss how the intersection between teacher and leader responsibilities occurs in collaborative planning and shared professional development, ensuring a cohesive and sustainable implementation of place-based learning in educational settings. The chapter offers a chance to think further about its content through the Conclusion and Key Takeaways and Reflection Questions sections. The chapter concludes with the Journey Log for writing down your thoughts and ideas.

What Does It Mean to Monitor and Assess the Efficacy of Place-Based Learning and to Build Capacity?

Instructional leaders—both in the classroom and in the main office—are essential in establishing effective monitoring and assessment mechanisms for place-based learning within the local context, ensuring alignment with learning goals. Monitoring and assessing the efficacy of place-based learning involves regularly evaluating student engagement, project outcomes, and the overall impact within the local context. This process ensures alignment with educational goals and allows for data-informed adjustments to instructional strategies. Building capacity in place-based learning requires fostering a culture of continuous professional development, integrating local knowledge, and scaling the approach to sustain its effectiveness across various grades and subjects.

How Do I Monitor and Assess the Efficacy of Place-Based Learning and Build Capacity?

To monitor and assess the efficacy of place-based learning and build capacity, consider taking the following actions.

- **Assess readiness and potential with a skill-will chart:** Gauge and customize individual support for teachers with a skill-will chart to best prepare to meet the needs of the adult learners who are embarking on this new methodology.
- **Use reflection and assessment tools to build capacity:** See how one organization co-created, scaffolds, and maximizes teacher capacity with a reflection and assessment tool.
- **Co-create an assessment and monitoring tool:** Encourage risk taking and vulnerability in teachers by using a process to design a place-based assessment tool in partnership.
- **Measure what matters: the student experience:** Learn more about alternative measurements of student growth and success that more accurately reflect the learning that is happening on a place-based campus.

Assess Readiness and Potential With a Skill-Will Chart

A *skill-will chart* is a tool for assessing an individual's ability (skill) and motivation (will) to complete a task or activity. In the context of monitoring and assessing the efficacy of place-based learning and building the capacity of teachers in the place-based learning classroom, a skill-will chart is a useful tool for assessing the readiness and potential of educators to implement place-based learning experiences effectively. *Skill*, in this context, refers to a teacher's ability to effectively apply their knowledge and expertise to facilitate learning and support student growth. *Will* refers to a teacher's motivation and drive to continuously improve their teaching and support their students' learning.

The skill-will chart is a simple two-axis chart that plots an individual's willingness to engage in an activity against their proficiency or skill level in that activity. Those who have high levels of both will likely excel in the activity, while those who have low levels of both may struggle. However, individuals who have high levels of will but low levels of skill may be motivated to learn and improve, while those who have high levels of skill but low levels of will may require additional motivation or incentives.

To define and align how we rank teachers and place them on a chart, we need to establish clear criteria for assessing both skill and will. Leaders can share these with teachers in the form of clearly communicated expectations and allowing teachers to self-assess and express the areas in which they would like to grow. This can include factors such as student outcomes, classroom observations, professional development participation, and feedback from colleagues, students, and parents. It's important to involve all stakeholders in the calibration process to ensure that assessments are fair, objective, and consistent. Additionally, ongoing professional development and support can help teachers improve both their skill and will and achieve greater success in the classroom. Figure 14.1 gives an example of a skill-will chart.

By identifying areas where teachers may require additional support or training, educators can take steps to improve their capacity and develop the skills needed to effectively teach in a place-based learning environment. Moreover, it can help in identifying those who are enthusiastic about the approach but require further skills development. Overall, the use of a skill-will chart, as depicted in figure 14.2, can assist in the ongoing assessment and refinement of place-based learning experiences, leading to greater effectiveness in achieving learning outcomes. Based on which quadrant of the skill-will chart that teachers land in, there are specific moves that leaders can take to provide differentiated support to the teachers.

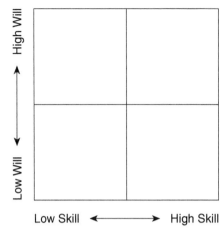

FIGURE 14.1: Blank skill-will chart.

*Visit **go.SolutionTree.com/instruction** for a free reproducible version of this figure.*

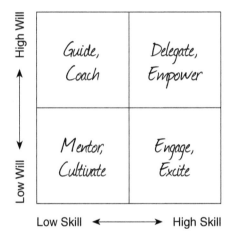

FIGURE 14.2: Skill-will chart with differentiated support.

- High-will, low-skill teachers receive more guidance and coaching.
- Low-will, low-skill teachers receive mentorship and cultivation of relevant skills as defined in the ranking criteria and expectations.
- High-will, high-skill teachers are delegated responsibilities that may help teachers in the three other quadrants, empowering them to grow and building capacity for place-based learning leadership.
- Low-will, high-skill teachers are engaged and excited intentionally by leadership.

Overall, the goal is to provide intentional support that moves teachers gradually. Ideally, educators will revisit this chart frequently to mark progress, with the goal of moving a critical mass of teachers to becoming empowered, high-will, high-skill place-based learning teachers.

Use Reflection and Assessment Tools to Build Capacity

Using a tool to self-assess and peer assess and giving feedback for growth early on in the process of building capacity for place-based learning are integral to short-term growth and long-term sustainability. One organization, the Technology Access Foundation (TAF), came to this realization when they took their school transformation model, STEMbyTAF, to schools beyond the two academies they co-created and manage with local districts. As their network and reach grew, it was imperative that the coaches working with schools making the shift to place-based learning had a way to reflect and assess their growth, individually and collectively goal-set, and measure progress over time.

Erin, who had taught at TAF's flagship academy and later became a coach of coaches, sat down at the table with the school's executive director of education and the director of school transformation and created a draft of that crucial reflection and assessment tool. What made it possible to even begin the task was TAF's direct and lived pledge, which is to:

> set high expectations of all our students, and through our STEMbyTAF model, students receive the tools, resources, supportive network, and 21st-century STEM education to achieve academic success. Even more, our model eliminates race-based and socioeconomic disparity so all students can thrive in anti-racist classrooms led by educators who reflect, value, and center the learning around their identities and cultures. (www.techaccess.org)

TAF knows who they serve, who they are, and where they are going. Clarity of mission is important in ensuring efficacy and sustainability, and in expanding place-based learning work. Once there is clarity of mission, we prompt you to follow TAF's example and name the attributes you want to see in teachers and instructional leaders, giving consideration to what a person in that role would demonstrate at the highest level, acknowledging it might take extensive time, and naming the ways your school will support people in getting there. What is the investment your school is willing to make to move everyone forward together in a collaborative way?

When the reflection and assessment tool is built (hopefully co-created with teachers and instructional leaders, which we'll talk more about later in this chapter, page 255) the impulse is to use it to evaluate, often in a top-down fashion. Fight the impulse. Building capacity is as much about building trust as it is about building skill. Scaffold use of the tool much as you would with students in the classroom. Begin with a self-assessment after a place-based learning experience, after a coaching cycle, or at the end of a quarter or semester. Ask the user to identify strengths and set goals.

The next time you use the tool, self-check progress on the goals and share with one supportive colleague. In the interim, colleagues can conduct professional observations (classroom or coaching) and give feedback, using the tool as the foundation. This cycle of self- and peer assessment should continue until everyone involved in the process agrees that a more formal assessment would be of benefit.

Inspect the following examples of a coach in the TAF network using the STEMbyTAF Transformational Coach Rubric to reflect and set goals for two criteria—equity and interdisciplinary project-based learning—and their corresponding indicators. Figure 14.3 shows the criteria for equity, and figure 14.4 (page 254) depicts the criteria for interdisciplinary project-based learning. A description of the levels of performance is provided after the sample. After you study the tool, begin to think about what a vision-aligned assessment tool bent toward capacity building would look like for your school. How would you begin the design process? How could it be inclusive of all users? How could it be employed? How could instructional leaders, coaches, and lead teachers use the tool, or how could it be used in a PLC setting? What information would it give you that traditional means of evaluation cannot?

Equity in Education	DEVELOPING	PROFICIENT	EXEMPLARY	Evidence
(1) Advocates for equitable academic, civic, and social-emotional outcomes to eliminate race-based disparity	X			**Evidence of growth**
(2) Recognizes and actively seeks to disrupt their own implicit biases		X		• Built a lot of great relationships and haven't had as big of an issue with compassionate unattachment as I thought.
(3) Practices self-reflection in service of professional growth, evidenced both verbally and in written form			X	• Have built strong relationships with teacher groups by listening, supporting ideas, and modeling positive relationships.
(4) Practices active and focused listening		X		• Compiled equity and culture-building resources and professional development; participated in a racial justice professional development.
(5) Builds trusting relationships with teachers (to enable discussion, reflection, and inquiry around teaching practices)		X		**Ideas for future**
(6) Encourages reflective dialogue by asking open-ended questions, and using problem and paraphrasing techniques		X		• I want to focus on building professional development and coaching systems directly connected to equitable practices and disrupting biases that inhibit learning for students.
(7) Practices compassionate unattachment; works for the good of the group, making sure to meet needs without getting caught up in difficult emotions and group dynamics	X			• I want to work to build cultures where it is the expectation that equitable practices are sought and used, not fought against.
(8) Exhibits a persistent focus on teacher and student learning outcomes by co-developing, aligning, and monitoring an equity-driven assessment system	X			• I hope that our schools and teachers can participate in race-based equity training in order to take steps to dismantle the iniquities that occur in our schools, in our classrooms, and within ourselves.
(9) Works with students to model for teachers what practices look like, using the role of warm demander (Bondy & Ross, 2008), while building relationships and trust		X		**Support needed**
(10) Engages all adults in change efforts that leverage assets and considers challenges in schools and communities		X		• What am I not foreseeing, and how can I get an idea of that and prepare?
				• Learn more about building cultures with adults where growth and improvement are the value (not isolation and independence).

Source: Adapted from Technology Access Foundation, 2020. Used with permission.

FIGURE 14.3: Equity in education example of STEMbyTAF Transformational Coach Rubric.

Interdisciplinary Project-Based Learning	DEVELOPING	PROFICIENT	EXEMPLARY	Evidence
(1) Speaks to impact of project-based learning on diverse learners and historically underserved learners		X		**Evidence of growth** • Release and support times. Teachers reaching out for strategies. • In a supportive role, I've helped push projects in project-based learning, and through generative work I've compiled project-based learning resources and strategies, along with research that has furthered my thinking. • Interdisciplinary project-based learning was new to me this year! I definitely grew in problem solving with teachers and in resource creation and gathering. • I have grown in listening to teachers and supporting their ideas. • Project-based learning release days have given a place for teachers to plan better projects and share ideas.
(2) Speaks with authority and accuracy about STEMbyTAF's vision for project-based learning, according to the *STEMbyTAF PBL Practitioners Rubric*	X			
(3) Supports teachers in their implementation of STEMbyTAF project-based learning		X		
(4) Assists teachers in analyzing student data and designing differentiated supports through the project design and implementation process	X			
(5) Works with teachers to co-create and solve solutions to challenges of project-based learning practice		X		**Ideas for future** • Buy-in and explicit modeling; transparency in our tools for assessment • Integrating equity within our project-based learning framework • Breaking down the project-based learning component for teachers so they are re-familiarized with each piece
(6) Actively utilizes literature, research, and knowledge of current educational reform when working with teachers		X		
(7) Continually collects and updates comprehensive wealth of practical project-based learning resources and strategies			X	**Support needed** • Moving teachers along the practitioner's rubric collaboratively • More support and ideas around which pieces to prioritize with "new to project-based learning" teachers

Levels of Performance	
Developing	The transformational coach is actively engaged in a cognitive process of unlearning, relearning, or learning to develop this competency.
Proficient	This competency is regularly demonstrated in the coaching practice.
Exemplary	In addition to the performance indicators above, this level indicates a high-leverage competency that leads to transformative work.

Source: Technology Access Foundation, 2020. Used with permission.

FIGURE 14.4: Interdisciplinary project-based learning example of STEMbyTAF Transformational Coach Rubric.

Co-Create an Assessment and Monitoring Tool

Co-creating an assessment and monitoring observation tool with teachers involves leaders collaborating with them to design an assessment instrument that captures their unique perspectives and experiences in the classroom. Shifting to place-based learning from a more traditional approach is vulnerable work, and teachers should be honored in their attempts. Co-creating the tool by which they will assess the practice is a means of respecting this attempt at making their work public, growing this new way of teaching and learning, and building the capacity of teachers across a campus. Here is an example of what this process could look like.

Let's say you are an instructional leader tasked with developing an observation tool to assess the effectiveness of a new place-based learning program in a school or district. Instead of creating the tool on your own, you decide to co-create the tool with a group of teachers who will be implementing the place-based learning program and design principles. Take the following steps.

1. **Invite** the teachers to a meeting where you explain the purpose and goals of the observation tool. During this meeting, you could also provide an overview of the place-based learning program, the place-based learning design principles, and the program's expected outcomes.

2. Collaboratively **brainstorm** assessment questions that align with the program goals, mission, and vision. Ask the teachers to share their thoughts on what should be included in the tool and why. Sample questions might include:

    a. To what extent has our place-based learning program increased students' understanding of local history, culture, and natural resources?

    b. In what ways has our place-based learning program supported students' development of 21st century skills, such as critical thinking, problem solving, and collaboration?

    c. How has our place-based learning program contributed to students' sense of community engagement and social responsibility?

3. **Create** a draft observation tool based on the questions and feedback from the brainstorming session. Share the draft tool with the teachers and ask for their input and suggestions for improvement.

4. **Revise** the tool based on the feedback and input of the teachers, ensuring that it reflects their perspectives and experiences in the classroom.

5. **Pilot test** the observation tool with a small group of teachers to gather feedback on its effectiveness. Use this feedback to further refine the tool until it meets the needs of the teachers and accurately captures the program's impact.

By involving teachers in the co-creation of an observation tool, you can ensure that the tool is effective in assessing the place-based learning experience's impact and that it reflects the experiences and perspectives of those who are implementing the program in the classroom. Empowering teachers through agency and co-creation gives them a sense of ownership over their work by involving them in the decision-making process. This approach recognizes the expertise and unique perspectives of teachers and allows them to contribute to the development of policies, practices, and curriculum.

Sharing power and creating positive interdependence through co-creation can lead to greater teacher satisfaction and engagement, as well as improved student outcomes. When teachers feel valued and involved, they are more likely to take ownership of their work and feel invested in the success of their students. This can also lead to greater collaboration and a sense of community among teachers as they work together to develop innovative solutions and share best practices.

By fostering agency and co-creation among teachers, educational institutions can create a more dynamic and responsive learning environment that is better suited to the needs of students and teachers alike. This approach can lead to greater innovation, collaboration, and engagement, ultimately resulting in improved outcomes for all involved.

Measure What Matters: The Student Experience

A reflection and assessment measure for adult learners in instructional leadership and teacher practice is a compass, pointing us toward an objective direction set from the vision of a school. Measuring the student experience is a barometer, gauging the atmosphere and forecasting the future of an endeavor like place-based learning. These data are a force for questioning everything we adults think we know about the way students move through our educational spaces and reside in our classrooms. If practitioner's rounds are taking place, then conducting the student experience triad gives recurring feedback on the student experience related to a single project. But what about a whole-school shift to place-based learning? How can one measure a change of that size?

Since the rise of high-stakes testing in the 1990s, schools that do things differently—whether they are project based, experiential, or somehow considered alternative—have been forced to use measurement and assessment tools built for traditional, comprehensive schools, and they are judged (harshly) by those results. Marked with a failing label, punished with loss of funding, taken over by state departments of education, or, in the case of charter schools, facing lost authorization, they are punished in ways that hurt students and families who have often been underserved and, in more than a few cases, traumatized by the traditional school system.

Leaders in schools engaged in change began to ask, "If the measurements used to assess and punish places that are trying to do things differently for students who have yet to experience success are not the right measurements (or shouldn't be the only measurements), is it possible to design an alternative that is more representative of the knowledge, skills, and dispositions students are learning?" One such tool was born out of this need, and various others have come since.

The *Hope Survey*, a diagnostic tool developed by Ron J. Newell and Mark J. Van Ryzin (2007), was at its inception meant to supply qualitative data to the EdVisions network of self-directed PBL schools, whose flagship site, MNCS, was mentioned earlier in this book. Teachers in EdVisions schools knew that something special happened in their spaces. They knew they had grown a profound sense of community on their campuses; they knew they had changed lives and entire communities; they knew that hope abounded in their schools; and if there were only a way to measure it and show that growth over time in schools newer to the project-based learning methodology, they would have a counternarrative to the one told solely by test scores.

The Hope Survey, drawing on the hope theory developed by Rick Snyder and Shane Lopez in 2010 in the field of positive psychology, measures, according to Sam Chaltain (2013) of *Education Week*, "whether aspects of the school climate support students' development of intrinsic motivation. It's about improving schools to support student development of intrinsic motivation, and making that an important, valued outcome."

The Hope Survey asks students about the quality of their relationships, their level of engagement and autonomy, and their sense of efficacy and how it connects to their academic performance and their goal orientation. There are seventy-five questions (which are public domain) covering six categories, as shown in table 14.1.

TABLE 14.1: Six Categories of the Hope Survey

Autonomy	Opportunity for self-management and choice
Belongingness	A measure of the depth and quality of my interpersonal relationships
Goal Orientation	The reasons behind my efforts to achieve
Engagement	My behavior and attitudes in school
Individual Hope	How I feel about my ability to make and reach goals in order to boost my confidence as a learner
Efficacy	The power I have to achieve results, alone or with a group

The survey, simple in its design, gives students a novel way to share their experience of school with adults who are ready to listen and respond by making tangible changes to school culture. Getting at the root cause of student underperformance takes trust, and a means for students to share their experience of school. According to Talent Enthusiasts (2021), "The Hope Survey results help teachers and leaders focus on why students may or may not be achieving so they can create environments for students and teachers to thrive. It is the missing half of the story." The results contribute balance to a school's overall data portfolio, and they're not just handed over; recommendations are made for actionable interventions and improvements that will raise engagement, raise hope, and ultimately raise achievement. Talent Enthusiasts (thetalententhusiasts.com) have been administering the Hope Survey in EdVisions schools for over a decade. As you move into systemic place-based learning, considering an alternative assessment tool like the Hope Survey can open up pathways to tell your school's story with student narratives at the center.

So what about the rest of the data portfolio for schools moving to place-based learning? Portfolios of student work are a common accompaniment, as are exhibitions where students showcase their process and learning to the community at large, getting feedback or as a means of celebration. Alternatives to high-stakes testing have also become more commonplace, forced into the mainstream in part due to the necessity to shift to online learning during the COVID-19 pandemic. Valerie Shute, a professor of education at Florida State University, coined the term *stealth assessment* to describe how companies like Khan Academy and SplashLearn record data every time a student answers a question in their system. In describing Shute's conception of stealth assessment, Open Colleges (2015) writes:

> The companies that develop this software argue that it presents the opportunity to eliminate the time, cost and anxiety of "stop and test" in favor of passively collecting data on students' knowledge over a semester, year or entire school career.

This adaptive testing, requiring no additional work on the teacher's part, means less formal assessment for students, fewer days lost to testing all students in the same content at the same time, and less test anxiety (because unfamiliar content need not be tested). As Anya Kamenetz (2015b) writes, "Stealth assessment doesn't just show which skills a student has mastered at a given moment. The pattern of answers potentially offers insights into how quickly students learn, how diligent they are and other big-picture factors." This manner of data collection moves at a pace agreed on by the teacher and student, and is only used to formatively assess, removing any concerns about transparency.

There are also a host of on-demand assessments (such as PowerSchool and IXL) that, when teachers are given the autonomy to administer them in tandem with content knowledge and skills gained through projects, can be a means of widening the view of student needs and learning:

> Born out of the competency-based model of assessment, on-demand assessments offer more flexible, on-demand opportunities for students to take tests. Instead of requiring every student to take the same test at the same time throughout the year, this alternative lets certain students take assessments when they are ready, and provides opportunities for them to revisit material that they have not mastered. (Open Colleges, 2015)

When measuring the student experience, there should be a recognition that their daily lives, from the time they enter the school building until the end of the school day, are as unique, expansive, and relational as they are, and can't be fully encompassed with any one tool. Place-based learning, blurring the artificial boundaries of siloed disciplines and units of instruction, of schools and community, makes traditional achievement tests even less reliable. Which tools will you use in your classroom and school to understand the atmosphere of learning, to be a barometer for the student experience?

What Is School Reform Through Place-Based Learning?

School reform refers to intentional efforts to improve the quality and effectiveness of education. It can involve a variety of strategies, such as changes to curriculum, teacher training, assessment methods, and school organization. The goal of school reform is to create a more equitable and responsive educational system that meets the needs of all students.

Place-based learning supports school reform by providing a framework for educational innovation grounded in the local context. By emphasizing the importance of connecting students with their environment and community, place-based learning encourages educators to tailor the curriculum to the unique needs and interests of their students. This can help create a more engaging and relevant educational experience, which can improve student outcomes and increase motivation to learn.

Moreover, place-based learning can help to promote educational equity by recognizing the diverse cultural and social contexts of students. By incorporating local history, culture, and ecology into the curriculum, place-based learning can help to create a more inclusive and culturally responsive educational environment. This approach can be particularly beneficial for students from historically marginalized communities, who may have been underserved by traditional educational models.

In addition, place-based learning can also foster greater community engagement and support for education. By connecting students with their local environment and community, this approach can help to build stronger relationships between schools and community organizations. This can lead to increased resources and support for education, as well as opportunities for students to engage in service learning and civic action.

Overall, place-based learning provides a powerful tool for school reform by promoting innovation, equity, and community engagement. By empowering educators to create a more relevant and impactful educational experience, this approach can help to improve student outcomes and create a more responsive and effective educational system.

Conclusion

Project five years into the future and think about what you want your students, your school, and your community to gain from place-based learning. Maybe words like *agency, empowerment,* and *compassion* come to mind. Now think about how you will know if you've succeeded in your endeavor. What are the tools by which you measure accomplishment? How will you know if you and your colleagues were ready for the change in the first place?

The examples and elaborations in this chapter helped you think preemptively about these questions, sharing a skill-will chart as a useful tool for assessing the readiness and potential of educators to implement place-based learning activities effectively. This chapter further helped you match your vision, what you want to measure, and the equitable means to design assessment tools to ensure that in five years you have the evidence to demonstrate lasting change. Finally, this chapter situated place-based learning within the larger school reform movement by providing a framework for educational innovation grounded in the local context, setting you up to have a panoramic view of the shift you are making and the direction you are going.

Key Takeaways and Reflection Questions

Consider this chapter's key takeaways and reflect on the following questions as you work to monitor and assess the efficacy of place-based learning and build capacity. Use the Journey Log to further reflect, brainstorm, jot down ideas, make observations, or plan.

- ◆ In place-based learning, examining the alignment between a classroom's values and its practices is a vital step in the process of sustaining the practice.
- ◆ Take your school's mission and vision and name the attributes you want to see in teachers and instructional leaders and name the ways your school will support people in getting there. Then build a vision-aligned assessment tool to support capacity building, like the example from TAF (pages 253 and 254).
- ◆ Empowering teachers through agency and co-creation of an observation and assessment tool gives them a sense of ownership over their work and a stake in the decision-making process.
- ◆ Using an alternative measurement for students that is more representative of their knowledge, skills, and dispositions gives a school a holistic data map that is inclusive of place-based learning. One such tool, the Hope Survey, was born out of this need, and various others have come since.

- ◆ What is the current alignment between your classroom's values and practices? Create a list of both and then see how many matches there are. What remains unmatched? What function does it serve? What might need to change?
- ◆ This chapter provided an overview of several tools, including the skill-will chart, the STEMbyTAF Transformational Coach Rubric, the process for co-creating an assessment and observation tool, and the Hope Survey. How did these tools or other examples you saw in this chapter move you to think about building capacity and sustaining place-based learning?

- Which tools will you use in your classroom and school to understand the atmosphere of learning?
- How have you intensified your understanding of how place-based learning is situated in the larger context of school reform? What actions does it inspire you to take?

Journey Log

Epilogue

*Land is life, and the connection between land and
our culture is vital to our survival.*
—PALAUAN PROVERB

As you come to the end of this book on place-based learning, liberatory education, and equity, we hope you are left with a profound understanding of the importance of connectedness in education. We have explored the ways in which learning can be grounded in the unique experiences and perspectives of communities, and we have seen how this can lead to a more equitable and liberatory education for all students. But the work is not done. As educators, we must take action to build on this understanding and create meaningful change in our schools and communities. We must commit to centering the voices and experiences of our students and their families, and to creating learning environments that are inclusive, culturally responsive, and relevant to the world in which our students live.

We must also recognize that this work cannot be done in isolation. We must work together as educators, families, and community members to create a more just and equitable society. We must engage in ongoing reflection and learning and be willing to challenge our own biases and assumptions. This call to action is not easy, and it will require us to take risks, to be vulnerable, and to be committed to the long-term work of creating a more just and equitable world. But we believe that this work is worth it. We believe that all students deserve a high-quality education that is grounded in their own unique experiences and that prepares each of them for the world in which they live.

Indeed, this work is a journey. It is a path that we must walk together, learning and growing along the way. As we embark on this journey, we must recognize that change will not be a quick fix or a one-time event, but rather will be a process of ongoing learning and reflection.

This book serves as a guide on that journey toward place-based learning, liberatory education, and equity. It provides a framework for understanding the importance of connectedness in education and offers practical strategies for implementing this approach in your own classrooms and schools. But this book is not the destination—it is a tool to use along the path. As you engage in this work, you will encounter challenges and obstacles, and you must be willing to adapt and adjust your approach as needed.

Through this journey, you will experience moments of joy and celebration as you see the positive impact of your work on your students and in your communities. And you will build connections with others who share your commitment.

Let us embrace this journey with open hearts and minds, knowing that it will not be easy, but that it is necessary. Let us continue to learn, to grow, and to work together to create a better future for our students and our communities. Let us commit to the ongoing work of place-based learning, liberatory education, and equity, and let us do so with courage, compassion, and a deep sense of connection to one another and to the world around us.

Appendix

In this appendix you will find blank reproducible versions of each part of the place-based learning project-planning tool—the community asset map and liberatory learning and assessment pathways. Please use these tools to conceptualize, develop, and, when needed, chart new directions in your place-based learning journey.

Community Asset Map

Who my students are

Ways of knowing, issues, and infinite capacities to connect to the community		
Ways of knowing:	**Issues:**	**Infinite capacities:**

Connecting academic, justice, and action standards	
Academic anchor standards:	**Justice anchor standards:** **Action anchor standards:**

Place-Based Learning © 2024 Solution Tree Press • SolutionTree.com • Visit **go.SolutionTree.com/instruction** to download this free reproducible.

Who, how, and what		
Who will be involved? (Primary community partners)	**How are they an asset? How will they be involved? How will we connect and reciprocate?**	**What learning will happen as a result of their involvement?**
Potential community product, service, or call to action		

Place-Based Learning © 2024 Solution Tree Press • SolutionTree.com • Visit **go.SolutionTree.com/instruction** to download this free reproducible.

Liberatory Learning and Assessment Pathways

Project title:			Grade:	Estimated duration:

Essential question:

Project sketch:

Community product or products *Presentations, performances, products, or services*	Ways of knowing (in student-friendly language) *Content and skills needed by students to successfully complete products*	Journey checks and formative assessments *To check for learning and ensure students are on track*	Culturally embedded teaching strategies for all learners *Provided by teacher, other students, experts; includes scaffolds, materials, lessons aligned to learning outcomes, and formative assessments*
			☐ **Incorporating Cultural and Historical Significance:** ☐ **Participatory Design:**
			☐ **Emphasizing the Power of Storytelling:** ☐ **Analyzing the Impact of Racism:**

Place-Based Learning © 2024 Solution Tree Press • SolutionTree.com • Visit **go.SolutionTree.com/instruction** to download this free reproducible.

Community product or products	Ways of knowing (in student-friendly language)	Journey checks and formative assessments	Culturally embedded teaching strategies for all learners
			☐ **Understanding the City Council's Cultural Values:** ☐ **Researching Community Needs:**
			☐ **Challenge the Stereotypes:** ☐ **Provide Access and Opportunity:**

Place-Based Learning © 2024 Solution Tree Press • SolutionTree.com • Visit **go.SolutionTree.com/instruction** to download this free reproducible.

Using the Quality Indicators

Quality Indicators	
Design Principle	**Quality Indicator**
Elevate ways of knowing	
Path to higher quality (How do I get there?)	
Build authentic community partnerships	
Path to higher quality (How do I get there?)	
Embed culture in teaching and learning	
Path to higher quality (How do I get there?)	

Place-Based Learning © 2024 Solution Tree Press • SolutionTree.com • Visit **go.SolutionTree.com/instruction** to download this free reproducible.

Design Principle	Quality Indicator
Facilitate purpose-driven Inquiry	
Path to higher quality (How do I get there?)	
Empower student ownership	
Path to higher quality (How do I get there?)	
Co-create an authentic community product	
Path to higher quality (How do I get there?)	

Place-Based Learning © 2024 Solution Tree Press • SolutionTree.com • Visit **go.SolutionTree.com/instruction** to download this free reproducible.

Design Principle	Quality Indicator
Engage in feedback, revision, and reflection	
Path to higher quality (How do I get there?)	

Place-Based Learning © 2024 Solution Tree Press • SolutionTree.com • Visit **go.SolutionTree.com/instruction** to download this free reproducible.

References and Resources

A:shiwi A:wan Museum and Heritage Center. (n.d.). *Collaborations: A:shiwi map art.* Accessed at http://www.ashiwi-museum.org/collaborations/ on July 26, 2023.

Adams, C. (2021, December 2). *Georgia destroyed a Black neighborhood. Now former residents want justice.* NBC News. Accessed at https://www.nbcnews.com/news/georgia-destroyed-black-neighborhood-now-former-residents-want-justice-rcna7148 on July 26, 2023.

Adichie, C. N. (2009, July). *The danger of a single story.* TEDGlobal. Accessed at https://www.ted.com/talks/chimamanda_ngozi_adichie_the_danger_of_a_single_story?language=en on January 30, 2024.

Adobe. (n.d.). *How Adobe continues to inspire great performance and support career growth.* Accessed at https://www.adobe.com/check-in.html on December 8, 2022.

Aguilar, E. (2018). *Onward: Cultivating emotional resilience in educators.* San Francisco: Jossey-Bass.

Alabama Youth Justice Alliance & Southern Poverty Law Center. (n.d.). *Unlocking your community's hidden strengths: A guidebook to community asset-mapping.* Accessed at https://www.splcenter.org/sites/default/files/d6_legacy_files/downloads/publication/communityassetmapping2.pdf on July 28, 2023.

Alaska Department of Education & Early Development. (n.d.). *Cultural.* Accessed at https://education.alaska.gov/standards/cultural on July 26, 2023.

Alderman, D. H., & Inwood, J. F. J. (2021, February 23). *How Black cartographers put racism on the map of America.* The Conversation. Accessed at https://theconversation.com/how-black-cartographers-put-racism-on-the-map-of-america-155081 on July 26, 2023.

Alderman, D. H., Inwood, J. F. J., & Bottone, E. (2021). The mapping behind the movement: On recovering the critical cartographies of the African American Freedom Struggle. *Geoforum, 120,* 67–78. Accessed at https://doi.org/10.1016/j.geoforum.2021.01.022 on April 22, 2024.

American Society for Quality. (n.d.). *Five whys and five hows. Learn About Quality* [blog post]. Accessed at https://asq.org/quality-resources/five-whys on May 8, 2024.

Amplify Africa. (n.d.). *The rich history of braids.* Accessed at https://www.amplifyafrica.org/the-rich-history-of-braids/ on July 26, 2023.

Anderson, S. (2018, July 10). *Place-based education: Think globally, teach locally.* Education Week. Accessed at https://www.edweek.org/teaching-learning/opinion-place-based-education-think-globally-teach-locally/2018/07 on July 27, 2023.

Ash, S. L., & Clayton, P. H. (2009). Generating, deepening, and documenting learning: The power of critical reflection in applied learning. *Journal of Applied Learning in Higher Education, 1*(1), 25–48. Accessed at https://files.eric.ed.gov/fulltext/EJ1188550.pdf on July 26, 2023.

Atkins, R., & Oglesby, A. (2019). *Interrupting racism: Equity and social justice in school counseling.* New York: Routledge.

Baron, D. (n.d.). *Realms of concern and influence.* Bloomington, IN: National Schools Reform Faculty. Accessed at https://www.nsrfharmony.org/wp-content/uploads/2017/10/realms_concern_influence_0.pdf on July 27, 2023.

Bean, H. (2022). An Indigenous sense of place. *University of Waterloo Magazine.* Accessed at https://uwaterloo.ca/magazine/fall-2022/feature/indigenous-sense-place on July 27, 2023.

Becton-Consuegra, D. (2019, May 20). *What you can do to advance culturally responsive PBL practice* [Blog post]. Accessed at https://www.pblworks.org/blog/what-you-can-do-advance-culturally-responsive-pbl-practice on July 27, 2023.

Becton-Consuegra, D. (2020, January 1). *Getting clearer: HQPBL as an equity imperative.* Getting Smart. Accessed at https://www.gettingsmart.com/2020/01/01/getting-clearer-hqpbl-as-an-equity-imperative/ on July 27, 2023.

Benner, D. (2021, October 7). *Six strategies for building empathy in the classroom* [Blog post]. Accessed at https://blog.tcea.org/what-empathy-how-practice-empathy-classroom/ on July 27, 2023.

Berger, R. (2003). *An ethic of excellence: Building a culture of craftsmanship with students.* Portsmouth, NH: Heinemann.

Berger, R., Rugen, L., & Woodfin, L. (2014). *Leaders of their own learning: Transforming schools through student-engaged assessment.* San Francisco: Jossey-Bass.

Beriont, L. (2020, May 4). *Decolonizing evaluation* [Blog post]. Accessed at https://www.emergencecollective.org/post/decolonizing-evaluation on July 27, 2023.

Bombay, A., Matheson, K., & Anisman, H. (2014). The intergenerational effects of Indian Residential Schools: Implications for the concept of historical trauma. *Transcultural Psychiatry, 51*(3), 320–338.

Bondy, E., & Ross, D. E. (2008, September 1). *The teacher as warm demander.* ASCD. Accessed at https://www.ascd.org/el/articles/the-teacher-as-warm-demander on July 27, 2023.

Bottone, E. M. (2020). *The "Green Book" and a Black sense of movement: Black mobilities and motilities during the Jim Crow era* [Doctoral dissertation, University of Tennessee]. Tennessee Research and Creative Exchange. Accessed at https://trace.tennessee.edu/utk_graddiss/5814 on January 9, 2024.

Bowen, R. S. (2017). *Understanding by design.* Nashville, TN: Vanderbilt University Center for Teaching. Accessed at https://cft.vanderbilt.edu/guides-sub-pages/understanding-by-design/ on August 12, 2022.

Brockwell, G. (2022, November 10). La. voters keep "slavery" at Angola prison, once and still a plantation. *The Washington Post.* Accessed at https://www.washingtonpost.com/history/2022/11/10/angola-prison-louisiana-slave-labor/ on July 27, 2023.

Brown, C. (2021, February 23). *Equity and assessment.* Center for Professional Education of Teachers. Accessed at https://cpet.tc.columbia.edu/news-press/equity-and-assessment on July 27, 2023.

Butterfoss, J. K. (2021, November 2). *Equity-focused leadership: What does it look like in action?* New Leaders. Accessed at https://www.newleaders.org/blog/equity-focused-leadership-what-does-it-look-like-in-action on July 27, 2023.

Camhi, T., Chávez, J., & Ligori, C. (2020, November 28). Indigenous peoples, in Oregon and beyond, are decolonizing maps. *OPB News.* Accessed at https://www.opb.org/article/2020/11/28/indigenous-peoples-in-oregon-and-beyond-are-decolonizing-maps/ on July 27, 2023.

Cause IQ. (n.d.). *Village Earth.* Accessed at https://www.causeiq.com/organizations/village-earth,841243878/ on July 31, 2023.

Cavey, T. (2022, January 30). Why schools must tell their stories. *Teachers on Fire Magazine.* Accessed at https://medium.com/teachers-on-fire/why-schools-must-tell-their-stories-d51f04d392f8 on July 27, 2023.

CBC News. (2021, February 9). *New locally-developed Black curriculum shifts focus from slavery to stories of kings and queens.* Accessed at https://www.cbc.ca/news/canada/kitchener-waterloo/guelph-black-heritage-society-lorraine-harris-curriculum-1.5906779 on July 27, 2023.

Center for Court Innovation. (2011, June). *Introduction to community asset mapping.* Center for Justice Innovation. Accessed at https://www.courtinnovation.org/publications/facilitating-community-asset-mapping-exercise on July 28, 2023.

Chaltain, S. (2013, December 16). *How to "bake" intrinsic motivation: A holiday recipe for your classroom or school.* Education Week. Accessed at https://www.edweek.org/education/opinion-how-to-bake-intrinsic-motivation-a-holiday-recipe-for-your-classroom-or-school/2013/12 on July 27, 2023.

Christoph, E. (n.d.) *The art of Harkness: Language around the table*. Accessed at https://www.exeter.edu/sites/default/files/documents/Revolution-The-Art-of-Harkness.pdf on May 8, 2024.

Clark, D. (2008, December). *Learning to make choices for the future: Connecting public lands, schools and communities through place-based learning and civic engagement*. Accessed at https://www.nps.gov/civic/resources/learning%20to%20Make%20Choices.pdf on July 27, 2023.

Costa, A., & Kallick, B. (2009). *Learning and leading with habits of mind: 16 characteristics for success*. Alexandria, VA: Association for Supervision and Curriculum Development.

Covey, S. (1989). *The 7 habits of highly effective people* (1st ed.). New York: Simon & Schuster.

Criser, R., & Knott, S. (2019). Decolonizing the curriculum. *Die Unterrichtspraxis, 52*(2), 151–160.

Curtis, P. (n.d.). *How does assessment in PBL classrooms differ from traditional classrooms?* New Tech Network. Accessed at https://helpcenter.newtechnetwork.org/hc/en-us/articles/360026690712-How-does-assessment-in-PBL-classrooms-differ-from-traditional-classrooms- on July 27, 2023.

Daily Good. (n.d.). *Counter mapping*. Accessed at https://www.dailygood.org/story/2052/counter-mapping-adam-loften-and-emmanuel-vaughan-lee/#:~:text=The%20Zuni%20maps%20are%20an,why%20this%20place%20is%20important on January 10, 2024.

The Daring English Teacher. (n.d.). *The danger of a single story activity for secondary ELA*. Accessed at https://thedaringenglishteacher.com/the-dangers-of-single-story-activity/ on July 27, 2023.

Deakin University Library. (n.d.). *Qualitative study design*. Accessed at https://deakin.libguides.com/qualitative-study-designs/narrative-inquiry on July 27, 2023.

DeGruy, J. (2017). *Post traumatic slave syndrome: America's legacy of enduring injury & healing*. Stone Mountain, GA: Joy DeGruy.

Delpit, L. (2013). *"Multiplication is for White people": Raising expectations for other people's children*. New York: The New Press.

Delpit, L. (Ed.). (2021). *Teaching when the world is on fire: Authentic classroom advice, from climate justice to Black Lives Matter*. New York: The New Press.

Demarest, A. B. (2015). *Place-based curriculum design: Exceeding standards through local investigations*. New York: Routledge.

Dose Team. (2017, March 6). *Music was the secret language of the Underground Railroad*. Medium. Accessed at https://medium.com/dose/music-was-the-secret-language-of-the-underground-railroad-e91b3981d21a on July 27, 2023.

Drake, R., & Oglesby, A. (2020). Humanity is not a thing: Disrupting White supremacy in K–12 social emotional learning. *Journal of Critical Thought and Praxis, 10*(1), 1–22. Accessed at https://doi.org/10.31274/jctp.11549 on April 25, 2024.

Education Northwest. (2016, April). *How Roosevelt High School is creating real writers*. Accessed at https://educationnorthwest.org/insights/how-roosevelt-high-school-creating-real-writers on July 27, 2023.

Educircles. (2019, October 23). *How to co-create rubrics with students*. Accessed at https://educircles.org/2019/10/23/how-to-co-create-rubrics-with-students-free-lesson-plan-handouts-slideshow/ on July 27, 2023.

Edutopia. (n.d.). *Top ten tips for assessing project-based learning*. Accessed at http://wylla.org/wp-content/uploads/2017/08/edutopia-10-tips-assessing-project-based-learning.pdf on July 27, 2023.

Edutopia. (2011, April 11). *Free resources and tools for replicating project-based learning*. Accessed at https://www.edutopia.org/stw-replicating-pbl-resources on August 12, 2022.

Eizadirad, A. (2022, June 5). *Ontario can close students' access and opportunity gaps with community-led projects*. Yahoo! News. Accessed at https://ca.news.yahoo.com/ontario-close-students-access-opportunity-122246366.html on July 27, 2023.

Elbaz, M. M. (2023). Place-based education: Community as a multidisciplinary learning environment. *Port Said Journal of Educational Research, 2*(1), 59–74.

EL Education. (n.d.). *Austin's butterfly: Building excellence in student work* [Video file]. Accessed at https://eleducation.org/resources/austins-butterfly on January 19, 2024.

Ellis, D., & Hughes, K. (2002, October). *Partnerships by design: Cultivating effective and meaningful school-family-community partnerships*. Portland, OR: Northwest Regional Educational Laboratory. Accessed https://educationnorthwest.org/sites/default/files/pbd.pdf on July 27, 2023.

Emdin, C. (2016). *For White folks who teach in the hood. . . and the rest of y'all too: Reality pedagogy and urban education*. Boston: Beacon Press.

Equal Justice Initiative. (n.d.). *Community Remembrance Project*. Accessed at https://eji.org/projects/community-remembrance-project/ on July 27, 2023.

Evans, C. (2021, September 9). *A culturally responsive classroom assessment framework: The intersections of equity, pedagogy, and sociocultural assessment*. Accessed at https://www.nciea.org/blog/a-culturally-responsive-classroom-assessment-framework/ on July 27, 2023.

Ferlazzo, L. (2020a, January 28). *Author interview with Dr. Gholdy Muhammad: "Cultivating genius"* [Blog post]. Accessed at https://www.edweek.org/teaching-learning/opinion-author-interview-with-dr-gholdy-muhammad-cultivating-genius/2020/01 on July 27, 2023.

Ferlazzo, L. (2020b, June 16). *Teaching that activates and leverages background knowledge is an equity issue* [Blog post]. Accessed at https://www.edweek.org/teaching-learning/opinion-teaching-that-activates-and-leverages-background-knowledge-is-an-equity-issue/2020/06 on July 27, 2023.

Fischer, F. (2020, November 2). *Leading liberated: Why liberation pedagogy is the heart and foundation of TAF's Network for Edwork*. Technology Access Foundation. Accessed at https://techaccess.org/leadingliberated/ on July 27, 2023.

Freitag, E., & Knight-Justice, N. (2020, December 2). *Rethinking Intervention. Instruction Partners*. Accessed at https://instructionpartners.org/2020/12/02/dr-gholnecsar-gholdy-muhammad/ on May 8, 2024.

Global Oneness Project. (n.d.). *Counter mapping*. Accessed at https://www.globalonenessproject.org/library/films/counter-mapping on January 9, 2024.

Goldsmith, M. (n.d.). *Try feedforward instead of feedback*. Accessed at https://marshallgoldsmith.com/articles/try-feedforward-instead-feedback/ on July 27, 2023.

Gonzalez, J. (2018a, December 2). *10 ways educators can take action in pursuit of equity* [Blog post]. Accessed at https://www.cultofpedagogy.com/10-equity/ on July 28, 2023.

Gonzalez, J. (2018b, January 21). *Moving from feedback to feedforward* [Blog post]. Accessed at https://www.cultofpedagogy.com/feedforward/ on July 28, 2023.

Goodreads. (n.d.). *Barack Obama quotes*. Accessed at https://www.goodreads.com/quotes/9609019-the-biggest-deficit-that-we-have-in-our-society-and on February 9, 2024.

Greenstein, L. (2021, September 7). *Equitable assessment*. Assessment Network. Accessed at https://www.assessmentnetwork.net/2021/09/equitable-assessment/ on July 28, 2023.

Greenwood, D. (2013). *A critical theory of place-conscious education*. In R. B. Stevenson, M. Brody, J. Dillon, & A. E.J. Wals (Eds.), *International handbook of research on environmental education* (pp. 93–100). New York: Routledge.

Gruenewald, D. A., & Smith, G. A. (Eds.). (2008). *Place-based education in the global age: Local diversity*. New York: Routledge.

Hammond, Z. (2020, April 1). The power of protocols for equity. *Educational Leadership*, *77*(7). Accessed at https://www.ascd.org/el/articles/the-power-of-protocols-for-equity on July 28, 2023.

Hammond, Z. (2021). Liberatory education: Integrating the science of learning and culturally responsive practice. *American Educator*, *45*(2), 4–11. Accessed at https://files.eric.ed.gov/fulltext/EJ1305167.pdf on July 28, 2023.

Hashem, D. (2017, October 24). *6 reasons to try a single-point rubric*. Edutopia. Accessed at https://www.edutopia.org/article/6-reasons-try-single-point-rubric/ on July 28, 2023.

Hawley Miles, K., Ferris, K., & Quist Green, G. (2017, May). *Designing schools that work: Organizing resources strategically for student success*. Watertown, MA: Education Resource Strategies. Accessed at https://www.erstrategies.org/cms/files/4004-designing-schools-that-work.pdf on July 28, 2023.

Henning, G. W., & Lundquist, A. E. (2018, August). *Moving towards socially just assessment*. Champaign, IL: National Institute for Learning Outcomes Assessment.

Henning, G. W., & Lundquist, A. E. (2020, June 8–19). *Using assessment as a tool for equity and inclusion* [Conference presentation]. Association for the Assessment of Learning in Higher Education Virtual Conference 2020. Accessed at https://aalhe.memberclicks.net/assets/Conference/Online2020/Proceedings_2020_Online_Conference/Lundquist_Henning_SJA_AALHE.pdf on July 28, 2023.

Hill, C. (n.d.). *equityXdesign 3.0: A working reprise*. 228 Accelerator. Accessed at https://static1.squarespace.com/static/5e84f10a4ce9cb4742f5e0d5/t/6345aa94e3a3986e5b6ddcdc/1665510038474/equityXdesign+3.0+-+Caroline+Hill.pdf on July 28, 2023.

The Historical Thinking Project. (n.d.). *Historical thinking concepts*. Accessed at https://historicalthinking.ca/historical-thinking-concepts on February 2, 2024.

hooks, b. (1995). *Killing rage: Ending racism*. New York: Henry Holt.

Houston, J. (1997). *The search for the beloved: Journeys in mythology and sacred psychology* (2nd ed.). New York: TarcherPerigee.

Howard, A. (2022). *Counter-mapping the material world of* The bone clocks: *A critical analysis through digital cartography* [Master's thesis, California State Polytechnic University, Humboldt]. Cal Poly Humboldt Theses. Accessed at https://digitalcommons.humboldt.edu/cgi/viewcontent.cgi?article=1631&context=etd on January 18, 2024.

Hoyt, S. (2016, August 26). *My wonder wall* [Blog post]. Accessed at https://sallyhoyt.blogspot.com/2016/08/my-wonder-wall.html on July 28, 2023.

Hughes, C. (2021, May 3). *Decolonising the curriculum*. Council of International Schools. Accessed at https://www.cois.org/about-cis/news/post/~board/perspectives-blog/post/decolonising-the-curriculum on July 31, 2023.

International Baccalaureate. (2023). The IB learner profile. Accessed at https://www.ibo.org/benefits/learner-profile/ on May 8, 2024.

Jacobs, R. (2020, October 26). *Decolonising assessment: Can we ever really assess for justice and equity?* [Speech transcript]. World Alliance for Arts Education Virtual Seminar 2020. Accessed at https://www.waae.online/uploads/1/2/9/2/129270960/waae_2020_rachael_jacobs.docx.pdf on July 28, 2023.

Judson, G. (2016, October 25). *Guidelines for assessment in place-based learning*. Getting Smart. Accessed at https://www.gettingsmart.com/2016/10/25/guidelines-for-assessment-of-place-based-learning/ on July 28, 2023.

Kamenetz, A. (2015a). *The test: Why our schools are obsessed with standardized testing—But you don't have to be*. New York: Public Affairs.

Kamenetz, A. (2015b, January 6). *What schools could use instead of standardized tests*. NPR. Accessed at https://www.npr.org/sections/ed/2015/01/06/371659141/what-schools-could-use-instead-of-standardized-tests on July 28, 2023.

Kamps, K. (2021, January 27). *Promoting a PBL mindset: The "dimmer switch" approach*. PBLWorks. Accessed at https://www.pblworks.org/blog/promoting-pbl-mindset-dimmer-switch-approach on July 28, 2023.

Karnovsky, S. A. (2020). *Learning the emotional rules of teaching: A Foucauldian analysis of ethical self-formation in pre-service teacher education* [Doctoral dissertation, Curtin University]. CU Doctoral Dissertations. Accessed at https://espace.curtin.edu.au/bitstream/handle/20.500.11937/81668/Karnovsky%20S%202020.pdf on January 18, 2024.

Kaul, M. (2019, June 4). *Keeping students at the center with culturally relevant performance assessments*. Next Generation Learning Challenges. Accessed at https://www.nextgenlearning.org/articles/keeping-students-at-the-center-with-culturally-relevant-performance-assessments on July 28, 2023.

Kelly, D., & Nicholson, A. (2022). Ancestral leadership: Place-based intergenerational leadership. *Leadership*, *18*(1), 140–161. https://doi.org/10.1177/17427150211024038

Kemp, S. M. (2017, November 17). The importance of school, community partnerships. *The Daily Journal*. Accessed at https://www.smdailyjournal.com/opinion/guest_perspectives/the-importance-of-school-community-partnerships/article_0320fcf4-cb3b-11e7-a8ee-83f57369e16c.html on July 28, 2023.

Klein, J. D. (2017). *The global education guidebook: Humanizing K-12 classrooms worldwide through equitable partnerships*. Bloomington, IN: Solution Tree Press.

Klein, J. D., & Ciotti, K. (2022). *The landscape model of learning: Designing student-centered experiences for cognitive and cultural inclusion*. Bloomington, IN: Solution Tree Press.

Kleinfeld, J. (1975). Effective teachers of Eskimo and Indian students. *School Review, 83*(2), 301–344.

Krikorian, M. (2022). *Higher education for the people: Critical contemplative methods of liberatory practice*. Charlotte, NC: Information Age.

Krishnan, A. (n.d.) *A system of stories: Weaving stories into organisations*. The Storytellers. Accessed at https://thestorytellers.com/a-system-of-stories/ on July 28, 2023.

LaFever, M. (2016). Switching from Bloom to the Medicine Wheel: Creating learning outcomes that support indigenous ways of knowing in post-secondary education. *Intercultural Education, 27*(5), 409–424.

Larmer, J. (2015, October 21). *Debunking 5 myths about project-based learning*. Edutopia. Accessed at https://www.edutopia.org/blog/debunking-five-pbl-myths-john-larmer on July 28, 2023.

Lathram, B. (2014). *The role of noncognitive skills for student success*. Providence, RI: Big Picture Learning. Accessed at https://books.apple.com/us/book/ the-role-of-noncognitive-skills-for-student-success/id904019800 on April 11, 2024.

Learning Forward Ontario. (2014). *The power of protocols*. Accessed at https://www.uen.org/literacyresources/downloads/Learning_Forward_Power_of_Protocols.pdf on July 28, 2023.

Leedy, B. (2019, May 7). *How to tell your school's stories: Learning how to turn your school's successes into engaging narratives that influence and engage*. School Webmasters. Accessed at https://www.schoolwebmasters.com/how-to-tell-your-schools-stories on July 28, 2023.

Liebenberg, L., Wall, D., Wood, M., & Hutt-MacLeod, D. (2019). Spaces & places: Understanding sense of belonging and cultural engagement among Indigenous youth. *International Journal of Qualitative Methods, 18*.

Lindsay Unified School District, Summit Public Schools, & Transcend, Inc. (2018, October). *An early inquiry into educator and leadership mindsets*. Accessed at https://transcendeducation.org/personalized-learning-tools/ on July 28, 2023.

Loften, A., & Vaughan-Lee, E. [Directors]. (2018). *Counter mapping*. Global Oneness Project. Accessed at https://www.globalonenessproject.org/library/films/counter-mapping on January 9, 2024.

Loria, R. (2018, March 26). A how-to guide for building school-community partnerships. *Education Week*. Accessed at https://www.edweek.org/leadership/opinion-a-how-to-guide-for-building-school-community-partnerships/2018/03 on July 28, 2023.

Love, B. L. (2019). *We want to do more than survive: Abolitionist teaching and the pursuit of educational freedom*. Boston: Beacon Press.

Lucas Education Research. (n.d.). *Key principles for project-based learning*. San Rafael, CA: George Lucas Educational Foundation. Accessed at https://www.lucasedresearch.org/wp-content/uploads/2021/02/Key-Principles-for-PBL-White-Paper-1.pdf on July 27, 2023.

Lundquist, A. E., & Henning, G. (2021, May 14). *Increasing awareness and reducing harm: A framework for equity-minded and equity-centered assessment*. Anthology. Accessed at https://www.anthology.com/blog/increasing-awareness-and-reducing-harm-a-framework-for-equity-minded-and-equity-centered on July 28, 2023.

Madden, E. J. (2016). *Place-based education: Educator perspectives on a critical pedagogy* [Master's thesis, Prescott College]. ProQuest Dissertations and Theses. Accessed at https://www.proquest.com/openview/c42e9c46d2cce48874429ec2fba4da09/1?pq-origsite=gscholar&cbl=18750 on January 18, 2024.

Martinez, V., & Waddell, B. (n.d.). The cultural triangle: Three dimensions of place-based learning at Hispanic serving institutions. *Community Works Journal*. Accessed at http://www.benjaminjameswaddell.com /wp-content/uploads/2016/03/Three-Dimensions-of-Place-based-learning_Final.pdf on July 31, 2023.

Mayes, R. D., Edirmanasinghe, N., Ieva, K., & Washington, A. R. (2022). Liberatory school counseling practices to promote freedom dreaming for Black youth. *Frontiers in Education, 13*(7). https://doi.org/10.3389 /feduc.2022.964490

Mayotte, C., & Kiefer, C. (Eds.). (2018). *Say it forward: A guide to social justice storytelling*. Chicago: Haymarket Books.

McDonald, M., VanCleave, B., Kim, C., Salesky, M., & Green, M. (2020). *GUS method*. K20 Center. Accessed at https://learn.k20center.ou.edu/strategy/76 on July 28, 2023.

McKittrick, K. (2011). On plantations, prisons, and a black sense of place. *Social & Cultural Geography, 12*(8), 947–963. Accessed at https://doi.org/10.1080/14649365.2011.624280 on April 25, 2024.

Miller, R. (2020, February 7). *Teaching Black history in culturally responsive ways*. Edutopia. Accessed at https:// www.edutopia.org/article/teaching-black-history-culturally-responsive-ways on July 28, 2023.

Minero, E. (2016, April 19). *Place-based learning: A multifaceted approach*. Edutopia. Accessed at https://www .edutopia.org/practice/place-based-learning-connecting-kids-their-community on January 18, 2024.

Mitchell, A. N. (2023, Spring). Survival, resistance and resilience. *Learning for Justice, 4*. Accessed at https:// www.learningforjustice.org/magazine/spring-2023/survival-resistance-and-resilience on July 28, 2023.

Mora, R. A. (2014). *Counter-narrative*. Washington, DC: Center for Intercultural Dialogue. Accessed at https:// centerforinterculturaldialogue.files.wordpress.com/2014/10/key-concept-counter-narrative.pdf on July 28, 2023.

Morrison, T. (2015, March 23). No place for self-pity, no room for fear. *The Nation*. Accessed at https://www .thenation.com/article/archive/no-place-self-pity-no-room-fear/ on July 28, 2023.

Muhammad, G. (2020a). *Cultivating genius: An equity framework for culturally and historically responsive literacy*. New York: Scholastic.

Muhammad, G. (2020b, December 2). *Rethinking intervention* [Video transcript]. Instruction Partners. Accessed at https://instructionpartners.org/2020/12/02/dr-gholnecsar-gholdy-muhammad/ on July 28, 2023.

Murphy, S. (2018, May 8). *Technology and the evolution of storytelling*. Medium. Accessed at https://medium. com/@shanemurphy_2728/technology-and-the-evolution-of-storytelling-90a533dc3037 on July 28, 2023.

Nā Hopena Aʻo (HĀ). (n.d.). In *Hawaiʻi State Department of Education online dictionary*. Accessed at https:// www.hawaiipublicschools.org/TeachingAndLearning/StudentLearning/HawaiianEducation/Pages/HA.aspx on July 18, 2022.

National Equity Project. (n.d.). *Developing community agreements*. Accessed at https://www.nationalequityproject .org/tools/developing-community-agreements on July 28, 2023.

National Geographic. (n.d.). *Here be dragons*. Accessed at https://education.nationalgeographic.org/resource /here-be-dragons/ on July 31, 2023.

National Museum of African American History & Culture. (n.d.). *Power of place* [Exhibition]. Accessed at https://nmaahc.si.edu/explore/exhibitions/power-place/ on July 28, 2023.

National School Reform Faculty. (n.d.). *Success analysis protocol with reflective questions*. Accessed at https:// www.nsrfharmony.org/wp-content/uploads/2017/10/success_analysis_reflective_0.pdf on July 28, 2023.

National School Reform Faculty. (2014). *Chalk talk protocol*. Accessed at https://www.nsrfharmony.org/wp-content /uploads/2017/10/ChalkTalk-N-1.pdf on May 8, 2024.

Niccolls, K., & Benedetto, A. (2023, January 16). *Assessment as revelation, not destination*. Getting Smart. Accessed at https://www.gettingsmart.com/2023/01/16/assessment-as-revelation-not-destination on July 28, 2023.

Oka, A. (2019, July 22). *Lessons from Hawaiian-focused charter schools featured in* Education Week. Kamehameha Schools. Accessed at https://www.ksbe.edu/article/lessons-from-hawaiian-focused-charter-schools-featured -in-education-week on July 28, 2023.

Okun, T. (2021). *What is White supremacy culture?* Accessed at https://www.whitesupremacyculture.info/what -is-it.html on February 8, 2024.

Onufer, L. (2018, December 12). Teaching at PITT: Making your assessments more equitable. *University Times.* Accessed at https://www.utimes.pitt.edu/news/teaching-pitt-making-your on July 26, 2023.

Open Colleges. (2015, November 21). *8 alternatives to high-stakes standardised tests.* informED. Accessed at https://www.opencolleges.edu.au/informed/features/8-alternatives-to-standardized-testing/ on February 9, 2024.

Parsons, C. M. (2016, December 16). *So, what can WE do? PLACE in action at the Whitney Plantation.* PBL Path. Accessed at http://www.pblpath.com/blog/so-what-can-we-do-place-in-action-at-whitney-plantation on July 28, 2023.

Penuel, W. R. (2021, November 29). Reimagining American education: Possible futures for equitable educational assessment. *Kappan, 103*(4), 54–57. Accessed at https://kappanonline.org/possible-futures-equitable -assessment-penuel/ on July 28, 2023.

Perkins, D. (2021, April 26). *Using authentic audience in PBL to unlock critical thinking.* Teach Thought. Accessed at https://www.teachthought.com/critical-thinking/authentic-audience-in-pbl/ on July 28, 2023.

Pieratt, J. (2020, February 16). *How to create a project based learning lesson.* Cult of Pedagogy. Accessed at https:// www.cultofpedagogy.com/project-based-learning-lesson/ on July 28, 2023.

Pisters, S. R., Vihinen, H., & Figueiredo, E. (2019). Place based transformative learning: A framework to explore consciousness in sustainability initiatives. *Emotion, Space and Society, 32,* Article 100578.

Pisters, S. R., Vihinen, H., Figueiredo, E., & Wals, A. E. J. (2023). "We learned the language of the tree" ecovillages as spaces of place-based transformative learning. *Journal of Transformative Education, 21*(1), 59–83. Accessed at https://doi.org/10.1177/15413446211068550 on April 25, 2024.

Place-Based Education Evaluation Collaboration. (2010). *Benefits of place based learning PEEC report, 2010.* Promise of Place. Accessed at https://promiseofplace.org/research-evaluation/research-and-evaluation /benefits-of-place-based-learning-peec-report-2010 on May 8, 2024.

Project Zero. (n.d.). *Project Zero's thinking routine toolbox.* Harvard Graduate School of Education. Accessed at http://www.pz.harvard.edu/thinking-routines on July 28, 2023

Project Zero. (2019a). *Circle of viewpoints: A routine for exploring perspectives.* Harvard Graduate School of Education. Accessed at https://pz.harvard.edu/sites/default/files/Circle%20of%20Viewpoints_0.pdf on July 28, 2023.

Project Zero. (2019b). *The power of stories.* Harvard Graduate School of Education. Accessed at https:// pz.harvard.edu/sites/default/files/The-Power-of-Stories_1.pdf on February 8, 2024.

Reibel, A. R. (2021, March 11). *Uncovering implicit bias in assessment, feedback and grading.* All Things Assessment. Accessed at https://allthingsassessment.info/2021/03/11/uncovering-implicit-bias-in -assessment-feedback-and-grading/ on July 28, 2023.

Rethinking Schools. (2014). The gathering resistance to standardized tests. *Rethinking Schools, 28*(3). Accessed at https://rethinkingschools.org/articles/the-gathering-resistance-to-standardized-tests/ on July 27, 2023.

Rhodes, R. J. (2019). Personal story sharing as an engagement strategy to promote student learning. *Perspectives on Urban Education, 16*(1). Accessed at https://urbanedjournal.gse.upenn.edu/volume-16-issue-1 -spring-2019/personal-story-sharing-engagement-strategy-promote-student-learning on July 28, 2023.

Right Question Institute. (2024). *What is the QFT?* Accessed at https://rightquestion.org/what-is-the-qft/ on May 8, 2024.

Ripp, P. (2019, February 24). *Using the single point rubric for better assessment conversations.* Accessed at https:// pernillesripp.com/2019/02/24/using-the-single-point-rubric-for-better-assessment-conversations/ on July 28, 2023.

Ritskes, E. (2012, September 21). What is decolonization and why does it matter? *Intercontinental Cry.* Accessed at https://intercontinentalcry.org/what-is-decolonization-and-why-does-it-matter/ on July 31, 2023.

Rodgers, C. (2002). Defining reflection: Another look at John Dewey and reflective thinking. *Teachers College Record, 104*(4), 842–866. https://doi.org/10.1111/1467-9620.00181

Rosales, J., & Walker, T. (2021, March 20). The racist beginnings of standardized testing. *NEA Today*. Accessed at https://www.nea.org/advocating-for-change/new-from-nea/racist-beginnings-standardized-testing on July 28, 2023.

Sanchez, E. (2023). Four stumbling stones in a first project and how to keep momentum. *PBL Works.*

Safir, S. (2015, November 4). *The power of story in school transformation.* Edutopia. Accessed at https://www.edutopia.org/blog/power-of-story-school-transformation-shane-safir on July 28, 2023.

Safir, S., & Dugan, J. (2021). *Street data: A next-generation model for equity, pedagogy, and school transformation.* Thousand Oaks, CA: Corwin.

Saltmarshe, E. (2018, February 20). *Using story to change systems.* Stanford Social Innovation Review. Accessed at https://ssir.org/articles/entry/using_story_to_change_systems# on July 28, 2023.

Selby, D. (2021, September 17). *How the 13th amendment kept slavery alive: Perspectives from the prison where slavery never ended.* Innocence Project. Accessed at https://innocenceproject.org/news/how-the-13th-amendment-kept-slavery-alive-perspectives-from-the-prison-where-slavery-never-ended/ on July 28, 2023.

Shannon, J. (2020, May 15). *Community GIS and the Linnentown Project: A collaboration* [Blog post]. Community Mapping Lab. Accessed at http://www.communitymappinglab.org/blog/community-gis-and-the-linnentown-project-a-collaboration on July 28, 2023.

Sheehan, M., & Neimand, A. (2018, May 10). *Science of story building: Master and counter narratives.* Medium. Accessed at https://medium.com/science-of-story-building/science-of-story-building-master-counter-narratives-1992bec6b8f on July 28, 2023.

Shepard, L. A. (2021). Ambitious teaching and equitable assessment: A vision for prioritizing learning, not testing. *American Educator, 45*(3). Accessed at https://www.aft.org/ae/fall2021/shepard on July 28, 2023.

Shute, V., & Ventura, M. (2013). *Stealth assessment: Measuring and supporting learning in video games.* Cambridge, MA: MIT Press. Accessed at https://library.oapen.org/viewer/web/viewer.html?file=/bitstream/handle/20.500.12657/26058/1004027.pdf on July 28, 2023.

Skills You Need. (n.d.). *Life skills.* Accessed at https://www.skillsyouneed.com/general/life-skills.html on July 28, 2023.

Smith, C. (2021a). *How the word is passed: A reckoning with the history of slavery across America.* New York: Little, Brown.

Smith, C. (2021b). I visited a former plantation to understand why people get married there. All I saw was pain. *Buzzfeed News.* Accessed at https://www.buzzfeednews.com/article/clintsmith/married-weddings-on-plantations on July 28, 2023.

Smith, G. A., & Sobel, D. (2010). *Place- and community-based education in schools.* New York: Routledge.

Smith, T., & Pham, J. (n.d.). *Understanding teacher bias.* Learning A–Z. Accessed at https://www.learninga-z.com/site/resources/breakroom-blog/understanding-teacher-bias#:~:text=Teacher%20bias%20has%20the%20power,pick%20up%20this%20learned%20behavior on January 26, 2024.

Snyder, C. R., Lopez, S. J., & Pedrotti, J. T. (2010). *Positive psychology: The scientific and practical explorations of human strengths* (2nd ed.). Thousand Oaks, CA: SAGE.

SOLVE. (2006). *Reaching out to community partners.* SOLVE Service Learning Tools Series.

Soper, S. (2017, October 13). *Making project-based learning authentic.* Getting Smart. Accessed at https://www.gettingsmart.com/2017/10/13/making-project-based-learning-authentic/ on July 28, 2023.

Southern Poverty Law Center. (n.d.a). *Social justice standards.* Accessed at https://www.learningforjustice.org/frameworks/social-justice-standards#:~:text=Justice%20Anchor%20Standards,level%20(e.g.%2C%20discrimination). on January 29, 2024.

Southern Poverty Law Center. (n.d.b). *Test yourself for hidden bias.* Accessed at https://www.learningforjustice.org/professional-development/test-yourself-for-hidden-bias on January 26, 2024.

Southern Poverty Law Center. (2012). *Unlocking your community's hidden strengths: A guidebook to community asset-mapping*. Accessed at https://www.splcenter.org/20121126/unlocking-your-community%E2%80%99s-hidden-strengths-guidebook-community-asset-mapping?gclid=CjwKCAjwv4SaBhBPEiwA9YzZvPXK-a-LqHq7mDk0wGcERkupmlx-s60MN2RplXnfexlJ_YrwPU2PPxoCZjoQAvD_BwE on February 9, 2024.

State of Michigan. (n.d.). *Place-based education*. Accessed at https://www.michigan.gov/leo/boards-comms-councils/mistem/stem-toolbox/place-based-education#WhatPBE on January 8, 2024.

StoryCorps. (n.d.). *Great questions*. Accessed at https://storycorps.org/participate/great-questions/ on November 16, 2023.

StoryCorps. (2017, July 22). *Four tips for an effective interview: A StoryCorps education tool* [Video file]. Accessed at https://www.youtube.com/watch?v=G70rR2vG5wY&ab_channel=StoryCorps on July 31, 2023.

Student reflection, Spring 2022, Community GIS Course, UGA. Acessed at https://storymaps.arcgis.com/stories/8c57971b20d7462c8868c4e480766ceb on April 25, 2024.

SUNY Faculty Advisory Council on Teaching & Technology 2. (n.d.). *Social justice assessment*. Accessed at https://online.suny.edu/innovativeassessments/social-justice-assessment on July 28, 2023.

Talent Enthusiasts. (2021, December 21). *The hope survey for schools!* [Video file]. Accessed at https://www.youtube.com/watch?v=WUeKILu7xNM&t=86s on July 28, 2023.

Technology Access Foundation. (n.d.). *STEM by TAF model*. Accessed at http://www.techaccess.org/our-approach on July 28, 2023.

Tikkanen, L., Anttila, H., Pyhältö, K., Soini, T., & Pietarinen, J. (2022). The role of empathy between peers in upper secondary students' study engagement and burnout. *Frontiers in Psychology, 13*, Article 978546. Accessed at https://doi.org/10.3389/fpsyg.2022.978546 on April 25, 2024.

Tredway, L., & Generett, G. (2015). *Community story-mapping: The pedagogy of the griot*. Washington, DC: Institute for Educational Leadership. Accessed at https://iel.org/wp-content/uploads/2015/04/Community_Story-Mapping_Guide-2015-04.pdf on July 31, 2023.

Treuer, A. (2012). *Everything you wanted to know about Indians but were afraid to ask*. St. Paul: Minnesota Historical Society Press.

Tuck, E., & Yang, K. W. (2012). Decolonization is not a metaphor. *Decolonization: Indigeneity, Education & Society, 1*(1), 1–40. Accessed at https://clas.osu.edu/sites/clas.osu.edu/files/Tuck%20and%20Yang%202012%20Decolonization%20is%20not%20a%20metaphor.pdf on January 25, 2024.

Tweit, S. J. (2009). *Walking nature home: A life's journey*. Austin: University of Texas Press.

Valenzuela, J. (2022, May 16). *Using frequent feedback cycles to guide student work*. Edutopia. Accessed at https://www.edutopia.org/article/using-frequent-feedback-cycles-guide-student-work on July 31, 2023.

Vander Ark, T. (2014, October 25). *13 barriers to education innovation*. Getting Smart. Accessed at https://www.gettingsmart.com/2014/10/25/13-barriers-education-innovation/ on July 31, 2023.

Vander Ark, T. (2016, July 28). *Genius loci: Place-based education & why it matters*. Getting Smart. Accessed at https://www.gettingsmart.com/2016/07/28/genius-loci-place-based-education-why-it-matters/ on July 31, 2023.

Vazquez, A. (2022, August 2). *How to mitigate your unconscious bias*. Gladstone Institutes. Accessed at https://gladstone.org/news/how-to-mitigate-your-unconscious-bias?gclid=CjwKCAiAhJWsBhAaEiwAmrNyqz-CEoO-83ERSnmotGvgLqw6sPUKKcQgLofsii7UJva9I5vBZCvZQBoCNboQAvD_BwE on January 26, 2024.

Village Earth. (2021a). *5 ways mapping can help empower your community and the tools you need to do it*. Accessed at https://villageearth.org/5-ways-mapping-can-help-empower-your-community-and-the-tools-you-need-to-do-it/ on July 31, 2023.

Village Earth. (2021b). *Welcome to Village Earth!* Accessed at https://villageearth.org/ on January 9, 2024.

Voice of Witness. (n.d.). *Our mission*. Accessed at https://voiceofwitness.org/about/ on July 28, 2023.

Washington, B. (2021, May 12). *Creating engaged citizens through civic education*. Teach Hub. Accessed at https://www .teachhub.com/teaching-strategies/2021/05/creating-engaged-citizens-through-civic-education/ on July 31, 2023.

Weiss, J. (2016, November 9). *Powerful school-community partnership brings learning to life*. Getting Smart. Accessed at https://www.gettingsmart.com/2016/11/09/powerful-school-community-partnerships-brings -learning-to-life/ on July 31, 2023.

White Supremacy Culture. (n.d.a). *What is White supremacy culture?* Accessed at https://www.whitesupremacyculture .info/what-is-it.html on July 28, 2023.

White Supremacy Culture. (n.d.b). *White supremacy culture characteristics*. Accessed at https://www.whitesupremacyculture .info/characteristics.html on July 28, 2023.

Wiggins, G., & McTighe, J. (2011). *The understanding by design guide to creating high-quality units*. Alexandria, VA: ASCD.

Wright, Z. (2019, October 3). We can't just teach about heroes and holidays and call it culturally responsive. *Ed Post*. Accessed at https://educationpost.org/we-cant-just-teach-about-heroes-and-holidays-and-call-it -culturally-responsive/ on July 31, 2023.

Yale Poorvu Center for Teaching and Learning. (2021). *Awareness of implicit biases*. Accessed at https:// poorvucenter.yale.edu/ImplicitBiasAwareness on May 8, 2024.

Zak, P. (2013). How stories change the brain. *Greater Good Magazine*. Accessed at https://greatergood.berkeley .edu/article/item/how_stories_change_brain on May 8, 2024.

Index

The Landscape Model of Learning
Jennifer D. Klein and Kapono Ciotti
Help students take the lead on reaching their personal highest level of success by shifting from the current paradigm of education. This essential guide offers the landscape model and its three elements: understanding what students bring to the ecosystem, defining the horizon, and charting the pathway. Access practical strategies for drawing on students' experiences and strengths to create a more meaningful and inclusive educational ecosystem.
BKG043

Real-World Learning Framework for Elementary Schools
Marge Maxwell, Rebecca Stobaugh, and Janet Lynne Tassell
Bring about deeper, self-directed learning in elementary school students. This book outlines opportunities teachers and students have to exercise cognitive complexity, engagement, and technology integration through real-world project-based instruction. Part one details the Create Excellence Framework, and part two offers sample lesson plans from real-world learning projects so educators can help students take more responsibility for and find more enthusiasm in their own learning.
BKF753

Real-World Learning Framework for Secondary Schools
Marge Maxwell, Rebecca Stobaugh, and Janet Lynne Tassell
Foster authentic learning in classrooms. Students desire to find meaning in what they learn and to exert creativity in their schoolwork. Using the Create Excellence Framework, educators can help students find greater fulfillment in learning, while also meeting the guidelines of curriculum standards. Explore the framework's main components, and understand how to use the framework for classroom, school, and district pursuits.
BKF656

Two-for-One Teaching
Lauren Porosoff and Jonathan Weinstein
Empower your students to make school a source of meaning, vitality, and community. *Two-for-One Teaching* offers 30 protocols, derived from contextual behavioral science, that embed student-centered, equity-driven social-emotional learning into every stage of an academic unit. Transform students' psychological experience of school by turning their lessons, assignments, and assessments into opportunities for them to explore and enact the values they want to live by.
BKF923

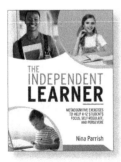

The Independent Learner
Nina Parrish
Teach students how to self-regulate with research-affirmed, teacher-tested strategies. Perfect for teachers in any grade level or content area, this book will give you the tools you need to equip students with metacognitive skills and the ability to take ownership of their learning. Support students as they learn how to build intrinsic motivation, emotional literacy, and problem solving skills—all essential for future success.
BKG017

a division of
Solution Tree

Visit SolutionTree.com or call 800.733.6786 to order.

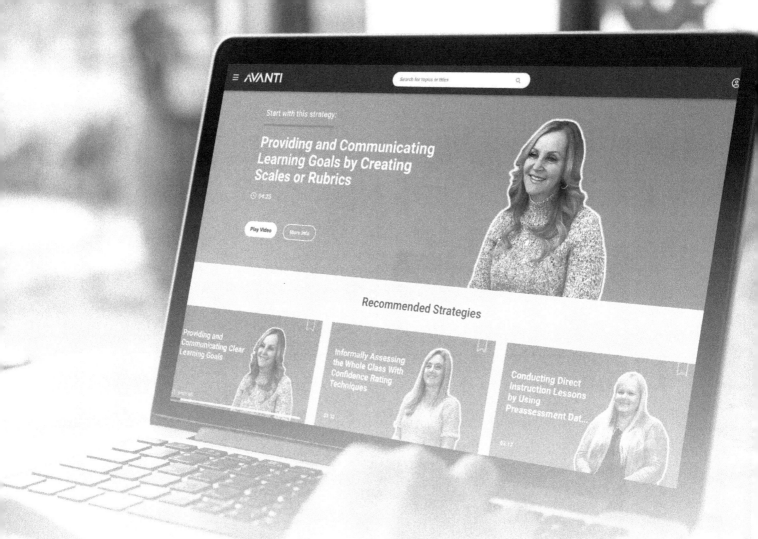

AVANTI

Grow your teacher toolkit by learning from other teachers

Take control of your professional growth and positively impact your students' lives with proven, ready-to-use classroom strategies. With Avanti, you'll get professional learning created by teachers, for teachers.

Learn more
My-Avanti.com/**GrowYourToolkit**